Venture Capital at
the Crossroads

Venture Capital at the Crossroads

William D. Bygrave
Jeffry A. Timmons

HARVARD BUSINESS SCHOOL PRESS   Boston, Massachusetts

Printed in the United States of America.
    96   5 4 3

Library of Congress Cataloging-in-Publication Data

Bygrave, William D., 1937–
   Venture capital at the crossroads / William D. Bygrave, Jeffry A.
Timmons.
       p.   cm.
   Includes bibliographical references and index.
   ISBN 0-87584-304-2 (acid-free paper)
   1. Venture capital.   I. Timmons, Jeffry A.   II. Title.
HG4751.B94   1992
332'.0415—dc20   92-2603
                                                         CIP

The paper used in this publication meets the requirements of the
American National Standard for Permanence of Paper for Printed
Library Materials Z39.48-1984.

To the spirit and memory of
the late Professor Georges Doriot,
father of classic venture capital
in America

Contents

Acknowledgments

This book represents the culmination of our research, curricula development, teaching, and practical involvement with venture capital and startup and growing companies for the past twenty-five years. Innumerable colleagues and friends have made important contributions to this effort. While it is impossible to acknowledge them all, a substantial number deserve mention here.

First, we are deeply appreciative to Carol Franco and Paula Duffy for recognizing the potential in this project and for encouraging us to write the book. Richard Luecke, our editor, deserves enormous thanks for his painstaking, and very thoughtful effort. His numerous ideas and suggestions helped us improve early drafts of the manuscript in a significant way. Thomas J. Soja, while serving as Jeffry Timmons' research associate at the Harvard Business School, was invaluable in gathering and analyzing data and trends, commenting on drafts, and developing graphic presentations. Tom also made a major contribution by elaborating on an earlier study by the authors (Chapter 10), "Venture Capital and Regional Economic Development." Another research assistant, Christine Remey, was a great help in winding up loose ends on the project. Lisa Lamoreaux of the Harvard Business School, as always, was extraordinarily organized and cheerful in helping us prepare chapters, meet deadlines, and follow through. At Babson College, Barbara Ward and Bonnie Pandya provided their usual exceptional support and covered our tracks on our numerous other projects while we tended to this one.

Our Harvard colleagues, Howard H. Stevenson and William A. Sahlman, encouraged us to write the book, made valuable suggestions on chapter drafts, and contributed their ground-breaking study of "Capital Market Myopia," to Chapter 5. We are also grateful to Harry A. Sapienza of the University of South Carolina, who allowed us to draw on his dissertation and other research work for our discussion of whether venture capitalists add value (Chapter 9).

It is a privilege to thank other associates who have worked with us: Michael Stein labored tirelessly on the study of venture-capital-backed IPOs (Chapter 7); Al Bruno, Joseph Rosenstein, Natalie Taylor, and Todd Packard contributed to our understanding of the value-added process (Chapter 9); Joel Shulman brought insights to the influence of the capital gains tax (Chapter 11); King Ng wrote the programs to calculate venture capital returns (Chapter 6) and to analyze co-investing patterns (Chapter 8); Audrey Smith made many computer analyses under the watchful eye of John McKenzie of Babson College who advised us on statistical due diligence.

Experienced venture capitalists Geoff Taylor and Gordon Baty reviewed the manuscript and provided numerous insights and suggestions that we have tried to incorporate into the book. Gordon inspired us to consider bolder prescriptions for the industry in Chapter 12. We also appreciate David Brophy's review and Jocelyn Desroches' thoughtful comments on the final draft.

Special thanks goes to the MBA Class of 1954 at Harvard Business School for its support of entrepreneurship through its endowed chair and particularly Bert Twaalfhoven. This support enabled Jeffry Timmons to pursue this project. Similarly, Frederic C. Hamilton endowed a chair in Free Enterprise Development at Babson College, which has been another crucial source of support to both authors who have held the chair over the course of the project.

We are also grateful for Jeffry Timmons' support by Dean John H. McArthur and the directors of research at the Harvard Business School, Jay W. Lorsch and Warren McFarlan, and by Neil C. Churchill, Allan Cohen, and Dan Muzyka at Babson. Special thanks also goes to Venture Economics for allowing us to quote some of its data and studies. Earlier Rubina Khoylian, Norman Fast, and Stanley Pratt collaborated with us in a National Science Foundation–funded study on the flows of venture capital;

Linda Vincent and William Yue developed the information on the rates of return; and Jane Morris has been continually supportive.

Finally, many practitioners have been important sources of ideas, insights, and knowledge which have contributed to our continuing education in this field. These include Brion Applegate, Ed Beanland, Bill Boyce, Les Charm, Bill Egan, Craig Foley, Bill Foxley, Joe Frye, Dan Garner (and partners and staff at Ernst & Young too numerous to list), Hoyt Goodrich, Bart Goodwin, Ted Horton, Dick Johnson, Bill Johnston, Doug Kahn, Paul Kelley, Richard Kimball, Brian Little, Ed Marram, Jos Peeters, Kirk Raab, Donald Remey, Arthur Rock, Ben Rosen, Ralph Sabin, Bill Spencer, Bob Sullivan and Paul Tobin, Bill Torpey, and Peter Wendell and Allyn Woodward.

CHAPTER 1

Venture Capital

W E BEGIN OUR STUDY of venture capital by examining—and then dispelling—these stereotypes about the venture capital industry: (1) all venture capital is "patient and brave" money that seeks out new and growing companies and invests for the long haul, that is, often ten years or more; (2) all venture capital firms are basically alike; and (3) the venture-capital investing process is highly organized and refined. We will also map the important historical roots and key developments in the industry to the present, thus setting the agenda for the subsequent chapters.

Since its inception after World War II, venture capital has had a little-known but profound impact on the U.S. and world economy. It has played a catalytic role in the entrepreneurial process: fundamental value creation that triggers and sustains economic growth and renewal. In terms of job creation, innovative products and services, competitive vibrancy, and the dissemination of the entrepreneurial spirit, its contributions have been staggering. The new companies and industries spawned by venture capitalists have changed fundamentally the way in which we live and work.

Consider the following examples:

- In 1957, American Research & Development (ARD) invested $70,000 for 77% of the common stock of a new company created by four MIT graduate students. By 1971, that investment had grown to comprise $355 million in common stock in

Digital Equipment Corporation (DEC), which today is a world leader in the computer industry, with one of its founders, Kenneth Olsen, still at the helm.

- In 1975, Arthur Rock, in search of innovative concepts "that change the way people live and work," invested $1.5 million in the startup of Apple Computer, Inc. At Apple's first public stock offering in 1978, that investment was valued at $100 million.

- After monthly losses of $1 million and more for twenty-nine consecutive months, a new company that launched the overnight delivery of small packages turned the corner. The $25 million invested had a valuation of $1.2 billion when Federal Express issued its stock to the public for the first time.

These legendary companies—started and built in the 1950s, 1960s, and 1970s—have been followed by other extraordinary new companies in the 1980s: Lotus Development Corporation, Genetics Institute, Sun Microsystems, Compaq Computer Corporation, Staples, Inc., and hundreds of others. In what may seem like a blink in time, many of these new companies have created and then become premier firms in their industries. They have become entrepreneurial legends, and in a single decade some have broken into the *Fortune* 500 business establishment.

What do all these "superstar" firms have in common? In a word, venture capital. Each received early venture capital backing to launch and propel its ambitious growth plans. This cream of the venture capital crop and hundreds of similar firms are noted for value creation through technological and market innovations and entrepreneurial genius. Their products and services have become household names. The $90+ billion personal computer industry is a good example, accounting for the largest legal creation of wealth in the United States in the past two decades.

Less well known is the role venture capital firms have played in the value creation process and their remarkable contributions to the overall economy. As catalysts and risk takers, these firms have played a unique role in the formation and commercialization of entirely new industries: personal computers, cellular communications, microcomputer software, biotechnology, and overnight delivery, to name a few. Some direct results of this participation have been the creation of hundreds of thousands of new jobs, new expenditures for research and development, increased export sales, and the payment of hundreds of millions of dollars in state and federal taxes. By mobilizing and later recycling scarce risk capital and entrepreneurial talent, venture capital firms have transformed our economy.

This profound economic impact has been documented in numerous studies, among them, a recent survey by Venture Economics, Inc., and Coopers & Lybrand of 1,650 venture-capital-backed companies.[1] The 235 companies that responded had been in existence an average of only 1.9 years but, for the years 1985 through 1989, had created 36,000 new jobs, $786 million in export sales, $726 million in research-and-development expenditures, and $170 million in corporate tax payments. The average firm employed 153 people, had $3.3 million in export sales, invested $3.1 million in R&D, and paid $723,000 in taxes. By any standard, these firms represent exciting and productive additions to the economy, with net growth far outstripping that of the majority of small businesses and giant corporations. In contrast to the *Fortune* 500 companies, which, on average, consumed $59,510 of equity capital per new job, these venture-backed companies required just $42,914 per job. What is more, their labor force consisted of more highly skilled professionals (53%) than does the labor force in general (13%), and they employed far fewer administrators (10%) than did the *Fortune* 500 (25%). These venture-capital-backed companies also generated nearly four times more export sales per dollar of equity than the *Fortune* 500 companies did.

Perhaps the archetype for the new venture environment is the neighborhood of East Cambridge, Massachusetts, recently termed "The Most Entrepreneurial Place on Earth" by *Inc. Magazine.*[2] According to the article, roughly 10% of Massachusetts software companies and nearly 25% of the state's 140 biotechnology companies are headquartered there. Not coincidentally, they are a stone's throw from the MIT campus. One of the East Cambridge superstars is Lotus Development Corporation, which went from a three-employee startup in 1981 (located elsewhere in Cambridge at the time) to the $500+ million giant it is today. The area is also home to the many service support groups that make new business formation possible: accounting firms, consultants, public relations firms, a day care center, and, of course, venture capitalists such as Zero Stage Capital and Founders Capital Partners. Some 17,000 new jobs have been created in that one-mile-square neighborhood since 1982.[3] (We will examine the role of venture capital in economic development in Chapter 10.)

Highly successful new ventures like the ones mentioned above have created inspirational role models for an entire generation of would-be entrepreneurs. Their swift, nimble, adaptive, and innovative approaches to markets and management have spawned a new generation of entrepreneurs and managers. Venture capital and new venture creation are considered by many to be the very core of the entrepreneurial process.

PATIENCE AND BRAVERY

One of the most durable stereotypes about traditional venture capital is that it is "patient and brave" money. We call this classic venture capital, the type pioneered by the father of U.S. venture capital, General Georges Doriot, who is profiled below. To understand it, one must first understand the fundamental business and financial requirements facing startup and early-stage companies.

Young, rapidly growing companies go through financial hell compared to existing, ongoing firms, small and large alike, with established customer bases, revenues, and, thus, cash flow streams. The faster a firm grows, the more voracious is its appetite for cash. Pre-startup investment in R&D, product development and testing, key team members, facilities, and specialized equipment is expensive. The costs of raw materials, components, sales and distribution capability, inventory of partially and fully completed products, hiring and training, trade shows, demos and samples, and marketing efforts quickly add up. A typical personal computer software start-up in the mid-1980s, for instance, often required $5 to $6 million, most of which was spent on product introduction, trade incentives to gain distribution, and the advertising and promotion essential to move the product off the shelf. Negative cash flows generally prevailed for a number of years before the original capital was recovered.

Figure 1-1 summarizes data for 157 companies all backed and owned by the Dutch firm Indivers.[4] The shaded area represents their cumulative cash flow. It took 30 months to reach a break-even cash flow and 75 months (into the seventh year!) to recover the initial equity investment. One can see why patience and bravery are necessary attributes of classic venture capital. Since founders rarely have the cash to fill such gaps, where does the capital come from? No bank or other institutional lender will agree to wait seven years for its first payment of interest or principal. Yet without this risk capital, such ventures are aborted, stillborn, or, worse, suc-

FIGURE 1-1 **Initial Losses by Small New Ventures**

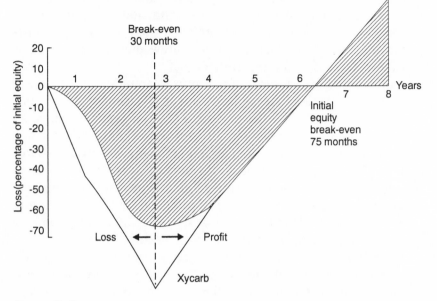

Source: Indivers.
Note: Average of 157 companies at various stages of development USA, 1972–1982.

cumb in early infancy. Equity investors who both understand the risks and possess the know-how to overcome them and achieve commercial success have historically filled this gap.

Risk capital is as critical today as it was when Ralph Flanders and General Doriot launched ARD, their venture capital fund, in 1946. It must be available to fuel the new firms that are, in essence, the molecules of economic growth itself. And, certainly, investments in startup companies like DEC and Apple are very rewarding, financially and emotionally. But, today, the stereotype of venture capital as patient and brave money is more myth than reality. Many of the new breed of venture capitalists have little in common with their predecessors of the pre-1980 era.

THE QUEST FOR THE SUPERDEAL

Another stereotype of venture capitalists is that they are very much alike. Contributing to this belief is a long-held axiom of investors: one must pursue the superdeal. The common notion has been that virtually all venture capitalists specialized in new, high-tech companies that aspired to superstar status in their industries. If you were not high tech, were not a startup, and could not achieve at least $50 million in sales in five years, then venture capitalists would not back you. This stereotype grew out of past triumphs and the people associated with them.

One of the most successful venture capitalists of all time is Arthur Rock, the lead investor not only in the triumphal launching of Apple Computer but in several other highly successful companies as well: Fairchild Semiconductor, Teledyne Corporation, Intel, and Scientific Data Systems, Inc. The last company was twice as large as DEC, a close rival, when it was sold to Xerox in 1969 for $1 billion. Rock's $257,000 investment had grown to $100 million. Teledyne's investment in about 125 companies returned an astonishing 25% compounded over the first twenty-five-year period—a record unmatched in the industry on a sustained basis.

Rock has a clear notion of what he is after: new concepts for products or services that will change the way people live and work. In a 1987 interview at the Harvard Business School, he summarized the importance he places on the lead entrepreneur and management team:

> If you can find good people, they can always change the product. Nearly every mistake I've made has been in picking the wrong people, not the wrong idea. . . . Most entrepreneurs have no problem coming up with a good strategy, but they usually need all the help they can get in developing and implementing the tactics that will make them successful in the long run.

Of course, a number of other criteria, especially market potential, are carefully evaluated before investors part with their money. These criteria differ considerably, depending on the investing strategy and focus of the particular venture capital firm. Startup investments, for instance, are evaluated differently from leveraged buyouts (LBOs).

Figure 1-2 is an attempt to profile the superdeal that classic venture capital investors dream about. Typically, this would be a startup company. Note the mission: build a highly profitable, industry-dominant company that can go public or be sold within four to seven years at a very substantial gain. Traditional venture capitalists are in the business of identifying, evaluating, financing, and nurturing highly successful, growth-minded companies. The key to achieving the high rates of return of an ARD or an Arthur

FIGURE 1-2 **Characteristics of the "Classic Superdeal" from the Investor's Perspective**

Mission
Build a highly profitable and industry-dominant company.
Go public or merge within four to seven years at a high price/earnings (P/E) multiple.

Complete Management Team
Led by industry superstar.
Possess proven entrepreneurial, general management, and P&L experience in the business.
Have leading innovator or technologies marketing head.
Possess complementary and compatible skills.
Have unusual tenacity, imagination, and commitment.
Possess reputation for high integrity.

Proprietary Product
Has significant competitive lead and "unfair" advantages.
Has product or service with high value-added properties resulting in early payback to user.
Has or can gain exclusive contractual or legal rights.

Large and Rapidly Growing Market
Will accommodate a $50 million entrant in five years.
Has sales currently at $100 million and more, growing at 25% per year.
Has no dominant competitor now.
Has clearly identified customers and distribution channels.
Possesses forgiving and rewarding economics, such as:
 –Gross margins of 40% to 50% or more.
 –Ten percent or more profit after tax.
 –Early positive cash flow and breakeven sales.

Deal Valuation and ROR
Has digestible first-round capital requirements (i.e., greater than $1 million and less than $10 million).
Able to return ten times original investment in five years at P/E of fifteen times or more.
Has possibility of additional rounds of financing at substantial markup.
Has antidilution and IPO subscription rights.

Source: J. A. Timmons et al., *New Venture Creation* (Homewood, IL: Richard D. Irwin, 1990), p. 428.

Rock lies in investing early, avoiding serious dilution, and picking companies with enormous upside potential. (In Chapter 6, we will examine in detail how venture capital funds have actually performed.) Notice also the other critical criteria: a complete management team led by an "industry superstar," a proprietary product or service with very high value-added qualities, a significant market with high growth potential, and a deal of digestible size (requiring $1–$10 million).

Sometimes, a lead investor is enthralled by the creative brilliance of a company's lead entrepreneur: a Mitch Kapor, a Steven Jobs, or a Fred Smith. Ideally, this entrepreneur—often a scientist, engineer, or programmer—has an extraordinary vision of what is possible, balanced by a clear recognition of what he or she does and does not know and a willingness to accept help in these areas. These entrepreneurs, if successful, often become celebrities— boardroom and campus, if not household, names. Some end up on the covers of *Inc. Magazine, Time, Business Week,* and *Fortune.* But before the fact, to all but a discerning few, they look a lot like thousands of other people who are trying to launch companies.

At other times, investors bet on the superb track records of the management team working as a group. One good example of this is found in the rapidly developing cellular car-phone industry. Two of the three people on the original management team of Cellular One in Boston had worked together previously at Satellite Business Systems Corporation. In five years, they built Cellular One from nothing into a business approaching $150 million in sales that was sold to Southwestern Bell Telephone Company in 1988 for an estimated $180 million. At its peak in 1990, the system had a market value in the vicinity of $1 billion. With backgrounds in general management, marketing, and the engineering aspects of wireless communications, the team attracted a fourth member in the financial and accounting area. Their outstanding early record in this infant industry led to venture capital backing by Boston's Burr, Egan, & Deleage to acquire rights to and build Cellular One in parts of Maine and New Hampshire. In less than two years, this system was built and sold to a public company, yielding a return of twenty-five times the original equity investment.

Significant market potential, especially in high-technology investments, often derives from a proprietary product with very high value-added properties, such as Lotus 1-2-3 software, or some legal or contractual license providing exclusive rights or territory. In the cellular phone industry, for instance, just two licenses are available in any single market—one for the existing telephone "wireline" company and one for an independent, or "non-wireline," firm. Having just one competitor is a useful advantage. Such a proprietary position coupled with a product that can pay for itself in a year or less translates into high margins and high profit potential. Software, computers, medical products, biogenetic engineering, telecommunications and information systems are examples of technologies in which high profit has been achieved.

Entrepreneurs and venture capitalists fall madly in love with products with rapidly growing markets and high gross margins of 50%, 60%, even 70% or more. They know that these margins will accommodate a multitude of management weaknesses, early mistakes, and the inevitable surprises that go with startup companies. The experience of R. Douglas Kahn, currently CEO of EASEL Corporation, is instructive. At age twenty-five, Kahn began to develop international marketing for McCormack & Dodge, Inc., a leading software firm acquired in 1983 by Dun & Bradstreet, Inc. From 1978 to 1983, he built this part of the business from zero to $17 million in sales; it contributed the bulk of the company's entire profits. The very high gross margins common in software at that time made it possible, in Kahn's words, "to make every conceivable mistake in the book (I'm too embarrassed to tell you all of them) and get away with it."

Finally, investors hope for returns of ten times or more on their invested capital. Ideally, they want to be in an investment for only four or five years but are prepared to stick it out if the promise and progress are there. Historically, this has meant an annualized rate of return of 50% and up. It has also meant deal structures that, in effect, gave investors a nearly perpetual "free option" to invest or abandon the deal. The lead investor usually cast the deciding vote on whether, when, and how to exit an investment, either through a public offering or through a sale to another company.

These kinds of investors have extremely high aspirations, and few investments fulfill them. A very sobering reminder of just how few was reported in a study compiled by the leading industry data source, Venture Economics, publisher of *Venture Capital Journal.* Just 6.8% of the 383 investments made in portfolio companies between 1969 and 1985 returned ten times or more on invested capital. And more than 60% of all these investments either lost money or failed to exceed savings account rates of return.[5] Judging by this, the label "risk and venture capital" is well deserved.

Despite the glorification of the superdeal of the 1960s and 1970s, the mentality of the industry has changed in recent years. There has been a perversion of both the superdeal focus and the patient and brave money that once dominated industry investing practices. Subsequent chapters will show how and why the investing focus has changed, from classic venture capital to a hybrid we call "merchant capital," consisting of venture capital, part LBO and management buyout (MBO) deals, more debt than equity, and a preference for investing in established ventures. Today's industry wears a different face. It is fragmented, differentiated, and more heterogeneous than is commonly believed. And today, ironically, the very strategies and investing targets that led to the DECs, Federal Expresses, and Apples account for a relatively small part of venture capital dollars and deals.

THE VENTURE CAPITAL PROCESS

A final stereotype that has entered industry folklore is that the investing process itself operates as a highly organized, rational, and methodical model of modern financial engineering. One envisions young MBAs, sporting colorful suspenders or the most fashionable "power" dresses, working day and night to grind out one financial spreadsheet model after another on their laptop computers, crafting elegant deal structures and forecasts. In fact, the industry has evolved through a lot of trial and error. Indeed, in many ways, it may be the most sophisticated cottage industry in the world today. Just how does the process work?

Venture capitalists and entrepreneurs—both winners and losers—are engaged in a process aimed at the longer-term creation and realization of value for themselves, their companies, communities, and other stakeholders. At the core of this process, they assume and manage the risks inherent in pursuing opportunities. It is fair to think of them as the bird dogs of economic development, catching the scent of innovations that will define the industries of the future.

With exceptional frequency, venture capitalists have been at the vortex of innovative, entrepreneurial activities, providing the scarce risk capital needed to fuel business inception and early growth (although, in recent years, this focus has broadened and changed significantly, which we shall discuss later). Their efforts have made possible entirely new industries: semiconductors in the 1960s, microprocessor-based ventures in the 1970s, and biotechnology and cellular communications in the 1980s, to mention a few. But who are the players and how does the venture capital process work?

Figure 1-3 represents the core activities of the venture capital

FIGURE 1-3 **Flows of Venture Capital**

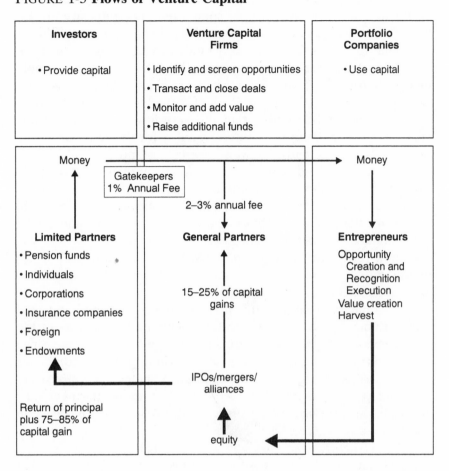

process. At the heart of this dynamic flow is the collision of entrepreneurs, opportunities, investors, and capital. The dominant legal structure for the process, which evolved in the 1970s, is not the corporation but the partnership for the venture capital fund. It originated in 1961 with Rock and his partner, Davis, who pioneered the concept and structure for a general partnership, including dividing the realized capital gains 80% and 20% to the limited and general partners, respectively. The partnership has two classes of partners: general and limited. The general partners act as organizers of the fund, shouldering the challenge of raising capital, accepting full personal responsibility and legal liability for fund management, and participating in any gains their investments produce. They typically contribute 1% of the capital in return for

15% to 25% of the realized capital gains and receive an annual fee of 2% to 3% of the total capital committed. The fiduciary obligations that rest squarely on the general partners create a significant economic incentive for them to achieve capital gains in the form of what is called the "carried interest." Carried interest is simply that portion of any gains realized by the fund to which the general partners are entitled. The suppliers of capital—institutional investors, pension funds, wealthy families—are limited partners. They play a passive role, enjoy "limited" liability for the activities of the fund, and, for tax and regulatory reasons, stand at arm's length from day-to-day fund management. They cannot become directly involved in the management and investing decisions of the venture capital funds in which they have placed money—to do so would jeopardize their limited liability and, in the case of pension funds, their nontaxable status. Typically, they contribute 99% of the capital in return for, usually, 80% (with a range of 75% to 85%) of the capital gains realized from the investments made by the general partners.

In some cases, management companies are formed and paid a fee to manage the funds for the partnership. The officers of the management company are normally the general partners. Since many groups would raise more than one venture capital fund over a number of years, this form of organization helped simplify structure and provide management continuity. Limited partners may also enlist the services of an investment adviser, who receives an additional annual fee of 1% to 2%.

Fee structures can vary considerably. Take, for instance, the contrast between funds we shall call Boston Four (BF) and BCI Growth (BCI). Each had raised funds in the 1980s and achieved attractive returns enabling them to continue raising funds in 1990. BF sought to raise $100 million with the help of an investment bank that would receive a 6% fee off the top. BF general partners proposed an annual 2% management fee, with a cost-of-living escalator, plus $1 million off the top of the fund for their financial advisory services. They would, as general partners, also be entitled to 20% of the capital gains. BCI, on the other hand, proposed a one-half of 1% annual management fee, with no cost-of-living escalator, 15% of the carried interest, a minimum threshold rate of return for limited partners before the general partners could participate in the gains, and no "off-the-top" fees. BCI closed its fund at $135 million in April 1990, while, at this writing, BF had failed to close its $100 million funding and abandoned the effort.

Clearly, venture capital today includes a more demanding institutional investor.

The main advantage of the partnership arrangement is that its life can be limited (typically to ten years) yet extended if the general partners and two-thirds of the limited partners agree to do so. Before, venture capitalists had a difficult time staying in the game long enough to see positive results. Often, investments were made one at a time, with the suppliers of the capital providing money on a deal-to-deal basis. Invariably, the failures cropped up first, usually in the first one or two years (it is often five years or more before a startup company is a real winner), and the outside backers simply would not step up for the next deal. It is simply said in the industry that the lemons ripen within two and a half years while the plums take seven or eight. The partnership form also has the advantage of avoiding the double taxation on profits that affects corporations and their shareholders. Probably the main disadvantage of the arrangement, which was not fully appreciated in the early 1970s, is the risk of litigation. Complicated issues concerning the valuation of carried interest in the event of a partner's withdrawal and partners' liability for bad investments have led to litigation among general partners and between general and limited partners.

No matter how they organize themselves as legal entities, venture capitalists collaborate with entrepreneurs to gather and provide equity financing for business opportunities that eventually can be harvested at profit. But, beyond the tasks of financing growth and reaping the benefits, venture capitalists who claim to descend from the likes of Doriot and Rock put something of themselves into the businesses they back. They are not passive providers of capital but active coaches and cheerleaders for the entrepreneurs with whom they work. This makes them venture capitalists in the classic sense.

A detailed examination of the classic venture-capital investing process is depicted in Figure 1-4. Venture capital firms seek to add value in several ways: identifying and evaluating business opportunities, including management, entry, or growth strategies; negotiating and closing the investment; and tracking and coaching the company; providing technical and management assistance; attracting additional capital, directors, management, suppliers, and other key stakeholders and resources. (We address the growing controversy about the amount of value actually added by venture capitalists in Chapter 9.) The process begins with the conception

FIGURE 1-4 **Classic Venture-Capital Investing Process**

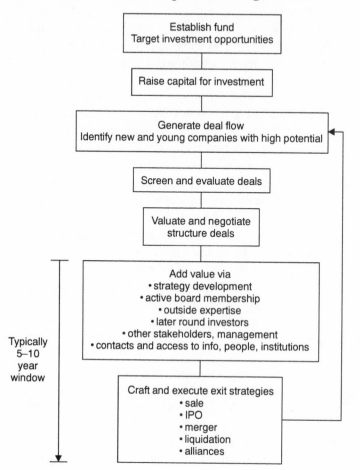

of a target investment opportunity or class of opportunities (e.g., PC software, biotechnology, energy, or materials specialization, or by stage of the venture or geography), which leads to a written proposal or prospectus to raise a venture capital fund. Once the money is raised, the value creation process moves from generating deals to crafting and executing harvest strategies and back to raising another fund. The process usually takes up to ten years to unfold, but exceptions in both directions often occur. For example, Lotus Development was founded by Mitch Kapor in mid-1981 and taken public in 1983. Lotus contrasts sharply with the seventeen-year cycle of the West Coast technology firm Boole & Babbage. B&B received its first venture capital in 1966, had several presidents replaced, and was finally able to make its initial public offering (IPO) in the very hot market of 1983.

Given the time necessary to build companies from scratch and to realize a gain and historical data indicating that only about one out of fifteen of these investments ever realize as much as ten times or more return on invested capital, these odds are daunting. (In Chapter 6, we will examine the actual performance, that is, rates of return, of venture capital funds.)

The venture capital process occurs in the context of mostly private, quite imperfect capital markets for new, emerging, and middle-market companies (i.e., those with $5–$100 million in sales). The availability and cost of this capital depend on a number of factors:

- perceived risk, in view of the quality of the management team and the opportunity
- industry, market, attractiveness of the technology, and fit
- upside potential and downside exposure
- anticipated growth rate
- age and stage of development
- amount of capital required
- founders' goals for growth, control, liquidity, and harvest
- fit with investors' goals and strategy
- relative bargaining positions of investors and founders

Figure 1-5 depicts the available private capital markets for risk and equity capital for companies with different sales goals and capital requirements, and at different stages of development. As can be seen, the various sources have preferences concerning how much money they will provide, when in the life of a company they are likely to invest, and the expected cost of the capital (or annual required rate of return). It is important to note that the dynamic character of this rather imperfect marketplace for capital is hard to appreciate from the static snapshot shown in Figure 1-5. Company valuations change from year to year, even from month to month or faster in turbulent periods and in different regions of the nation and the world, and for different companies. It is also evident from this figure that there are competing alternatives to venture capital.

Unfortunately for the economy, the vast majority of investing today is not the high value-adding, classic venture capital described

FIGURE 1-5 **Financing Life Cycles**

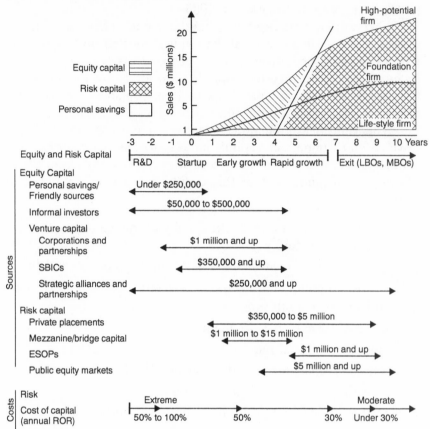

Source: J. A. Timmons et al., *New Venture Creation* (Homewood, IL: Richard D. Irwin, 1990), p. 408.

here, even though there has never been a greater need for capital to fund startup entrepreneurs with business ideas whose time has come.

ROOTS OF VENTURE CAPITAL

The roots of venture capital in the United States can be traced to the 1920s and 1930s, when wealthy families and individual investors provided the startup money for companies that would later become famous: Eastern Airlines, Xerox, and others. Most industry followers agree that the landmark event in venture capital occurred in 1946 with the formation of ARD, the first firm, as opposed to a private individual, to provide risk capital for new and rapidly growing firms, most of which were manufacturing and technology oriented. According to Patrick Liles, who has analyzed the firm in great detail, venture capital was the idea of Ralph E. Flanders, then president of the Federal Reserve Bank of Boston. Concerned about the lack of new company formation and the inability to tap institutional capital locked up in fiduciary funds by corporations, insurance companies, and other institutions, Flanders offered a unique proposal in an address to the National Association of Security Dealers in Chicago on November 16, 1945. At a time when there was no public institutional source of capital for new and young companies, Flanders argued in favor of freeing fiduciary funds from the restrictive requirements of the Investment Act of 1940, thereby enabling them to invest up to 5% of their assets in the equity of new enterprises. Wealthy families, such as the Paysons, Whitneys, and Rockefellers, had created private funds managed by individuals to seek out high-potential investment opportunities. As he put it:

> American business, American employment and the prosperity of the citizens of the country as a whole cannot be indefinitely assured under free enterprise unless there is a continuous birth of healthy infants in our business structure. We cannot depend safely for an indefinite time on the expansion of our old big industries alone. We need new strength, energy, and ability from below. We need to marry some small part of our enormous fiduciary resources to the new ideas which are seeking support.[6]

Flanders's views were supported by General Georges Doriot. Doriot, a professor at the Harvard Business School, was a long-time student and advocate for new and promising companies, and for years his course on the subject was one of the most popular at .Harvard Business School. He, Flanders, and a few colleagues believed that a great deal of the technology developed at MIT during World War II held great promise for commercial application. By tapping the pool of funds within financial institutions, they were certain they could create a private and independent entity—without government assistance—that could transform such technological research into viable enterprises. This entity—ARD—was organized under Massachusetts law on June 6, 1946. Its MIT roots were evident: Flanders and Doriot were joined by the entrepreneur Frederic C. Blackall, a director of the Federal Reserve Bank of Boston and member of the Corporation of MIT; Bradley Dewey, co-founder of Dewey and Almy Chemical Company and president of the American Chemical Society; Horace S. Ford, treasurer of MIT; Carl T. Compton, president of MIT; Edward R. Gilliland, professor of chemical engineering at MIT; and Jerome C. Hunsaker, head of MIT's Departments of Mechanical and Aeronautical Engineering. Distinguished lawyers and financiers were also among the founding group.

Raising the initial $5 million for this closed-end investment company proved to be a formidable challenge. Imagine trying to raise that sum today for an unproven concept. Imagine further the enormousness of the task if, despite numerous attempts, you have been unable to convince an underwriter to raise the money on any terms, none of the founding management team would be working full time, the key management team was led by a professor who planned to continue teaching, the prospectus and presentations made little mention of profit-making objectives, and, last, your primary mission seemed to be "to help build the economy." Most people experienced in such matters would say it could not be done.

Eventually, the officers and two investment bankers attempted to raise the funds, on a best-effort basis only, through the sale of 200,000 shares at $25 each. By late October 1946, the Dow Jones Industrial Average had fallen to 165, and only 139,930 shares of the offering had been sold, nevertheless netting $3.5 million—$500,000 more than the targeted minimum—for ARD. Of this sum, $1.8 million came from institutional investors. By the end of 1947, insurance companies (including John Hancock Mutual Life Insurance Company), investment companies (including Massachusetts Investors Trust), and universities (MIT, the University of Pennsylvania, and the University of Rochester) owned 49.6%, and the ARD directors and officers owned 45%. The three universities bought a total of 9,000 shares in order to provide a "means for their faculties to engage in outside activities which would be of direct financial benefit to the universities."[7] The fact that they exceeded the targeted minimum of $3 million is a testimony to the great vision behind this simple idea.

The principal sources of ARD's deals reflect its close ties to the Harvard and MIT communities, as well as the kinds of technology-based ventures that eventually transformed the economy of Boston through the birth of Route 128 (called America's Technology Highway). Its first investment, High Voltage Engineering Corporation (HVE), founded by five physicists and engineers from MIT, became one of the very first venture-capital-backed high-technology firms listed on the New York Stock Exchange. This deal was followed by Tracerlab and Circo Products, and by the end of 1947, ARD had invested in six startups and two existing ventures. This growth continued into the 1950s and led to the inevitable: negative cash flows in the fund and its cash-hungry portfolio companies, lack of both profitability and liquidity, lack of capital gains early on, and the inability to pay dividends. Throughout these first few years, says Liles, the "management and directors made no effort to generate enthusiasm over the firm's prospects."[8] Their communications to shareholders stated bluntly that they would not start showing earnings until the fourth year of operations and that "shareholders should understand and appreciate this."[9]

Continued active investing, negative cash flows, and conservative valuations of their portfolio companies led to other inevitabilities: a discounted price for ARD stock, a struggle over how to value the investments in such young, private companies, the need to raise more capital, and the initiation of fees for consulting to help cover staff salaries totaling $9,000 a year. Increasingly, Doriot and his advisers and directors became closely involved with their portfolio companies, providing technical and management assistance to help them grow. Doriot was quoted as saying that, in the early years, most of his portfolio companies had been "close to sudden death at least once," and that ARD's role was "to watch, push, worry, and spread hope."[10]

ARD sought additional capital in 1949, and its prospects looked promising after a cover story on General Doriot and ARD in *Business Week* and favorable articles in *Barron's* and *Fortune* appeared. Still, no underwriter could be found, and, by year end, 57% of the $4 million offering of 166,500 shares remained unsold, the balance having been sold privately.

There are enormous similarities between the learning curve of ARD in those formative years and what any new fund that concentrates on seed-stage, startup, and early-stage companies goes through today. The big difference, of course, is that in 1946 the concept of public venture capital had not been proven. Not until its fifth year, at the end of 1951, had ARD gained sufficient strength and liquidity to continue investing. By then, ten of its portfolio companies were operating at a profit; even so, its share price had dropped to $19. Understandably, by 1954, there was a discernible shift in ARD's philosophy to include a concern for profitability and an awareness of the need to pay dividends.

The single most decisive event in ARD's history was its

investment in 1957 in Digital Equipment Corporation (DEC), a company whose eventual success forever changed the future of the U.S. venture capital industry. The extraordinary success of DEC, the Massachusetts minicomputer manufacturer, rocketed venture capital into a new orbit and the modern era. Just under $70,000 gave ARD a 77% ownership position in the firm. DEC's meteoric rise, which increased the value of ARD's holdings by 5,000% by 1971, set the standard for venture capital in the 1970s and 1980s. This extraordinary achievement, and the similar successes of others that began to mimic DEC's ascent, radically extended the boundaries of what was possible in venture capital investing.

Little is known of how the investment was made and some of the reasons behind it. One version of the story suggests that General Doriot was not at all enthusiastic about making even a small investment in four MIT graduate students, all in their twenties, with an idea about computing. But Bill Congleton, a young associate and former student, was very excited about the venture's prospects. According to industry lore, the general thought that DEC presented an opportunity for young Congleton to learn some important lessons about the difficulties of picking winners. The early failure of a small investment would be instructive for his associate. Judging from the success of DEC, Congleton, who went on to form his own venture capital fund in Boston, never had to learn the lesson.

DEC's progress by 1960 enabled ARD to convince Lehman Brothers to underwrite an offering at $74.10 per share (a good deal more than the original $25 in 1947), which netted $8 million for the company. During the next ten years, with a very robust economy and buoyant stock market, DEC skyrocketed in value. By 1971, ARD's shares were valued at $355 million, and a year later ARD was sold to Textron, Inc., a large conglomerate, for the equivalent of $813 per original share. Since its inception, ARD had achieved a 14.7% compounded rate of return (ROR). Without DEC, the percentage would have been only 7.4%. Note the overwhelming impact of just one superstar investment on total portfolio return.

As a postwar catalyst of business development the policy has been a major influence in the transformation of areas such as Boston and Silicon Valley into high-technology economies. It proved the importance of and potential economic payoff in providing private venture capital and active assistance for fledgling companies. Doriot's underlying conviction about the need of fostering new enterprises as the key to further economic growth is as valid today, we believe, as it was in 1946.

ARD's approach was classic venture capital in the sense that it used only equity, invested for the longer term, and was prepared to live with losers and negative cash flows in the short term.

SMALL BUSINESS INVESTMENT COMPANIES

A second watershed event took place in 1958 when the Small Business Administration (SBA) established small business investment companies (SBICs). Inspired by the example of ARD and other private venture-capital funds, demand grew for the federal government to play an active role in mobilizing risk capital and improving small-company–building know-how. The SBIC Act was intended to create government-licensed and -regulated pools of venture capital to encourage the formation and development of new and early-stage ventures. While these funds were regulated by the Small Business Administration, investment decisions remained in private hands.

Legislation allowed organizers of SBICs to leverage four low-interest government dollars for each dollar they invested. The resulting capital structure has been both an anchor and an albatross for SBICs. Debt service requirements and the need eventually to repay federal government loans led to investing practices and philosophies very different from those pioneered by ARD. In order to meet their obligations to the government, SBICs structured their deals with a substantial amount of debt, as opposed to the all-equity route espoused by ARD, and confined their investing activities to established, more stable smaller firms with less volatile cash flows and earnings.

The instant availability of cheap government money brought financial entrepreneurs out of the woodwork. Many should have stayed there. By 1962, 585 SBICs were licensed, and by the mid-1960s the nearly 700 organized dominated the U.S. supply of risk and venture capital. The very difficult, cash-consuming, hands-on challenges described by Doriot in working with smaller companies were greatly underestimated by these new entrants into the venture capital arena. The inevitable result was reminiscent of today's shake-outs in the savings and loan industry. By 1966–1967, 232 SBICs were classified as problems, a major disaster by any standard. Charges of incompetence and even fraud tarnished the fledgling industry. New regulations were imposed to reduce the number of SBICs to 250, and by 1978 they accounted for only 21% of the available venture capital in the United States. One by-product of their demise was the emergence of private venture-capital funds, which, by 1968, surpassed the SBIC industry in total capital under management.

Another powerful force that contributed to some of the euphoria and excesses of SBICs was the soaring over-the-counter stock prices in 1968–1969, which fueled the hottest new issues market ever. Even the great binge of 1983 pales in comparison: nearly 1,000 small companies offered their stock to the public in 1968–1969. Underwritings of small company stocks reached $1.4 billion. This unprecedented activity reinforced the appealing logic that truly exceptional returns were possible for investors in the newly formed private venture-capital funds. After all, look at what General Doriot had done with DEC, argued those seeking to raise funds. The logic was irresistible in those heady times. Money poured in on the heels of these grand expectations—more than $200 million in 1969 alone (roughly equivalent to $700 million in 1990 dollars). Opportunities to invest in early-stage private companies, with prospects for cashing out with a public offering, seemed boundless.

But the stock market soured rapidly by late 1969, and thinly traded stocks of small companies led the pack in a downward spiral. Recessionary pressures and significant tax increases to fund the Vietnam War spelled catastrophe for the venture capital industry, and its death was reported in leading business publications. The frenzy of investing activity in the late 1960s, especially in newer companies, led to precisely the same traumatic difficulties experienced by ARD in the early days: negative cash flows in both the parent firm and in the portfolio companies; losses and the need for more cash; and some failures. But there was a big difference: ARD and other private venture-capital funds specialized in all or nearly all-equity investments, thus sparing themselves the additional burden of debt service in the early going. After all, it had been proven time and time again since ARD's inception in 1946, that the task of spotting and building successful small companies was an extremely hazardous trade, time- and cash-consuming, and management intensive.

The recession triggered by the oil embargo in 1974–1975 could not have come at a worse time for many SBIC-backed companies with debt-laden capital structures, declining sales, and negative cash flow. Clearly, the early 1970s was not a good time to be a publicly traded venture-capital firm like ARD. Part of the decision to sell out to Textron in 1972 was undoubtedly motivated by the signals being read and anticipated by ARD. Initial public offerings for small companies totaled only $16 million in 1975, a small fraction of the 1968–1969 boom. Faced with a dormant new-issues market, investors began to search elsewhere for opportunities—in expansion financing and eventually, in management and leveraged buyouts. Capital commitments to the venture capital industry dropped steadily through 1977 to $50 million a year and less. The number of venture capital professionals and their activities shrank. Especially hard hit were startup and early-stage investing, which were nearly nonexistent through the mid-1970s. Institutional investors questioned the viability of long-term investing and the inevitable illiquidity associated with it. ARD watchers, once awed by its success, developed misgivings about the appropriateness of publicly owned entities carrying on such investing activities, because of the high visibility associated with being a public firm. Many observers feared that the venture capital industry could not survive in its existing form. Such a fate held profound implications for investors, entrepreneurs, and, less appreciated at the time, the vitality and competitive resiliency of the U.S. economy itself.

The lessons of the SBIC movement and ARD provided an impetus to create a new industry structure, more durable and less subject to short-term evaluation, that could truly engage in equity-based venture-capital investing. This led to the evolution in the late 1970s and 1980s of the ten-year, private partnership structure that we know today. Besides, as the ARD experience had proven, finding the one DEC that will distinguish your entire fund performance is, at best, a risky, specialized, and very difficult type of investing, and, at worst, a random event.

A NEW ERA

As noted earlier, the U.S. venture capital industry all but shut down between 1970 and 1977. Looking back it seems inconceivable that this ever happened: the 1980s were remarkably buoyant for venture capital, and today's $30+ billion pool of venture capital in the United States alone, plus another $30 billion in Western Europe, indicates continued strength. Fortunately, 1978 was the first of the four most critical years in the eventual explosion of the global venture-capital industry. Working diligently throughout the 1970s to revive the comatose industry, venture capitalists, entrepreneurs, and sympathetic members of Congress and the Carter administration led the way to a more favorable climate. With echoes of Flanders's and Doriot's call for less restrictive securities and tax legislation reverberating on Capitol Hill, five monumental legislative initiatives were enacted that dramatically altered the genetic code of American venture capital. Figure 1-6 summarizes these and other key legislative changes, but five merit further discussion here:

- The *1978 Revenue Act* reduced the prevailing capital gains tax rate from 49½% to 28%, thereby creating the first major tax incentive for long-term equity investments since the late 1960s. This resulted in a tenfold increase in capital commitments for venture capital funds during the following year.

FIGURE 1-6 **Legislative Impact on Venture Capital Investment**

Small Business Act of 1958	Increased the availability of venture capital for small business.
Employment Retirement Income Security Act (1974)	Discouraged plan fiduciary incentives for high-risk investments.
1978 Revenue Act	Provided capital gains tax incentive for equity investments. Capital committed increased by 556 million from previous year.
ERISA's "Prudent Man" Rule (1979)	Clarified investment guidelines for pension investors to allow for higher risk investments.
Small Business Investment Incentive Act (1980)	Redefined venture firms as business development companies, eliminating the need for registering as an investment advisor.
ERISA's "Safe Harbor" Regulation (1980)	Stated that venture managers would not be considered fiduciaries of plan assets.
Economic Recovery Tax Act (1981)	Lowered capital gains rate. Capital commitments doubled to $1.3 billion in 1981.
Tax Reform Act of 1986	Reduced incentive for long-term capital gains.

Source: T. A. Soja and J. E. Reyes, *Investment Benchmarks: Venture Capital* (Needham, MA: Venture Economics, Inc., 1990), p. 202.

- The 1979 ERISA *"Prudent Man" Rule* governing investment guidelines for pension fund managers was revised and clarified to allow for higher-risk investments, including venture capital arrangements.
- The 1980 *Small Business Investment Incentive Act* redefined venture capital firms as business development companies, removing the need for them to register as investment advisers with the Securities and Exchange Commission (SEC). Fewer reporting requirements and the elimination of the risk of violating investment adviser regulations gave investors more flexibility.
- The 1980 ERISA *"Safe Harbor" Regulation* stated clearly that venture-capital fund managers would not be considered fiduciaries of pension fund assets invested in the pools (venture capital partnerships) that they managed. This gave venture capitalists more freedom and removed a serious risk exposure in accepting pension funds as limited partners.
- The 1981 *Economic Recovery Tax Act* lowered further the capital gains tax rate paid by individuals from 28% to 20%, causing a twofold increase in commitments to venture capital funds in 1981.

Singularly and collectively, these five pieces of legislation completely revamped the venture capital industry, both immediately and throughout the next decade to the present, resulting in a tenfold increase in the size of the U.S. venture capital pool. The stage was set for the dawn of a new, unprecedented era in venture capital. Ignition and lift-off would occur in 1979, and the venture capital industry would rocket into the 1980s.

THE 1980s: VENTURE CAPITAL TURNS BALLISTIC

All the gloom and doom of the 1970s was reversed as suddenly as the stock market had gone south in 1969. Figure 1-7 shows just how quickly the flow of new capital commitments turned around: a tenfold jump in 1980, then double that in ensuing years, rising to a peak of nearly $5 billion in 1987—a rate of new capital formation nearly fifty times greater than that of the 1970s.*

---

*Throughout the book, we refer to the money that limited partners supply to venture capital funds for general partners to manage and invest as "capital commitments." Monies general partners invest in portfolio companies we call "disbursements."

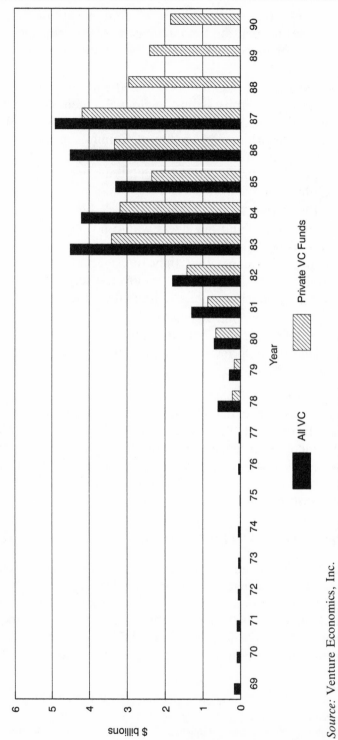

FIGURE 1-7 New Venture Capital Commitments, 1969–1990

Source: Venture Economics, Inc.
Note: Numbers after 1987 were reported only for independent private funds.

Accompanying this astonishing growth came a rush of entrepreneurial activity—from raw startups, to leveraged and management buyouts, to initial public offerings—that was totally unprecedented in the history of American enterprise. Invisibly to most, the U.S. venture capital industry in 1978 was beginning a radical metamorphosis. From the outside, the industry appeared to be small (about 225 firms), tightly knit, quite homogeneous in strategy and practice, and unusually cooperative in doing deals. Competition for deals was weak, since few financing alternatives existed and the number of players in the business was limited. Venture capitalists shared deal flow and information concerning due diligence and co-invested frequently. They shared board seats together. The sanguine described them as "the ultimate old-boy network," while cynics said they were "like sheep following sheep."

Before 1980, venture-capital investing activities could be called dormant: just $460 million was invested in 375 companies in 1979.[11] But at its peak in 1987, the industry had ballooned to more than 700 venture capital firms, which invested $3.94 billion in 1,729 portfolio companies (see Figure 1-8). The sleepy, cottage industry of the 1970s was transformed into a vibrant, at times frenetic, occasionally myopic, and dynamic market for private risk and equity capital in the 1980s. Even the SBIC industry had rebounded

FIGURE 1-8 **Venture Capital Investment by Year, 1979–1989**

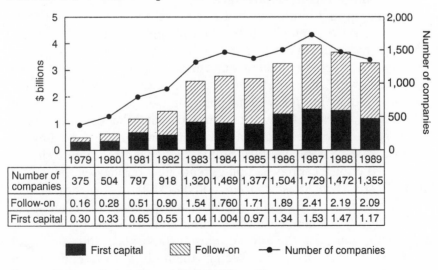

	1979	1980	1981	1982	1983	1984	1985	1986	1987	1988	1989
Number of companies	375	504	797	918	1,320	1,469	1,377	1,504	1,729	1,472	1,355
Follow-on	0.16	0.28	0.51	0.90	1.54	1.760	1.71	1.89	2.41	2.19	2.09
First capital	0.30	0.33	0.65	0.55	1.04	1.004	0.97	1.34	1.53	1.47	1.17

■ First capital   ▨ Follow-on   —●— Number of companies

Source: Venture Capital Journal (July 1990), p. 14.

and expanded—by the late 1980s, it consisted of 450 firms. (However, it had also become a less significant supplier of venture capital, accounting for only 1% by 1989.)

THE 1990s: THE INCREDIBLE SHRINKING VENTURE-CAPITAL INDUSTRY

By 1990, the venture capital rocket had sputtered and fallen back to earth. Consider some of the following observations, gathered at industry and board meetings and elsewhere from 1989 to 1991:

- "Venture capital has changed forever, and when the shake-out is over, it won't return to the good old days."
- "Venture and risk capital have increasingly become less available to deserving startup and growth companies."
- "Venture capitalists have become increasingly greedy."
- "Returns, both overall and to the limited partners, do not match the 20% to 50% per annum range the investors have come to expect."

Yet another crisis struck the SBIC movement. Since the program's inception, almost one-third of all SBICs had gone into liquidation. By mid-1990, 159 were reportedly in liquidation, owing Uncle Sam $476 million. One SBA study shows potential SBIC losses of more than $800 million.[12]

Compared to the pre-1980s, we are looking at a radically altered venture-capital industry. According to one entrepreneur, "Savvy entrepreneurs will avoid some venture capitalists at any cost, while carefully seeking out certain highly credible venture capitalists with the reputation for bringing unusual know-how, business judgment and wisdom, and contacts to the companies in which they invest." Others have noted that "the venture capital industry has been restructuring itself in a way that is eroding its historic role."[13] One venture-capital-backed entrepreneur simply stated, "Venture capitalists don't create new businesses, they steal them." *The Wall Street Journal* noted a shift in the earlier role: "Traditional venture capital concerns will provide a smaller share of the money for new businesses, compared with the 1980s."[14]

Even some of the oldest, most established, and successful firms in the industry are seeing themselves differently these days. Take, for instance, one of the country's true megafunds, TA Associates:

TA Associates is no longer, strictly speaking, a venture firm. Its new brochure doesn't even mention the once-magic phrase on its cover. Instead, the more ambiguous phrase, "private equity capital" is employed. TA has been moving off into what looks suspiciously like a variation on the theme of merchant banking.[15]

At the October 1990 Venture Forum, TA managing partner C. Kevin Landry's perspective on the current state of the industry was that "this is not the first time we have had a shake-out and it will not be the last, but it is not going to be as easy or as pleasant as the last, 1975–1976."

Despite the current pessimism, other enterprising investors like Ben Rosen, lead investor in Lotus Development Corporation and Compaq Computer Corporation, see opportunity ahead: "Conventional wisdom holds that . . . there is a lull in the industry and that there is no new technology and the returns are lousy. I'm a contrarian and I believe conventional wisdom is always wrong, whether in the stock market or in venture capital."[16]

John Doerr of San Francisco's Kleiner Perkins Caufield & Byers, one of the most successful funds ever, also discounted the current gloom. Speaking at the 1990 Venture Forum, he noted that the business press and others are reporting that "the game is over" and that "we have gathered here to mourn the ending of an era." He went on to contend that such pessimism is all wrong because the business is not a zero-sum game and several significant trends will create opportunities for billion-dollar companies in the 1990s. Doerr believes the most promising opportunities include instrumentation for human gene screening, the development of more effective pharmaceutical products for the aging population, a new generation of audiovisual, pen-based computing, new discoveries in neurobiology, and automated designer chemicals. There have been some twelve hundred biotechnology companies started with a mean survival time of eighteen months before they need additional funding; he sees many opportunities in this and related fields. Particularly revealing was Doerr's comment that "the biggest shortage is the people [i.e., entrepreneurs and investors] with the know-how [to build the companies], not the capital."

CONCLUSION

The aim of this chapter was to provide an overview and introduction to venture capital. This will provide a context for subsequent chapters, which examine some of the recent trends, developments, and practices that characterize the industry today and look at what the future holds for the industry, suppliers and users of risk capital, and the nation's economy.

One clear conclusion about the venture capital industry emerges: it is at a new crossroads. Facing turmoil, a period of transition, and a search for a new vision, the "incredibly shrinking venture capital industry"[17] of the 1990s is very different from what it was ten or twenty years ago. Ironically, while the investment environment and stream of opportunities are the best in years, the number of partnerships, deals, and dollars under management in private venture-capital partnerships peaked in 1987 and is declining for the first time since the late 1970s. The 1990s unfold on the heels of an unprecedented industry shake-out.

CHAPTER 2

Where Is the Venture in Venture Capital?

IN BOTH SIZE AND MENTALITY, today's venture-capital industry is light years away from its predecessor of just ten years ago. And not all the changes are good news. We argue that two dominant forces have led to major changes. First, classic venture-capital skills that add value in company forming, building, and harvesting have been largely replaced by financial engineering know-how, which emphasizes deal making, transaction crafting and closing, and fee generating and is obsessed with short-term gains. A more appropriate label for this neoventure capital might be "merchant capital," a hybrid that combines the seed, startup, and early-stage investing of classic venture capitalists with expansion, growth, and development financing reminiscent of merchant banks and with the investment-banking transaction mentality of many LBO and MBO specialists. These changes extend far beyond the tremendous increase in the total pool of money in the United States (around $33 billion by 1990).

DUAL FORCES TRANSFORM AN INDUSTRY

Profound changes have taken and are taking place that we believe are here to stay. Internal and external forces have led to a transformation of the venture capital industry. Some of these changes will make for a healthier and more profitable industry in the 1990s. Still other changes pose danger signals with troubling implications for the nation, and point to a need for both alternative sources of venture capital, a more constructive national policy toward entrepreneurship, and a revival of classic venture capital. We offer some fresh ideas for how this can be done in the final chapter, but do not advocate a monolithic national industrial policy board.

The collision of two sweeping forces transformed the venture capital industry in the 1980s. First, the industry experienced significant shifts in investing strategies and practices and in the basic structures and boundaries that, till then, had been reasonably stable and predictable. Second, these internal changes collided with substantially altered market factors. The effect of each of these upon the other was compounded, and dramatic. A new industry resulted. Figure 2-1 summarizes what we believe to be the causes of this transformation.

Why has there been a perversion of classic venture capital, a wellspring of both innovation and extraordinary rewards? There are new boundaries, know-how, and strategic purpose in the now global, $80+ billion venture capital industry. What does this mean for the nation and the industry?

DOMINANT INTERNAL FORCES: STRATEGIES AND STRUCTURES

Five distinct internal forces were at work in the U.S. venture capital industry during the 1980s. Individually, they are significant; collectively they constitute a major development.

Classic Venture Capital Deemphasized and Avoided

The venture capital industry apparently rose from the dead in the 1980s, but was it the same after its visit to the underworld? Consider the trend in startup and early-stage investments. On average for the three years from 1978 to 1980, 58 startups were reported by Venture Economics, Inc. Ten years later (in 1989), just 146 startups were reported, far behind the overall venture-capital industry growth rate. What was worse, from 1985 through 1989, the number of investments made declined steadily from 255 to 146. During the same period, the dollars invested also declined sharply from $329.4 million to $286.7 million. (Given that the 1989 figure would have had to have been $419 million just to keep up with an annual inflation rate of 5%, the decline was even worse than it appears at first.) Startup financings peaked in 1983, accounting for 43% of the deals done, then, as Figure 2-2 shows, declined steadily from 1985 on, accounting for only 10% of the 1,437 companies that received financing and just 9% of the total capital invested in

FIGURE 2-1 Transformation of the U.S. Venture Capital Industry, 1980–1990

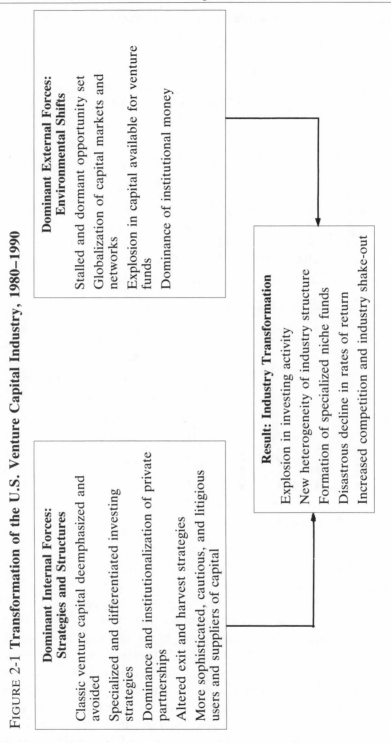

Dominant External Forces: Environmental Shifts

Stalled and dormant opportunity set

Globalization of capital markets and networks

Explosion in capital available for venture funds

Dominance of institutional money

Dominant Internal Forces: Strategies and Structures

Classic venture capital deemphasized and avoided

Specialized and differentiated investing strategies

Dominance and institutionalization of private partnerships

Altered exit and harvest strategies

More sophisticated, cautious, and litigious users and suppliers of capital

Result: Industry Transformation

Explosion in investing activity

New heterogeneity of industry structure

Formation of specialized niche funds

Disastrous decline in rates of return

Increased competition and industry shake-out

FIGURE 2-2 **Disbursements by Financing Stage, 1985–1989**

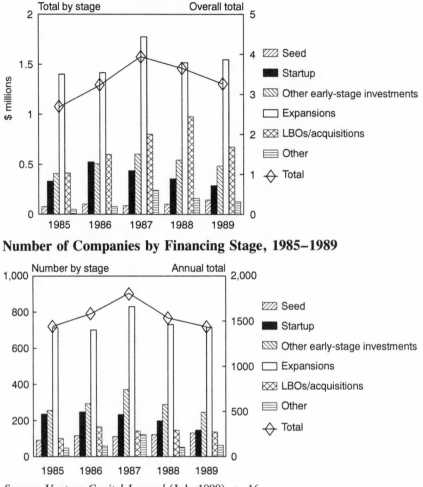

Number of Companies by Financing Stage, 1985–1989

Source: Venture Capital Journal (July 1990), p. 16.

1989. (The same pattern is true internationally as we shall see in Chapter 3.)

Other early-stage investing also declined, though not as severely. The number of deals declined slightly from 255 in 1985 to 245 in 1989; the dollar amount grew, but at less than a 5% inflation rate. By 1990, just 5% of the *Inc.* 500 fastest-growing companies in America were backed by venture capital. In the meantime, from 1985 to 1989, the number of deals and dollars for expansion financing, LBOs, acquisitions, and other investments continued to grow. Expansion financing grew steadily until 1987, when it accounted for 46% of the deals and 45% of the dollars invested.

LBO and acquisition financing, a new domain for the 1980s, peaked in 1988, representing 10% of the deals and 27% of the dollars invested. This is nearly the reverse of the pattern of the decade before.*

Targeted investments have shifted as well, moving away from the ground-breaking computer hardware technology areas. In Figures 2-3 and 2-4, we combined 1978 to 1980 and 1987 to 1989 data, showing the dollars and number of deals done in different industry sectors. In the more recent period, computer hardware, long an

---

*Industry data are subject to some recent definitional changes so it is not possible to do further apple versus apple comparisons with the late 1970s.

FIGURE 2-3 **Venture Capital Investment by Industry Sector, 1978–1980 ($1.354 billion invested)**

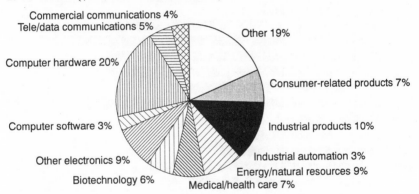

Venture Capital Investment by Industry Sector, 1978–1980 (2,646 investments)

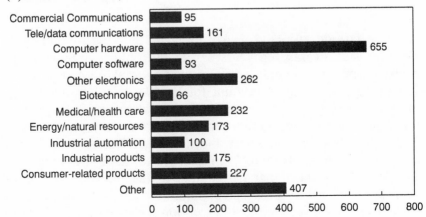

Sector	Investments
Commercial Communications	95
Tele/data communications	161
Computer hardware	655
Computer software	93
Other electronics	262
Biotechnology	66
Medical/health care	232
Energy/natural resources	173
Industrial automation	100
Industrial products	175
Consumer-related products	227
Other	407

Source: Venture Economics, Inc.

FIGURE 2-4 **Venture Capital Investment by Industry Sector, 1987–1989 ($10.855 billion invested)**

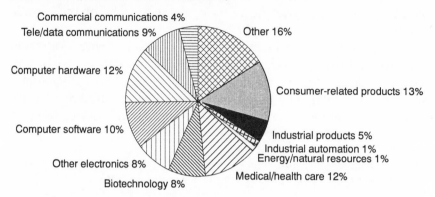

Venture Capital Investment by Industry Sector, 1987–1989 (15,351 investments)

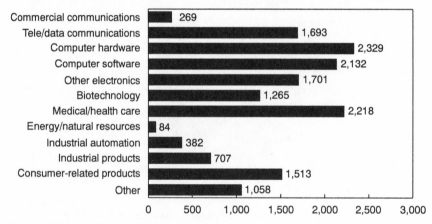

Source: Venture Economics, Inc.

industry darling, attracted nearly the same number of dollars as were invested overall ten years earlier but only four times more deals, despite the tenfold increase in the total pool of capital. Several reasons seem to account for this decline. For one thing, the great microprocessor technology wave of the 1970s has yet to find a successor in the computer industry. For another, blood baths in the hard-disk–drive industry and, to a lesser extent, in personal computers such as Osborne Computer, have made investors gun-shy. We also suspect that newcomers to the industry may have been seduced by the prospect of relatively easy money in later-stage and LBO investments, a perception fueled by the junk bond euphoria of the mid- to late 1980s. Certainly, these had to look a lot more appealing than the time-intensive, painstaking, hands-on involvement so characteristic of classic venture-capital investing. Certainly, evaluating and investing in an established business with some track record and in-place management was more understandable than trying to figure out if a scientist, computer wizard, or engineering genius could turn an untried concept into a growth business.

Large increases have occurred in computer software, with about twenty-three times more deals done compared to 1978–1980, and in biotechnology, with a nineteenfold increase. Medical/health care and tele- and data communications (including cellular) kept pace, with tenfold increases in the number of deals done in these fields. These were the new growth industries of the 1980s, and technology breakthroughs and new commercial applications in all of these fields continue today. An aging population will continue to create robust demand for medical services, health care, and the products of biotechnology, while many experts believe telecommunications is still in its infancy. Even with the spectacular growth of the cellular industry, the market penetration in 1990 was a scant 3½%! As has always been the case, venture capitalists do have a nose for new opportunities, and placing their bets in the industries of the future is in the tradition of classic venture capital.

The number of "other electronics" and consumer-related deals increased almost seven times, respectively, in this same period. The growth in consumer-related deals—utterly ignored historically as an investment target—was surprisingly significant: from 4% in 1980 to 13% in 1988. This trend continued in 1989 and 1990, as the consumer area tied for the largest sector. Note also that the medical/health care area had become one of the hottest fields by 1990.

Ironically, given current uncertainties in world energy prices, the biggest loser of all was "energy/natural resources," which all but disappeared from the range of venture capital activities, despite the tenfold increase in money available.

Specialized and Differentiated Investing Strategies

The pre-1980s industry was characterized by strikingly similar investing strategies and criteria. There was a homogeneity anchored in the quest for the superdeal described in Chapter 1. As the 1980s unfolded, a new phenomenon appeared in the form of focused and specialized investment strategies. Especially in terms of the strategic focus and the stage of investment the fund was seeking, a major shift evolved. For the first time, entire funds devised strategies quite different from classic venture capital's. Some targeted LBO deals only, while others focused on mezzanine investing or seed-stage deals. Others sought industry or technology areas where they believed they could achieve competitive edges. These included biotechnology, waste and environmental technologies, and, for the first time, retail and service businesses. A new breed of uniquely skilled specialists began to craft strategies to match their strengths to the investment opportunities they knew best.

Dominance and Institutionalization of Private Partnerships

A significant structural change, begun in the 1960s and early 1970s, became the standard legal form of venture capital funds in the 1980s: the ten-year partnership. The dominance of the private partnership in the 1980s paved the way for one of the important external forces of the decade: the emergence of institutional inves-tors, especially pension funds, as the primary source of capital for venture funds. The ten-year partnership offered both a tax-friendly structure and enough longevity to attract institutional investors for longer-term commitments. As investors and their lawyers became familiar with this legal form, it gained acceptance, which helped accelerate the pace at which funds could be raised and closed. Theoretically at least, the ten-year life of each fund enabled general partners to take a truly long-term perspective, resisting any pres-sures for short-term performance. (As we shall see, in practice, this did not always hold true.)

Altered Exit and Harvest Strategies

Venture capital liquidity is quite sensitive to the health and vibrancy of the over-the-counter (OTC) stock markets, as our research has demonstrated empirically (see Chapter 7). Historically, the ability to harvest an investment depended heavily on a hot new-issues market. Such was the case in the great IPO binge of 1983, when nearly 700 small companies had initial public offerings and raised nearly $6 billion (see Figure 2-5). The strong rates of return of funds formed in the 1970s were undoubtedly bolstered by 1983's buoyant IPO market. Another robust year by historical standards was 1986, though it wasn't nearly as strong as 1983.

All this ended suddenly with the October 19, 1987, stock market crash. The OTC markets for new issues essentially shut down in 1988 and 1989, dropping to barely a quarter of the activity

FIGURE 2-5 **Amount Raised by IPOs, 1969–1988**

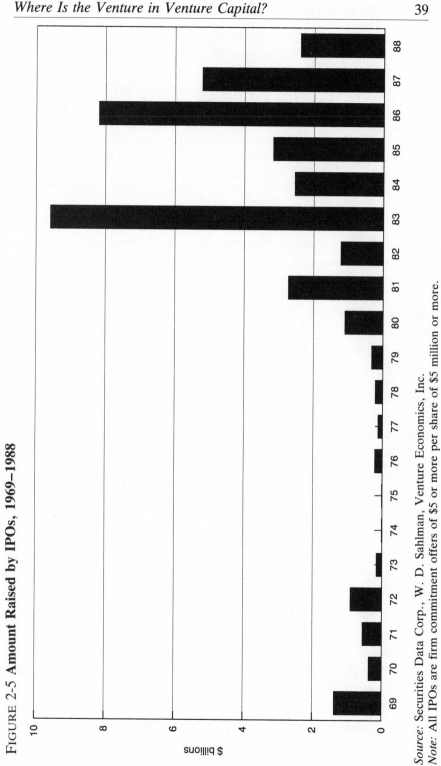

Source: Securities Data Corp., W. D. Sahlman, Venture Economics, Inc.
Note: All IPOs are firm commitment offers of $5 or more per share of $5 million or more.

in 1983 and one-third of that in 1986. The problem was not a lack of small companies ready for the market. The burst of startup activity in 1982–1985 (recall that 43% of all deals done in 1983 were startups) had created the biggest ever pipeline of growing companies. By 1987, many were in registration to go public. There was a parallel increase in new companies not backed by venture capital, nearly tripling the pool of candidates for IPOs.

This pattern recurred after the August 2, 1990, invasion of Kuwait by Iraq. What had been the best year since the 1987 crash for new issues suddenly turned sour. Only one of sixteen offerings of one active underwriter—Robertson, Stephens—succeeded in going public: EASEL Corporation went public but with a substantially reduced number of shares and price. By winter, the market was still dormant, although in 1991 it rebounded significantly, especially for biotechnology issues.

With the evaporation of the traditional IPO exit route, new and alternative exit strategies and mechanisms surfaced, principally in the form of acquisitions by private and public companies. In 1989, acquisition exits outpaced exits via IPOs for the third year in a row (see Figure 2-6).[1]

Foreign investors provided American venture capitalists with exit opportunities in the late 1980s and into the 1990s. Cash-rich Japanese companies, riding the wave of a strong yen, saw higher valuations (by U.S. standards) as bargains and sought access to vital technology that could bolster their strategic position.[2] Kubota, the tractor and farm equipment company, made aggressive strategic moves to acquire venture-capital-backed high-technology companies in the United States, among them:

- $26 million for 20% of MIPS Computer Systems, Inc., the Sunnyvale developer of the RISC-based microprocessor
- $10 million for 15% of Rasna Corporation, a San Jose, California, manufacturer of mechanical engineering programs
- $6 million for 9.2% of Exabyte Corporation, the Boulder, Colorado, manufacturer of high-capacity cartridge-tape subsystems for data storage
- $12 million for 25% of an optical-storage joint venture in San Jose, California
- $20 million for an outright purchase of Akashic Memories Corporation, the Santa Clara, California, producer of thin-film magnetic storage disks

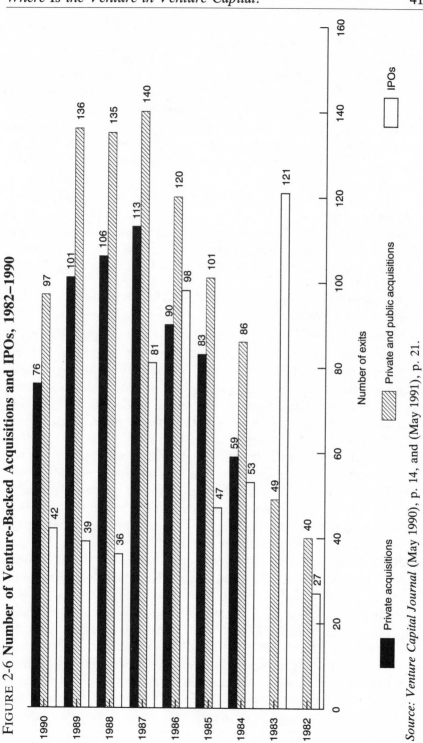

FIGURE 2-6 **Number of Venture-Backed Acquisitions and IPOs, 1982–1990**

Private acquisitions

Private and public acquisitions

IPOs

Number of exits

Source: Venture Capital Journal (May 1990), p. 14, and (May 1991), p. 21.

Kubota's acquisitions provided exits and higher valuations for venture capital investors and management.

Major U.S. firms were also active acquirers of venture-backed companies, including, among others, in 1989: Hewlett-Packard Co.; M/A COM, Inc.; Daisey Systems Corporation; Novell, Inc.; Bellsouth; Blockbuster Entertainment Corp.; Lear Seigler Holdings Corp.; K mart Corp.; Abbott Laboratories; AT&T Co.; and Paramount Communications Inc., to note some. (For a detailed summary of the 1989 activity, see *Venture Capital Journal* [May 1990], pp. 16–29.)

During the spring of 1991, the IPO market began to experience a healthy revival, led by biotechnology stocks. Until such time as it stages a complete rebound, however, acquisition-minded larger firms, especially Japanese, German, and British firms, will likely continue to be a major source of exits for U.S. venture capitalists.

More Sophisticated, Cautious, and Litigious Users and Suppliers of Capital

A by-product of the explosive growth of the venture capital industry is a much more savvy and sophisticated group of suppliers (especially the institutional investors and pension fund managers) and users (the entrepreneurs and companies) of capital than existed in 1979. Institutional investors now demand tougher terms and conditions for placing their money with a new group, starting with negotiations over the carried interest. In the 1970s, the eighty–twenty split between the limited partners and general partners was a given. Today, it is negotiated and can be closer to eighty-five–fifteen or, in rare instances, as high as 25% for the general partners. Increasingly, limited partners may insist on a minimum threshold rate of return (say, the thirty-year Treasury bill rate) before the general partners are entitled to any distribution of gains. Further, they are demanding management fees lower than the traditional 2.5% to 3% of the total capital raised. The stark reality is that a smaller fund of less than $40 to $50 million simply cannot provide the hands-on, management-intensive, value-added company-building role with anything less than 2.5%. Limited partners may tighten the screws on a fund and get the general partners to agree to less, but the deck is then stacked against ever achieving the high returns the limited partners were seeking in the first place. And many limiteds are unwilling to index the fees to inflation. Armed with a more sophisticated band of lawyers and advisers who have gained their savvy in venture capital in the 1980s, today's investors are a warier bunch.

Similarly, the entrepreneurs and companies who seek capital from the venture funds are also more sophisticated. Bill Egan of Burr, Egan & Deleage recently put it this way: "Ten years ago if entrepreneurs approached us with a complete, well-done business plan it gave them a real competitive advantage. Today it doesn't matter nearly as much since they all have great business plans." Entrepreneurs have become more knowledgeable and informed about the ins and outs of raising venture capital. They have learned where and how to search for capital; which are the funds to look for and look out for; how to identify the best lawyers, consultants, and accountants and which ones to avoid. This awareness has been propelled by America's "silent revolution" of entrepreneurship during the past twenty years.[3] A plethora of know-how became available through books, videos, college and adult education courses, seminars, and conferences and from a growing cadre of entrepreneurs, venture capitalists, and other professionals who make a living in the entrepreneurial process. Groups such as the American Electronic Association, *Venture Capital Journal,* MIT Enterprise Forum, the Babson College Entrepreneurial Exchange, Harvard Business School New Enterprise Club, Silicon Valley Entrepreneurs Club, and others have created networks and information exchanges for entrepreneurs and investors alike. The largest Big Six accounting firm, Ernst & Young, even has an entire nationwide department of entrepreneurial services (on an equal footing with the audit, tax, and special industries department) devoted to new and middle-market companies.

DOMINANT EXTERNAL FORCES: ENVIRONMENTAL SHIFTS

Externally, four major changes in the 1980s contributed significantly to the industry's transformation by decade's end. Combined with the strategic changes within the industry just noted, a powerful momentum began that reshaped the competitive rules of the game and its performance.

Stalled and Dormant Opportunity Set

An extraordinary burst of new technology-based ventures that began in the 1970s and continued well into the 1980s rode the crest of the microprocessor-based technology wave. Applications of the microprocessor made possible radical productivity breakthroughs, the personal computer industry, and a host of other microprocessor-based product innovations in nearly every industry sector from consumer electronics to automobiles to medicine to tele- and cellular communications. Biotechnology provided another impetus for new-company formation. In essence, the 1980s was working with an entirely new opportunity set, unlike anything the venture capital industry had experienced previously.

Yet, during the decade itself, and as the 1990s began, these opportunities had become dormant. This is not to say that new technologies and product innovations have stopped. Rather, there was no dominant new technology wave upon which new venture creation and capital formation could ride. Further, stalled technology inevitably depressed investing activity and rates of return, contributing to the shift away from classic venture capital.

Globalization of Capital Markets and Networks

One of the most dramatic developments over the past ten years has been the global growth of venture capital to over $80 billion by 1990. In 1979, venture capital was virtually nonexistent outside the United States. In 1988, the annual statistics told a different story: Europe and the United Kingdom exceeded for the first time ever the total amount of capital raised by venture funds in the United States ($4.1 billion versus $2.95 billion). Even more astonishing, in 1989, $6.28 billion of new capital flowed into the European venture capital pools, while U.S. commitments continued to decline. Further, the total venture capital pool in Europe was rapidly approaching the size of the U.S. pool: $24.8 billion versus $33.4 billion. Canada, Australia, and a host of other countries in Asia, South America, and Africa have also experimented with or created substantial venture-capital industries. And the former Soviets have a great interest in how the American venture-capital industry works.

This startling reversal globally has important implications in helping to spread free-market democracy to the rest of the world and to mobilize capital in Europe. It also raises the question of when the United Kingdom and European shake-out will begin. If there was a shortage of talent in the industry in America in the 1980s, then there must be an even greater shortfall of knowledgeable and experienced venture capitalists abroad.

Explosion in Capital Available for Venture Funds

Capital became available after 1979 in quantities even the industry gurus found mind numbing. As shown earlier, capital trickled into the industry at a paltry rate of $50 million or less by the mid-1970s. Stunningly, in 1980, commitments reached $1 billion, exceeded $2 billion in 1982, and surpassed $4 billion in 1983.

Never in the industry's short history had capital been available in such quantities. There seemed to be no end in sight to this bonanza. Any astute observer who subscribes to the theory that excesses beget excesses that beget imprudence can envision how the seeds of self-immolation began to be sown unknowingly in the industry in the early 1980s.

Dominance of Institutional Money

Historically, wealthy families and individuals had been the dominant source of money for venture capital pools, accounting for 32%, for instance, in 1978, when pension funds were a distant fourth, accounting for just 15% of the capital committed to venture funds in that year (see Figure 2-7). But legislative changes effected in 1978 profoundly altered sources of money for venture capital funds. By 1988, pension funds had become by far the dominant source of capital, accounting for 46% of the total that year (see Figure 2-8). Most conspicuous by their absence were the individuals and families of wealth, plummeting to about one-sixth of their

FIGURE 2-7 **Distribution of Venture Capital Sources, 1978 (new funds: $216 million)**

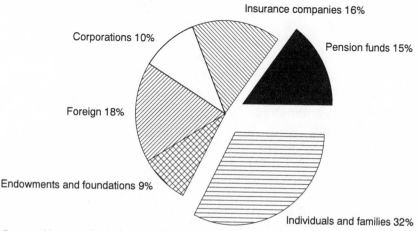

Insurance companies 16%

Corporations 10%

Pension funds 15%

Foreign 18%

Endowments and foundations 9%

Individuals and families 32%

Source: Venture Capital Journal.

FIGURE 2-8 **Distribution of Venture Capital Sources, 1988 (new funds: $2.95 billion)**

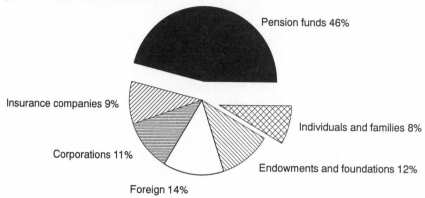

Pension funds 46%

Insurance companies 9%

Individuals and families 8%

Corporations 11%

Endowments and foundations 12%

Foreign 14%

Source: Venture Capital Journal.

earlier importance with just 8% of the total in 1988. Interestingly, foreign investors accounted for the second greatest proportion of new funding sources in both 1978 and 1988, illustrating the attractiveness of U.S. companies and their markets.

Nineteen eighty-nine was a down year for new commitments in general; all sources—except corporations and insurance companies—cut back their funding of private venture-capital partnerships. Still, foreign investors committed $499 million, ranking them fourth, just behind insurance companies at $303 million. Most notably, pension funds reduced their commitments by 36% in 1989, as their managers sought alternative investment opportunities.

In less than a decade, venture capital formation in the United States had become almost entirely dependent on institutional investors, both domestic and foreign, and with it pressures that have contributed to the perversion of classic venture capital.[4]

As funds grew larger, tripling over the decade on average from $18 million in 1979 to $49.5 million in 1989, the average size of deals and the minimum dollars invested also escalated. Funds simply could not invest monies in anything smaller than large chunks and make investments pay. This, by definition, pressured venture capitalists to move away from startups to later-stage financings that required more funds per deal. Larger funds were the first to move away from very-early-stage deals. To exacerbate the situation, the explosion in LBOs fueled the appetite for bigger deals and shorter holding periods. One venture capitalist summed it up this way: "Every venture capitalist is feeling the need to generate quick returns." Knowledgeable investors were keenly aware that it could take five or more years for a startup to reach a harvest stage, while a more mature company could deliver a product within six to eighteen months and be profitable in a year or two, and sometimes sooner. This reality is also reflected in the risk : reward ratio of startup and early-stage versus expansion-type financing.

The institutionally based limited partners who supplied most of the capital that venture capitalists invested may have unwittingly sabotaged the industry's most valuable contribution to the economy with their pressures for earlier liquidity. Institutional limited partner investors sought the liquidity of getting in and out of an LBO in two to four years, instead of the five- to ten-year window of "patience and bravery" typical of classic startup and very-early-stage investing. Their money was encumbered by a pair of invisible handcuffs that counseled the new breed of fund managers to be less risk tolerant, less patient and brave with their capital, than the wealthy individuals and families they had replaced as the main providers of risk capital. Moreover, their investing policies may have substantially eroded, if not eliminated, both the formation rate and growth of high-potential technology-based ventures in the United States. Historically, the best investors focused first and foremost on the quality of entrepreneurs and their ability to work effectively with them in building a company. By doing this, investors acquired reputations as value adders and thus were able to attract other highly talented entrepreneurs. Today, that focus on the entrepreneur has blurred. Would-be entrepreneurs in the forthcoming generation may have to look elsewhere for startup capital.

The new dominance of institutional money in the industry has had a profound effect. We were struck at a recent industry gathering by this phenomenon. In the opening plenary session, industry gurus bemoaned the reluctance of institutional suppliers to continue investing in their funds. During the two days of the meeting there was scant mention of the entrepreneurs and companies as the focal point of the process. There was one exception: a pre-conference seminar on seed investing featuring speakers from the tradition of classic venture capital—Reid Dennis, Brent Rider, and Henry Morganthaler—stressed the need for the fundamentals of classic venture investing.

Institutional investors have also altered the ground rules and terms governing the venture funds. Lead institutional investors willing to place $5 million, $10 million, $25 million, or more to kick off a new fund have powerful negotiating leverage with general partners. Their requirements for earlier and more frequent cash distributions, lower fees, a minimum threshold return, quarterly reporting, active advisory boards to help monitor valuations, and the like are causing a fundamental restructuring of the business.

The mismatch of interests between the long-term discipline of classic venture-capital investing and the requirements of institutional suppliers is growing larger. In fact, one venture capitalist we talked with was very proud of the fact that he had no institutional sources of money in his sizable fund in order to avoid just this mismatch. Another noted with irony how pressures from institutional investors for the earliest possible distributions of gains can actually backfire. In one instance, a limited partner wanted stock shares distributed well before the IPO of the stock because the valuation of the investment was rising on a quarterly basis as the company began to succeed. The general partners believed such a distribution would be premature because they were convinced that the stock would have even greater value downstream. They were right: $108 million of the $180 million gain from the investment occurred after the IPO of the stock. If the investors had had their way, they would never have seen almost two-thirds the eventual gain. Who can know better the future value of a company than the venture capital backers and management that are closest to it? Venture capitalists argue that such foresight is what they are paid for.

U.S. VENTURE CAPITAL IN THE 1980s

In every way imaginable, from the magnitude of investing activity, to industry structure and strategies and rates of return on invested capital, the industry has fundamentally changed.

Explosion in Investing Activity

The explosive growth in the flow of new money into the venture capital pools was evident in every measure of the magnitude and level of activity. Funds raised by existing venture-capital firms expanded rapidly, and a host of new groups of general partners (many of whom spun off from existing venture-capital funds) entered the picture. The extent of new-fund formation is summarized in Figure 2-9. During each year of the peak period of 1983–1987, as many as one hundred groups or more were seeking to raise new funds. This is quite staggering considering just 225 venture capital firms existed in 1979.

FIGURE 2-9 **New Venture Fund Formation and Amount Raised by Private Independent Venture Capital Firms**

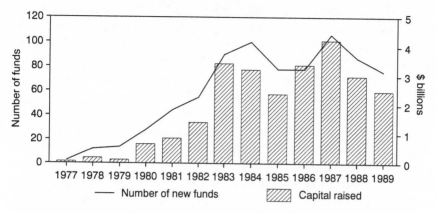

Source: Venture Economics, Inc.

Word has gotten around among institutional investors about the extraordinary returns realized by Rock's investments in Teledyne and SDS. Later on, returns from Apple Computer, Federal Express, Biogen, Lotus Development, and Genentech reinforced the potential seen in venture capital. Aggressive fund-raising prospectuses urged that rates of returns in the midtwenty percentages were replicable. Even the respected *Venture Capital Journal* reported such high returns from studies it had conducted on venture funds in its database. Bloodied by real estate investments in the 1970s and still reeling from oil embargoes, credit shortages, a prime rate at 18%, and double-digit inflation, institutional investors were hungry for such attractive yields.

Simultaneously, the nature of ownership of the capital under management in the industry changed. Earlier in 1978, corporate venture-capital firms controlled 34%, and SBICs, 21%, of the money in the industry, while private venture-capital funds managed just 45%. By 1989, private firms had expanded their base to 81% of the money under management, at the expense of the corporate venture-capital firms whose share declined to 19% and the SBICs' to less than 1%.

The overall explosion in the volume of available capital had important consequences.[5] On the bright side, there was never a more exciting period in the brief history of the industry. In 1983, for example, investors faced an amazing deal flow. Previously, the difficulty of getting managers to leave the comfort and security of their corporate stock options, bonuses, and generous benefits for the great uncertainty of a startup and the privilege of paying over 50% in taxes on any eventual gains was overwhelming. But this changed in a hurry. Corporate managers, university professors, and engineers changed from employees to entrepreneurs with business plans to start and grow companies. Investors had never seen more deals or deals of higher quality. The frenzy remained strong until the stock market crash of October 1987.

This flurry of entrepreneurship had a powerful impact on the general culture of America. The American dream was possible again, and the business of business was respectable—even exciting. Stephan Jobs was only twenty-one when he, Armas "Mike" Markkula, Jr., and Steve Wozniak launched Apple Computer, and if a former disk jockey could create Lotus 1-2-3, a lot of things seemed possible that previously had been inconceivable. Confidence in the economy and the nation were being restored. Ronald Reagan pronounced it the "decade of the entrepreneur."

But the rebirth of venture capital had a dark side. It took on some of the speculative fever and crowd madness associated with gold rushes and real estate booms. To the sanguine observer, the vision of more than one hundred groups seeking to raise a total of $2 or $3 billion must have looked like so many lemmings rushing to the sea. The period from 1983 to 1986 saw a number of half-baked proposals from organizers seeking to raise millions of dollars for their new funds. Fortunately, most of these did not get far. But the industry became top-heavy with newcomers and wunderkinder. By the end of 1983, half of the venture capitalists in the industry had three years of experience or less. At one fund closing in the frenzied summer of 1983, one newcomer, scarcely eighteen months in the business, casually bragged of a 1000% on-paper return in his fund *so far*. (It was politely suggested that he report back in 1993 and let us know what the realized return was then.) Such tales only fueled the frenzy further.

Still, some newcomers amazed veterans with seemingly overnight spectacular successes. Ben Rosen was one of those neophytes, yet his first two deals as lead investor are legends: Lotus Development and Compaq Computer. It is noteworthy that after initially trying to invest as minor players in the syndication of others' deals that did not work out—including Osborne Computer—he and L. J. Sevin decided on a strategy as lead investors. Lesser-known names like Peter Wendell of Sierra Ventures brought years of computer industry experience with them and early on began to distinguish themselves. Young but veteran investor Bill Egan hit staggering home runs with investments in Federal Express and Continental Cablevision. Overall, however, the supply of capital far outstripped the acumen of its handlers and the capacity of the industry to invest it wisely.

In retrospect, this pattern of inexperience had a lasting negative effect on the venture-capital screening and investing process. Experienced investors in the tradition of General Doriot, Arthur Rock, Don Valentine, Dan Gregory, and Peter Brooke had done their homework carefully and formulated investing strategies that enabled them to say no to many deals. It could take weeks, often months, for them to get to know the management of a new company and determine its market potential. This changed in the 1980s. The "normal" investing cycle was compressed. Time and again, extensive due diligence began to have a perverse consequence: the more dedicated you were to doing careful screening, the more likely you would be outbid at the twelfth hour by an impulsive competitor from a new fund. In the great frenzy of mid-1983, a venture capitalist of our acquaintance had this experience. After investing months of effort in evaluating a deal, he proposed an offer to the company founders. They told him that they also planned to talk with other venture capital firms. Just a few days later, he was informed that they had decided to accept money from a competing firm. It would have been impossible to conduct reasonable due diligence in that very short time period. The other investor's explanation was simple: if he did the due diligence and made the company an offer, that's good enough for me!

This compression in the investing process inaugurated a self-destructive competitive pattern in the industry. Patience and thorough due diligence, so characteristic of traditional venture capital, went out of favor in the early and mid-1980s. For entrepreneurs, in the near term at least, this was a joyful development. Valuations soared. Money had never been easier to raise—at one venture capital fair in Atlanta in 1983, seventeen small companies presented their business plans to a gathering of nearly 125 venture capital firms. Entrepreneurs and investors had never seen anything like this.

At its peak, such investing triggered a pattern of capital market myopia, epitomized by the overcrowding and subsequent debacle in the Winchester hard-disk–drive industry. In the end, what appeared to many in 1982–1983 to be an investing bonanza proved to be short lived, and the industry is still paying the price for its excesses.

A New Heterogeneity of Industry Structure

The 1980s demolished the stereotype that venture capital is venture capital is venture capital. Prior to 1979–1980, there was an accepted generalization about the homogeneous nature of the 200+ firms in the industry. They shared far more similarities than differences: fund sizes, investing strategies, preferred businesses, types and amounts of investments (typically common stocks), stages of the companies they sought to invest in, sources of capital, their roles as lead investors, and the like. The most common perception among entrepreneurs, the media, and industry observers was that venture funds were all alike. While this stereotype did little justice to the subtle differences that have always existed in the industry, it was not inaccurate.

Yet by 1980, early signs began to appear that the rules of the venture capital game were changing. By the end of the decade, a careful analysis revealed a substantially restructured, heterogeneous industry, strikingly different from the industry homogeneity at the outset of the decade (see Figure 2-10). Instead of a small, very similar group of about 225 funds, the new industry of nearly 700 firms can be sorted into five quite distinct groups.*

Megafunds (95) These funds are private and independent (by independent, we mean not associated with a bank, corporation, or financial institution), with an average of $200+ million under management, seeking national and global equity investments of at least $1 to $3 million in a first round. Most of their investments are in expansion financings, LBOs, and later-stage deals, with an occasional startup. Some groups have raised funds for a special role, such as a mezzanine financing, while still making startup and early-stage investments from other monies under their management. In other megafund firms, subgroups specialize in, for example, telecommunications, software, or other areas where a competitive advantage is seen. These funds typically prefer to be lead investors, have board seats, and also frequently syndicate

---

*Note that when we say "fund" in the following discussion, we are referring to firms that may have more than one fund under management.

deals, usually with other mega- or mainstream funds. Typically, these investments are in return for common stock or, increasingly during the last decade, preferred stock with a cumulating dividend and the right to convert to common and a subordinated debt instrument with a 10% to 12% coupon plus warrants to bring the total return up to the 20% to 30% return range.

Megafunds frequently have strong ties to venture capital firms in other countries through jointly created venture funds and limited partners in their U.S. funds. Examples of this are TA Associates, Burr, Egan, & Deleage Co., and Advent International. Their backers are often some of the more well-known national and international institutional sources, corporations, and universities. By 1989, these 95 funds dominated the industry. Though representing just 14% of all firms, they controlled 59% of the total U.S. venture capital pool by 1989 (see Figure 2-11).

Mainstream funds (200 +)   These are mainly private and independent (but include some large institutional SBICs), with $25 to $99 million under management. They seek regional and national equity investments of $1 million or less for a first round. Among the largest 211 in this group, the average capital under management was $49.3 million in 1989, and they controlled 31% of all the venture capital available (see Figure 2-12). Their instruments, sources of funding, preferences as to lead investorship and active board roles, and syndications are similar to those of the megafunds.

Second-tier funds (150–175)   These are mostly SBICs but include some private, independent firms. They are smaller with less than $25 million under management, investing $500 to $750 thousand per round, mostly as subordinated debt. Their backers are wealthy individuals and some smaller institutions. They tend to prefer solo investing to co-investing. We could identify 91 that made equity investments. They tend to have a local or regional market focus and often have an eclectic taste for deals, ranging from high technology, when available, to supermarkets and bottling businesses, to service businesses. Historically, they have filled a gap in providing capital for businesses generally overlooked by the rest of the venture capital industry. However, as the target markets in the industry have themselves become more diverse and heterogeneous, this group has faced increased competition.

Niche funds (40–50)   These are private and independent, with up to $25 million under management, and specialize in seed and startup

FIGURE 2-10 New Heterogeneous Structure of the Venture Capital Industry*

	Megafund funds	Mainstream funds	Second-tier funds	Niche funds	Corporate financial and corporate industrial funds
Estimated number and type (1988)	95 Predominantly private, independent funds	200+ Predominantly private and independent; some large institutional SBICs and corporate funds	150–175 Mostly SBICs; some private independent funds	40–50 Private, independent	85 & 84, respectively
Capital under management	$100M+	$25–99M	Below $25M	$3–25M	$25–50M+
Typical investment (first round)	$1–3M	$500K–1M	$500–750K	$50–200K	Larger $10–15M deals possible
Stage of investment	Later expansion, LBOs, startups	Later expansion, LBOs, some startups; mezzanine	Later stages; few startups; specialized areas	Seed and startup; technology or market focus	Later
Strategic focus	Technology; national and international markets; capital gains; broad focus	Technology and manufacturing; national and regional markets; capital gains;	Eclectic—more regional than national; capital gains, current income; service	High-technology national and international links; feeder funds; capital	Windows on technology; direct investment in new markets and suppliers;

	more specialized focus	businesses	gains	diversification; strategic partners; capital gains
Balance of equity and debt	Predominantly equity; convertible preferred	Predominantly debt; about 91 SBICs do equity principally	Predominantly equity	Mixed
Principal sources of capital	Mature national and international institutions; own funds; corporations; insurance companies; pension funds; institutions and wealthy individuals; foreign corporations and pension funds; universities	Wealthy individuals; some smaller institutions	Institutions and foreign corporations; wealthy individuals	Internal funds
Main investing role	Active lead or co-lead; frequent syndications; board seat	Less co-investing, with some solo investing	Initial or lead investor; outreach; shirt-sleeves involvement	Later stages, rarely startups; direct investor in funds and portfolio companies

*The authors are most appreciative of the assistance of Jane K. Morris, vice president of Sales and Marketing, Venture Economics, Inc., in providing some of the data for this table.

Source: J. A. Timmons et al., *New Venture Creation* (Homewood, IL: Richard D. Irwin, 1990), p. 427.

Note: Target rates of return vary considerably; depending on stage and market conditions. Seed and startup investors may seek compounded after-tax rates of return in excess of 50%–100%; mature, later stage investors seek returns in the 30%–40% range. The rule of thumb is realizing a gain of five to ten times the original investment in five to ten years, which is a common expectation.

FIGURE 2-11 **The Largest 95 Megafund Firms . . . ($100+ million under management)**

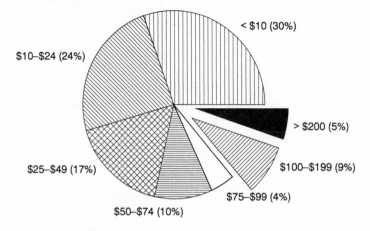

. . . Controlled 59% of the Venture Capital Pool in 1989 (average size: $207 million/firm)

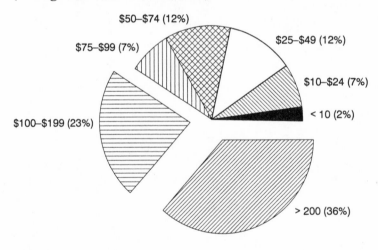

Source: Venture Economics, Inc.

investments or a special-technology/market focus, i.e., materials, environmental, and biotechnology. Typical first-round equity investments are $50,000 to $250,000.

Corporate financial (85) and corporate industrial funds (84)   These two types of funds, owned by large corporations, have $25 to $50

FIGURE 2-12 **The Mainstream Firms . . . ($25–$99 million under management)**

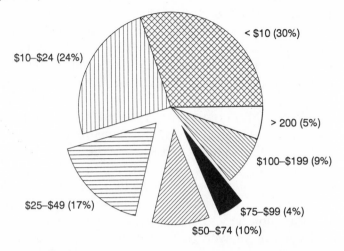

$10–$24 (24%)

< $10 (30%)

> 200 (5%)

$100–$199 (9%)

$75–$99 (4%)

$50–$74 (10%)

$25–$49 (17%)

. . . Controlled 31% of the Venture Capital Pool in 1989 (average size: $49.3 million/firm)

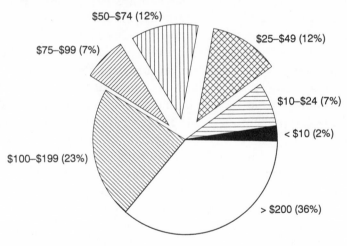

$50–$74 (12%)

$75–$99 (7%)

$25–$49 (12%)

$10–$24 (7%)

< $10 (2%)

$100–$199 (23%)

> $200 (36%)

Source: Venture Economics, Inc.

million under management. They seek later-stage, larger deals. As the entrepreneurial revolution of the 1980s gained steam, large corporations and financial institutions got the sense that much of it was passing them by. After all, the spectacular success stories of the 1980s were not spawned inside America's largest companies or financed by the largest and most prestigious money sources. Rather, these new economic miracles were parented and funded by obscure, unknown entrepreneurs and backers. With a multitude of aims— windows on technology, strategic diversification, alliances, and others—large corporations and financial institutions joined the fray.

By 1990, the 90% dominance in the marketplace for risk and venture capital by the megafunds and mainstream funds stood in stark contrast to the share controlled by the approximately 368 venture capital firms with less than $50 million under management (see Figure 2-13). When one considers that the 205 smallest firms (nearly a third of the total number of venture capital firms), with less than $10 million under management, account for a scant 2.4% of the total pool, or an average of $3.9 million per firm (see Figure 2-14), it becomes clear that this group will be the hardest hit by the current shake-out.

It is fair to conclude that the venture capital industry has evolved into three tiers: the megafunds, mainstreamers, and the rest. This reality has important industry, market, and competitive implications. For one thing, it contributed to a dramatic shift in relative bargaining power from the venture capitalists to the entre- preneurs. Just a few years earlier, probably 40 to 50 of the 225 firms in the industry did the lion's share of significant deals. They knew each other well through gatherings of the National Venture Capital Association (NVCA) and from information in *Venture Capital Journal*. For investors, this informal network was advan- tageous, enabling them to avoid destructive bidding for deals or investing in too similar or competing ventures. But in the 1980s the rules of the game changed. The new competitive structure broke down the old patterns of collaboration and deal sharing, and, for entrepreneurs, it became, for the first time, a seller's market.

Larger and larger funds had another important impact on the industry. The tripling of fund size meant that more capital had to be invested per general partner each year. Later-stage deals and LBOs fit the megafunds' needs for larger average investments. After all, it took no more time to analyze and invest in a $10 million deal than in a $1 million deal, and in many cases the startup, smaller deals were more difficult to assess. Established companies did not require the active involvement of the lead investor, so one

FIGURE 2-13 **The Rest of the 368 Firms . . . (< $25 million under management)**

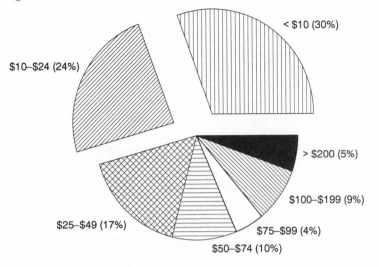

< $10 (30%)

$10–$24 (24%)

> $200 (5%)

$100–$199 (9%)

$25–$49 (17%)

$75–$99 (4%)

$50–$74 (10%)

. . . Controlled 9.9% of the Venture Capital Pool in 1989 (average size: $9.0 million/firm)

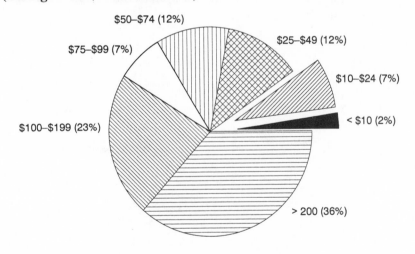

$50–$74 (12%)

$75–$99 (7%)

$25–$49 (12%)

$10–$24 (7%)

$100–$199 (23%)

< $10 (2%)

> 200 (36%)

Source: Venture Economics, Inc.

partner could make larger per-round investments in twice as many companies.

Finally, many of the larger funds that owed their success to their investments in the 1960s and 1970s became spawning grounds for the new generation of venture capitalists. As had happened at

FIGURE 2-14 **The Smallest 205 Firms . . . (< $10 million under management)**

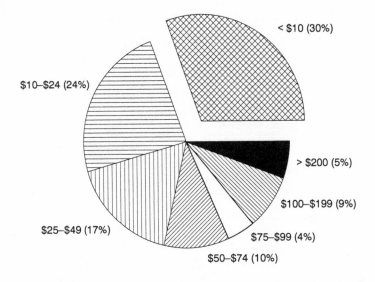

. . . Controlled 2.4% of the Venture Capital Pool in 1989 (average size: $3.9 million/firm)

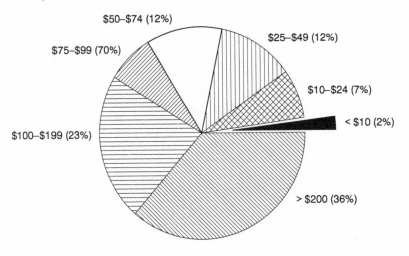

Source: Venture Economics, Inc.

ARD, partners from all over began to leave to launch their own new funds, further intensifying competition.

Formation of Specialized Niche Funds

The one bright light amid the industry changes has been the surprisingly strong showing of "seed" investing, which increased steadily over the decade to about 9% of the deals done in 1989 (although this accounted for only 4% of the investable funds, mainly because of the small size of these investments—$50,000 to $250,000). One of the most encouraging current trends is the creation of specialized niche funds that are providing important financing for R&D stage and other startup ventures that might otherwise fail to attract funding.

Zero Stage Capital and First Stage Capital, two sister funds in Cambridge, Massachusetts, exemplify this group of funds. Originally organized in 1983 with just $5 million, Zero Stage has played a significant role in adding value to fledgling innovators and in demonstrating the feasibility of such specialized investing. Funds similar to Zero Stage were created in Maryland and in Pennsylvania. First Stage Capital was organized with $15 million to back the more promising Zero Stage–backed companies as they grew from their embryonic stages, thus avoiding the ravages of dilution. In 1990, this same group of general partners was in the midst of pioneering yet another new fund concept in response to investor wariness about declining returns of venture funds. Their $50 million Assurance Fund proposed a Treasury bill floor on the rate of return for institutional investors while preserving the option for these limited partners of substantial upside gains through investments in startup and early-stage companies.

Other specialized funds were being formed even in 1990 in such fields as materials and environmental services. For example, the Beacon Fund intended to specialize in materials-related seed and startup companies that may never require large amounts of capital. Companies that offer products or services with very high value-added characteristics enable them to set prices aggressively and still have happy customers. Coupled with creative financial strategies that minimize asset ownership and maximize early cash flow, such investments can be accomplished.

Specialization has not been limited to technology-related ventures. There have been funds that focus on specialty retailing, cellular communications, and software and on providing liquidity vehicles for private family companies, such as the recently formed

Legacy Fund. Others have been created to concentrate entirely on bridge capital, LBOs, and buyouts. Niche funds seem to be a natural market evolution as the venturing industry matures and general partners seek competitive advantages by identifying various niches.

The movement toward niche funds is important for the nation. For one thing, seed and startup funds perform the classic venture capital role. In the financing domain, this is the best way to stimulate and accelerate the birth rate of new enterprises. Such a process is vital to the development of regional and the national economy and to long-term international competitiveness. In Chapters 4 and 10 we discuss the mounting evidence of the crucial rule such early investing plays in accelerating the birth of industries and in the revival of economic regions.

Disastrous Decline in Rates of Return

The darkest side of the venture capital story in the 1980s was the dismal performance of so many of the new funds raised in the early part of the decade. Very high rates of return had been reported for funds formed in the 1960s and 1970s—typically, in the mid-20% compounded range. These aroused even higher expectations among investors as the 1980s began, expectations that by and large would not be fulfilled by 1990. Many funds only achieved single-digit rates of return, and for the first time funds actually lost capital. Some are likely to be liquidated at values below original invested capital. This has come as grim news for the industry and accounts for the recent disenchantment among institutional investors and their reduced investing activity.

Despite the generally bad news on rates of return, there are some exceptions. Surprisingly, a group of funds achieved very high returns in the 1980s, even well above the mid-20% rates reported at the beginning of the decade. Such extraordinary returns defy prevailing expectations and point to the reality that this is truly a business of exceptions.

These major developments are of such importance to the industry, both suppliers and users of capital, and have such profound implications, that we devote an entire chapter (6) to a larger discussion of the performance of venture capital funds.

Increased Competition and Industry Shake-out

The changes of the 1980s have led to a more competitive, less rewarding, and sometimes punishing environment for venture capital. Evidence of the mayhem in the industry is manifested in the emergence—for the first time in the industry's history—of a secondary market for venture capital portfolios, as underperforming and poorly performing funds are pressured by substantial majorities of their limited partners to liquidate. Several hundred million dollars in such transactions occurred in 1990, most at a discount from the original capital invested.

Other evidence of declining industry performance was presented in the fall of 1988 at a venture capital seminar at the Harvard Business School by our colleagues Michael Porter, William Sahlman, and Howard Stevenson, all of the Harvard Business School. They provided an analysis of the industry and the deleterious effect of the many changes just described on its profitability. Figure 2-15 is a schematic of this analysis.

Porter's analytical framework of competitive forces and industry structure can be usefully applied to the venture capital industry. The sharp increase in competitive rivalries during the 1980s was a product of four dominant forces: (1) the threat of new entrants, (2) the bargaining power of suppliers and (3) the users of capital, and (4) the threat of substitutes.

With no technological, regulatory, legal, or capital requirements barriers to impede them, new entrants flocked to the industry in the 1980s. Entry was also fairly swift. Funds were raised and brought into play in a year or less—in contrast to the lengthy periods needed to bring other businesses to a state of operational effectiveness. The rate of increase in the opportunity set available did not keep pace with the amount of money available. This led to very high valuations, which made it very difficult to achieve high rates of return.

We saw earlier that the increased bargaining power of institutional investors resulted in more stringent terms for the venture capitalists—lower management fees and shares of the profits. At the same time, the bargaining power of companies in search of venture capital increased. More knowledgeable and more sophisticated, customers enjoyed more alternative funding sources and substitutes than ever, escalating further the valuations and leading to the eventual decline of returns. Angels, foreign investors, and corporations became increasingly active in providing capital to these companies.

The net effect of all this was intensified rivalry among firms in the industry. As we have noted, there was a breakdown of the earlier networks and norms of close communication, cooperation,

FIGURE 2-15 **Determinants of Venture Capital Industry Profitability**

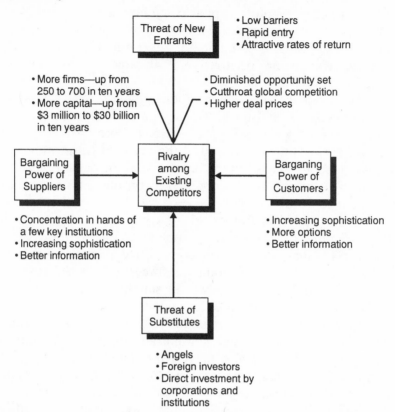

Source: M. Porter, W. Sahlman, and H. Stevenson, 1988. Based on theory presented in Michael E. Porter, *Competitive Strategy* (New York: Free Press, 1980).

and deal sharing. Old ties and syndication patterns have persisted, but many of these relationships were tested as never before by aggressive new players. For the first time, the industry has seen litigation among general partners and between limited and general partners, and we have not seen the end of this. Competition in the 1980s became intense for the U.S. venture-capital firms domestically and globally.

Another effect is that the profit potential for investments eroded and, with it, access to future funds. Earlier, a partnership would raise a new fund, concentrate on investing for the next two years, and then raise another fund. By 1990, this cycle had doubled to four years, even for the most experienced partnerships. The greater selectivity and withdrawal, or at least moratorium, of institutional investors limited access to funds after the 1987 peak. By 1991, their commitments were still declining, with no sign of future reversal.

On the bright side, expectations of 30% to 40% or more rates of return have been abandoned for more realistic targets in the 15% to 20% per annum range. Interestingly, most venture capitalists say they expect the industry to achieve rates of return of 14% to 16% but believe their own funds will do a bit better, closer to 20%.

Chapter 12 will revisit the industry as it appeared in 1991 and apply the Porterian analysis. This will provide a quite different, and certainly more encouraging picture than the industry snapshot of the late 1980s.

CONCLUSION: WHERE HAS ALL THE VENTURE GONE?

Today's venture-capital investing is clearly no longer the classic venture-capital investing of the past. One painful development is what venture capitalist Ben Rosen refers to as "the venture-capital gap": "No doubt there is a hole in the system for new, small and mid-sized businesses."[6] We argue that classic venture-capital investing is the maternity ward and incubation center for the entire economy. One Commerce Department study found, for instance, that 95% of all radical innovations since World War II have come from new and small companies, rather than large, established ones. Without new entrants, any economy is destined for long-term decline. The retreat of the former Soviet Union and East Germany almost to the economic status of third world countries since 1945 has no doubt stemmed in part from their failure to foster and develop a diversity of budding enterprises.

The venture capital industry faces a number of tough issues in the 1990s. With the collapse of the junk bond markets, the LBO and merger and acquisition business has headed south. A recent report by Merrill Lynch indicates that the average merger and acquisition in 1988 was about $55 million, whereas for the first nine months of 1990 this had dropped to about $25 million. Such sizable decreases affect the private capital markets, resulting in lower valuations for companies seeking venture capital. Lower valuations create improved opportunities for venture capitalists to add value to companies in search of capital for startup, growth, and recapitalization, but too few are stepping up to the challenge.

It is unlikely that newer funds can attain anything like 15% to 20% rates of return without classic venture-capital skills. We doubt, too, that they will succeed in raising additional funds in view of the dismal performance of so many funds, global competition, and the soft domestic economy. Until the next technology wave creates an opportunity set for the investor comparable to the semiconductor and microprocessor, we are unlikely to experience a replay of the "roaring eighties."

Extraordinary rewards for society, entrepreneurs, and investors have come from the patience and bravery of those who truly add value to the new-venture–creation and company-building process. The irony for startup entrepreneurs and the nation in the 1990s is that the industry may be losing the unique company-building skills that have been so vital to the entrepreneurial process, as classic venture-capital investing know-how has been replaced with financial engineering skills over the last ten years. What is worse, this has occurred at a time when the economy needs that know-how the most. If the seeds of the 1990s are to produce great harvests in the new century, a rebirth of classic venture-capital investing skills is vital today.

A new set of challenges faces the industry in the 1990s: how to craft a competitive strategy that enables a fund to differentiate itself in the marketplace for private capital. With the new competitive structure of the industry, failure to create that differentiation will undoubtedly result in a failure to achieve the rates of return now sought in the industry.

CHAPTER 3

Global Venture Capital

IN THIS CHAPTER, we document the explosive worldwide growth of venture capital since the 1970s and show how radically different venture-capital markets have evolved. We argue that while the suppliers of venture capital exist globally, their actual investing activities are local and domestic. Further, we argue that the rest of the world has never developed classic venture-capital investing know-how and instead has practiced a form of the merchant capitalism currently in vogue in the United States.

In 1980, formal venture capital was virtually nonexistent outside the United States. The number of firms actually investing in classic venture capital—that is, equity, not debt or quasi-debt, in new and budding companies—could be counted on one hand. No other country in the world had an organized venture-capital industry, although the first entrants were already in development stages or just under way in the United Kingdom, Sweden, and on the Continent.

A decade later, the situation had changed entirely: by 1990, over half of all the $80 billion of venture capital under management worldwide was outside the United States.[1] In 1988, more capital was committed to venture capital pools in the United Kingdom and Europe than in the United States. And in 1989, an astounding $6.28 billion of new venture capital flowed into the European venture capital pool. *Venture Capital Journal* summed it up this way in a December 1989 special report:

> The venture capital industry has entered the global village. Like the industries it supports, venture capital is crisscrossing national borders and moving into marketplaces around the world. U.S. firms are financing European corporations with funds raised from Japanese limited partners. Japan has become a major investor throughout the world; Korea, Taiwan and other Pacific Rim nations are gaining economic might; borders are breaking down in western as well as eastern Europe; and U.S.-based businesses are rushing to capture market share around the globe. The venture capital industry—in the U.S., Europe, and the Pacific Rim is now an international enterprise.[2]

This had been unimaginable ten years before.

The data we compiled and analyzed for the United States, Europe, Canada, and Australia concerning when in the life cycle of a portfolio company venture capitalists actually invest are revealing. The question raised in the previous chapter—"Where Is the Venture in Venture Capital?"—could apply to the European and Canadian experience as well. There is just not much classic venture-capital investing in Canada and Europe. In the previous chapter, we showed how the U.S. industry structure had changed radically, even describing one trend as the redefinition and deemphasis of classic venture capital. This trend is even more noticeable in Europe and the United Kingdom.

Cumulatively, from 1986 through 1989, fully 84% of all invested capital in Europe went to LBOs, acquisitions, and expansion financing, compared to 66% in the United States (see Figure 3-1). In Canada, the comparable figure for 1987–1989 was 65%. (Moreover, by 1990, the enthusiasm for LBOs had abated in the United States.)[3]

This is vivid confirmation of our contention that venture capital has evolved into merchant capital. Certainly, its current practitioners are operating far downstream from the stage of business evolution at which Apple Computer, Federal Express, and Lotus Development Corporation received the attention of venture capitalists. Mature companies, where opportunities for MBOs, management buyins (MBIs), LBOs, and expansion financing exist, are their preference. They have less and less appetite—and fewer skills—for startup investing. This investing approach characterizes over 85% of the capital currently under management in the world. Even 3i, the dominant player in the United Kingdom, has with-

FIGURE 3-1 **Portion of Dollars Invested by Stage, 1986–1989 USA ($14.08 billion)**

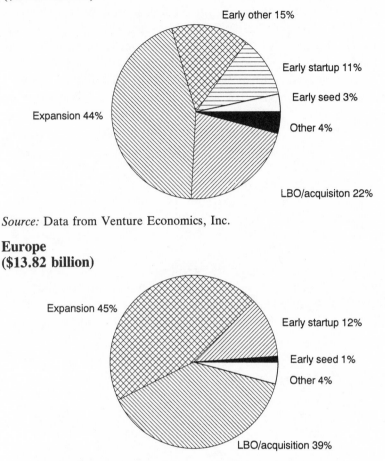

Source: Data from Venture Economics, Inc.

Europe ($13.82 billion)

Source: Data from *EVCA Yearbook,* 1989, 1990.

drawn from startup investing and has repositioned itself in early 1991 as a "development capital" firm. The result is an arena of increasing opportunity in the 1990s. Investors with the startup and operating know-how that can add value in the company-building process will find more opportunities and less competition than at any time since the early 1970s.

A WORLDWIDE PHENOMENON

The growth in the supply of worldwide venture capital in the past ten years is astonishing. In 1980, the industry was embryonic outside the United States, not unlike the situation here in the mid-1950s. But from that point the picture changed dramatically (yet another reflection of a flowering of entrepreneurship worldwide). Between 1986 and 1990, the worldwide venture-capital pool doubled, mostly because of explosive growth in Europe, where it increased from $8.95 billion to $29 billion. Figure 3-2 highlights recent patterns in Europe (including the United Kingdom), Japan, Canada, Korea, and the United States. By the end of 1990, because of the U.S. shake-out and Europe's ascent, the total pool in Europe would be nearly as large as that in the United States.

The growth of venture capital in the rest of the industrialized world has paralleled the U.S. pattern of the 1980s in many ways. We shall see subsequently that in many instances the industry was a U.S. export with many American venture funds having close linkages with new funds in other parts of the world. Yet, as one might expect, important differences have evolved from country to country.

As the industry outside the United States has developed, professional organizations such as the British Venture Capital Association (BVCA) and the European Venture Capital Association (EVCA) have formed. Publications such as the *European Venture*

FIGURE 3-2 **Worldwide Venture Capital Growth**

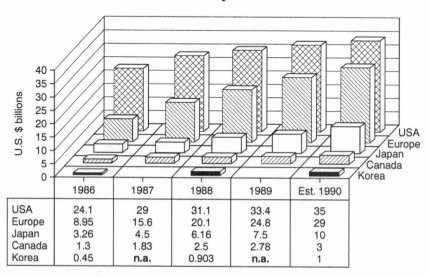

	1986	1987	1988	1989	Est. 1990
USA	24.1	29	31.1	33.4	35
Europe	8.95	15.6	20.1	24.8	29
Japan	3.26	4.5	6.16	7.5	10
Canada	1.3	1.83	2.5	2.78	3
Korea	0.45	n.a.	0.903	n.a.	1

Source: Data from *Asian Venture Capital Journal, EVCA Yearbook,* and *Venture Capital Journal.*

Capital Journal, the EVCA's annual summary of financing activity *Venture Capital in Europe,* and the *Asian Venture Capital Journal* track and report on important industry developments.

What is generally not well known is that Europe is on its second attempt at the development of a venture capital industry. Earlier efforts were made in the early 1960s by none other than General Doriot. The budding success of ARD in the United States and the general's own French connection led to the establishment of the European Enterprises Development Company S.A. (EED), with offices in Luxembourg and Paris. Its array of institutional stockholders was impressive: Aktiebolaget (Sweden), Banco Español, Banque Nationale pour le Commerce de Paris, Continental International Finance Corporation (Chicago), Credit Lyonnais, Dresdner Bank A.G., Lehman Brothers, Morgan Guaranty International Finance Corporation, Rotterdamsche Bank N.V., Société Générale (Paris), M. M. Worms & Cie. (Paris), and others. EED directors represented some of these same institutions.

The Canadian Enterprise Development Corporation Limited was launched at about the same time, with offices in Montreal and Vancouver. Preeminent Canadian financial institutions were among its twenty-seven institutional stockholders, including a dozen leading insurance companies and the Bank of Montreal, Dupont of Canada Limited Pension Fund, the Royal Trust Company, the Toronto-Dominion Bank, and others.

Despite the prestigious backing of both efforts, venture capital in Europe and Canada never gained a foothold in the 1960s. Disappointing investments were followed by the economic doldrums of the 1970s. But after this false start, the industry's current vigor would startle even General Doriot.

Annual Capital Commitments

The flow of new capital into venture funds outside the United States continued nearly unabated throughout the 1980s, especially in Europe, as summarized in Figure 3-3. In 1989, European commitments exceeded the strongest year in the United States ($4.18 billion in 1987) by 50%! Leading this surge was the United Kingdom, which raised £1.7 billion, more than double the commitment of any previous year.[4] And Japan may even outstrip the United States in its annual commitments to venture capital funds in the early 1990s, something that would have been unthinkable a year or two ago.

FIGURE 3-3 **Worldwide Venture Capital Commitments**

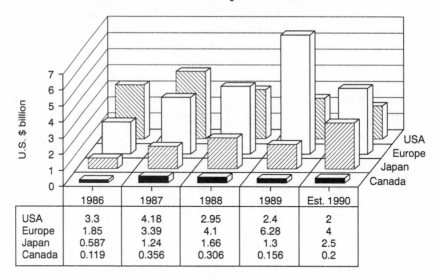

	1986	1987	1988	1989	Est. 1990
USA	3.3	4.18	2.95	2.4	2
Europe	1.85	3.39	4.1	6.28	4
Japan	0.587	1.24	1.66	1.3	2.5
Canada	0.119	0.356	0.306	0.156	0.2

Source: Data from *Asian Venture Capital Journal, EVCA Yearbook,* and *Venture Capital Journal.*

Annual Capital Disbursements

The amount of capital invested in portfolio companies showed a similar pattern (see Figure 3-4), growing throughout the 1980s, with Europe's $4.06 billion in 1988 surpassing the $3.65 billion of the United States. Indeed, nearly 65% of the global disbursements in venture capital in that year were non-American. This dramatic decline in the relative magnitude of U.S. venture capital is yet another sign of the radical changes in the industry's competitive structure during the past decade. The emergence of the European Economic Community and the opening of Eastern Europe and the former Soviet Union to more entrepreneurial and market-oriented economic policies should create new opportunities for the 1990s and the first decade of the twenty-first century. True to form, private venture-capital investors are at the forefront in anticipating, spotting, and investing in new opportunities. Take Germany, for example. Until now, Germany has been a sleeping giant on the European venture-capital scene. In 1990, however, BVK, the fifty-three–member German venture-capital association, reported a 25% increase in investments made by its members in 1989, with a 6%

FIGURE 3-4 **Worldwide Venture Capital Disbursements**

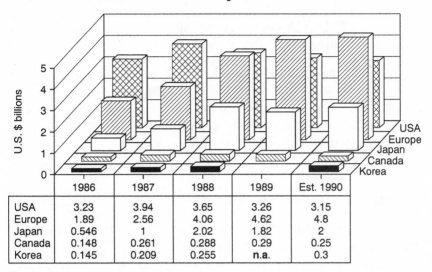

	1986	1987	1988	1989	Est. 1990
USA	3.23	3.94	3.65	3.26	3.15
Europe	1.89	2.56	4.06	4.62	4.8
Japan	0.546	1	2.02	1.82	2
Canada	0.148	0.261	0.288	0.29	0.25
Korea	0.145	0.209	0.255	**n.a.**	0.3

Source: Data from *Asian Venture Capital Journal, EVCA Yearbook,* and Venture Economics, Inc.

increase in the number of deals done. BVK has also set up a group to focus on investing and joint ventures in the former East Germany.

A CAUTION: WHAT IS MEANT BY VENTURE CAPITAL?

The growing size of these non-U.S. venture-capital pools can be quite misleading if one translates venture capital as "classic U.S.-style venture capital." Yet, we contend that these data are misleading. For one thing, a few very large LBO funds account for much of the pool. Further, the largest player, 3i plc, is repositioning itself away from startup and early-stage investing toward more mature companies. Moreover, their definition of startup includes firms up to three years old—hardly a startup in the United States. In fact, the twists, variations, and types of investments included in these numbers range even farther afield than what has evolved in the United States in the last decade. Even the leading industry tracker, *Venture Capital Journal,* cautioned readers in December 1989 that "there is no accepted definition of venture capital even within a single country, let alone worldwide."[5] We also suspect that the definitions used may overstate the amount of seed and startup investing since these numbers also include early-stage companies that are post-startup.

The 1990 EVCA yearbook defines venture capitalists as organizational units or persons

> who can prove substantial activity in the management of equity or quasi-equity financing for the startup and/or development of small and medium-sized unquoted enterprises that have significant growth potential in terms of products, technology, business concepts, and services;
>
> whose main objective is long-term capital gains to remunerate risks; and
>
> who can provide active management support to investees.[6]

The number of non-U.S. activities that fit this definition is very limited. In fact, 80% to 85% of the capital in the EVCA itself goes to management buyouts and buyins and LBOs and to restructuring and expansion financings.

ECONOMIC IMPACT ON EUROPE AND THE UNITED KINGDOM

The development of venture capital in Europe and the United Kingdom is of enormous importance not just for European economic progress but for the world's. Until the 1980s, this region had a far greater proportion of private companies and far more limited access to risk capital than did the United States. It also had (and still has in many areas) a tradition of state ownership, private cartels, and near monopolies that are the antithesis of an entrepreneurial economy. But fiat enterprise is generally in retreat, and the spirit of privatization is growing. The recent unprecedented mobilization of private risk and venture capital is tremendously important for the entrepreneurial process to take hold. There is growing evidence, for instance, that the new combination of entrepreneurial talent and venture-capital investing know-how is at the vortex of economic restructuring from state-dominated to private ownership and from monopolistic or at least quasi-monopolistic industries to more competitive industry structures. What may have even greater significance is the new role for government: creating sources of opportunities, rather than creating or protecting staid, anticompetitive oligopolies and cartels.

One good example of this nascent entrepreneurial spirit is

reflected in the new British regulations limiting brewery monopolies. Three British venture funds, Electra Investment Trust, County NatWest Ventures, and the giant 3i plc fund arranged for equity finance to back a plan by Northumbria Inns to develop fifty independent public houses in the northeast region of England in 1990. These pubs were to be acquired and refurbished to operate as "free houses"—not tied to a single brewery or brand of beer. Thus, venture capital funds will play an even more active and vital role in providing the risk capital and financing know-how for the restructuring of heretofore sedentary and monopolistic-like industries in the United Kingdom and EEC.

In 1989, according to the EVCA, 1,130 (20.7%) of the 5,439 investments made by its members went to seed (117) and startup (1,013) investments. What might this mean over the ten- to twenty-year period it will take for them to mature? Studies in the United States suggest that about 1% to 3% of these new firms (11–34) are likely to become extraordinary successes, with roughly $100 to $200 million or even $1 billion or more in sales, that will be the pioneers in the leading new industries of the decades ahead. Another 4% to 7% are likely to be very successful, achieving $25 to $50 million or more in sales. Add all these dollars up and the potential contribution of venture capitalism to the region's economy becomes obvious, not to mention the solutions to priorities in society such as medical and health care needs, job creation and tax payments, and the benefits to be derived from the innovations it finances. What is more, of the remaining pool of 1,000 candidates, if history repeats itself, 25% to 40% are likely to disappear, but the rest will stay in business. They will not be superstars, but they will employ tens of thousands of people, pay taxes, and function as important vertebrae in the economic backbones of their communities. What is not well known is that their founders and management will also likely fill a very disproportionate share of leadership roles in their communities as elected representatives and as directors on the boards of educational institutions, hospitals, churches, other companies, and nonprofit organizations.

All of the above may understate the total potential economic effect of venture-capital-backed companies in view of the following: not all venture-capital firms belong to the EVCA; new venture-capital firms are yet to be launched; startup investing may increase over time; and venture funds from the United States and elsewhere will continue to become more active in the region in the coming decade.

GLOBAL AND REGIONAL COMPARISONS

The venture capital industry's rapid growth the world over is also evident in the number of firms in Europe and the United Kingdom (440), Asia (245), and Canada (63). A country-by-country breakdown of the EVCA's 1990 membership for all of Europe shows the dominance of the United Kingdom in terms of numbers of firms (115, 55 of which belong to EVCA), followed by France (29), the Netherlands (28), and Belgium (22). Indeed, European venture capital is almost "Channel capital": more than 80% of the total pool rests in those four countries bordering the English Channel. The remaining twelve member nations of the EVCA account for a minuscule part of the total. In the Far East, the *Asian Venture Capital Journal* reported that Japan has the largest number of firms (86), followed by Australia (70).

Breaking our data down further reveals some distinct patterns and sharp differences among the countries of each region. Take, for instance, the striking data for 1989. The United Kingdom, with $13.8 billion, accounted for more than one-half of all the available venture capital in the sixteen countries in the region and nearly three times that of its closest rival. France, number two, which experienced a 60% increase in new venture-capital commitments, had a pool of $4.7 billion, followed by the Netherlands with $1.5 billion and Italy with $1.2 billion. Surprisingly, West Germany placed a distant fifth, with just $930 million, a match for Korea but barely more than Australia's $800 million, less than tiny Hong Kong's $1 billion, and dwarfed by Japan's $7 to $8 billion in 1989. (Note that these dollar figures reflect the exchange rates at the time.)

Venture capital was poised for takeoff in Spain, Portugal, and Italy, while Germany was just starting to come alive. Scandinavia experienced little growth from 1988 to 1989. One of the early very active countries in the 1980s, Finland experienced a disaster when its largest and oldest venture-capital firm went through bankruptcy, and Sweden was suffering from consolidation and decline. It had more than fifty venture-capital firms by the mid-1980s, but by 1989 the number had shrunk to a dozen.

Overall, the European picture from 1988 to 1989 was positive, as EVCA members' disbursements increased 24%, and realized gains increased 63%. First-time investments accounted for 77% of amounts invested. The largest growth segment was in management buyouts, which rose by 45%. The number of seed investments went from 77 to 113 but still accounted for little more than 2% of the total. Startup investing showed a slight decline.

The current size of the venture capital pools in most European and Asian nations may not seem impressive next to the $33.4 billion in the United States and the United Kingdom's $15.1 billion. However, when placed in the context of an industry only ten years old, these amounts are more impressive: the aggregate U.S. pool was only $3 billion at the end of the 1970s. To place data on a more even footing, we translated them into a per capita measure. By this measure, the United Kingdom was first (with $251), followed by Canada ($150), the United States ($134), France ($78), and Japan and Australia ($53 each).

The maturation of the industry in Europe by the end of the 1980s was most evident in the United Kingdom. A common cry was "too many funds, too much money chasing too few good deals, and too many inferior deals." The overheated market of 1986 to 1988 resulted in an oversupply of capital and a dissatisfaction with declining and poor rates of return. France mimicked the U.K. pattern in about three years. Most investments were in established low- and no-tech businesses. Private companies were often valued at low price/earnings multiples of four and then sold on the first unlisted securities market (*second marché*), established in 1982, at multiples of fifteen to twenty, spurring further investor frenzy. Two or three years later, Germany followed, with banks dominating the scene. Most investments were in LBOs and established companies. (It is estimated that only a half-dozen classic U.S.-style venture-capital firms exist in Germany today.)

There have been efforts to spread the venture capital concept in the developing world. Through efforts of the World Bank and the International Finance Corporation, initiatives have been supported in Kenya, Brazil, the Philippines, and other nations. Each faces unique challenges in its development process and lacks many of the supporting structures, know-how, and resources that we often associate with a healthy entrepreneurial process and venture capital industry. All told, these countries accounted for an estimated $350 million in 1988—about 0.5% of the world total reported by the *Venture Capital Journal.*[7]

There appears to be little relief in sight from the growing competitive pressures facing U.S. venture capital. And the American shake-out now under way will undoubtedly be felt in Europe and Asia. To make matters worse for the United States, the European industry is now in its second decade; presumably the valuable lessons they have learned will make them formidable global competitors. Yet, the vast majority of their learning in the 1980s came from doing LBOs, MBOs, MBIs, and later-stage investing. Competition for these deals is likely to intensify in the 1990s, and the few firms that have accumulated the relevant knowledge and experience to do startup and early-stage investments will likely face less severe competition.

It is not hard to envision a new Germany with several billion marks of new venture capital to exploit restructuring opportunities in former East Germany and the Eastern bloc. We noted earlier that the German venture-capital association has already established a group to examine this possibility. If Japan begins to see the fruits of its early efforts, another $10 to $15 billion is possible there. And who could be better positioned than the already dominant British venture-capital community to seize opportunities in the new Europe after 1992?

THE MONEY SUPPLIERS

One of the most significant changes in the U.S. venture-capital industry in the 1980s, noted in Chapter 2, was the altered sources of its money. Some very different patterns have evolved on the global scene. Consider a recent composite of European data (see Figure 3-5). Quite unlike the United States, in Europe banks are the dominant source of venture capital's money pools, having contributed 31% of the 1989 total. Banking laws and regulations in the United Kingdom and on the Continent allow for direct equity investment and ownership in a company to which a bank already has lent money. In the United States, this can only be done by a separate legal entity, such as a bank-owned SBIC or venture capital company that can conduct business at arm's length. U.K. and Continental banks have far-ranging networks, access to deals, and economic influence that have important implications for venture capital strategy, practice, and competitive options.

Another major contrast between Europe and the United States is the role of pension funds as suppliers of venture capital: in Europe, they provide less than half of the 36% of their U.S. counterparts. And government agencies provide 5% of the venture capital in Europe, while the U.S. government role, except in loans to SBICs, is nonexistent.

Detailed data on all eighty-six Japanese funds were not available, but the largest single pool, JAFCO, with $2 billion or one-

FIGURE 3-5 **European Venture Capital Sources, 1989 (new funds: $6.283 billion)**

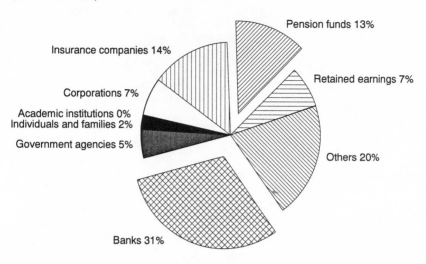

Source: Data from *EVCA Yearbook.*

quarter of the total, is dominated by corporations (37%) and financial institutions (36%), as shown in Figure 3-6.

In Europe and Japan, individuals and families account for 2% and 7%, respectively, of the total, as compared to the 6% U.S. figure. Yet they played very different roles in the early gestation of the venture industry in both areas. In the early days of American venture capital, wealthy individuals were the dominant suppliers and initiators of the industry and remained so through the 1970s. In contrast, the money roots in Europe and Japan have been far more institutional in nature.

Australia, on the other hand, has enjoyed funding from both institutions (44%), and individuals and families (34%), while corporations have contributed slightly, (2%) in 1987, a fairly representative year. The heavy role of individuals in Australia is quite reminiscent of early patterns in the United States.

The Canadian situation also has paralleled that in the United States, as reflected in the 1987 sources. Pension funds are by far the largest single source at 37% (compared to 46% in the United States). Individuals and families are second with 17%, followed by corporations (15%) and insurance companies (11%).

While there are similarities, what is striking is the considerable differences from region to region and country to country in who

FIGURE 3-6 **JAFCO's Shareholders, 1988 (Assets: $2 billion)**

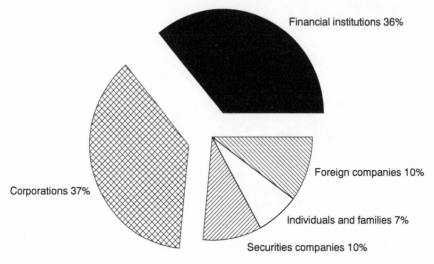

Source: Data from *Asian Venture Capital Journal.*

are the suppliers of money for venture funds, and their relative roles. It is quite apparent that the differences in the money sources between regions are a product of their unique regulatory conditions and financial markets. And, clearly, there seems to be no single "cookie cutter pattern" in the sources of funding around the globe.

As a generalization, in the less-developed countries where venture capital is embryonic, governmental initiatives have played a much larger role. Most of this has been through the efforts of the International Finance Corporation, a development banking arm of the World Bank. What is not known is whether—and how long it will take—classic venture capital will take root in these parts of the world. The entrepreneurial roots, and the requisite frontline experience and perspective that are acquired by actually helping companies to start and grow can take a generation to become established.

THE MONEY MANAGERS

While private, independent firms have emerged as the dominant conduits of venture capital in the United States, a quite different pattern has evolved abroad, where corporate- and government-related venture-capital firms play a much larger role. To illustrate, corporate firms accounted for 30% and Crown-related firms for 16% of the venture capital under management in Canada in 1989. Independent private firms accounted for the remaining 54%. We know from the American experience that a fund dominated by institutional sources or the government does not have the investing independence and flexibility of a fund with a sizable number of smaller private investors. Three or four general partners in such a fund can evaluate investments, make decisions, and close deals on a consensus basis faster than a fund that is part of a bank or corporation. For example, the one-time head of the venture capital arm of the large U.S. chemical company, Monsanto, told us, "We cannot make decisions fast enough to compete in today's fast-moving market even though we report right to the top of the company." He has since left to form his own fund.

There is substantial variation in disbursement patterns and practices around the world, probably more than one might suspect. Venture capital means different things in different countries. The following will outline the general characteristics of venture capital management in different countries: firm sizes; the typical size of investments made in companies at different stages of their growth; the industry sectors that have attracted venture capitalists in recent years; and the extent of investing activity at different business stages.

Firm Size

We have argued that venture capital may be the "ultimate cottage industry." By any measure venture capital firms (with some notable exceptions) are tiny, very labor/management-intensive, craft businesses. There are no formal training programs for would-be practitioners. It is a business learned by apprenticeship and by doing. Commonly, one general partner exists for each $10 to $15 million of capital under management, although less if the fund is involved in startup and early-stage companies and more if later-stage and LBO/MBO/MBI deals. Given the average size of venture capital firms around the world in recent years—that is, $40 to $50 million (see Figure 3-7), one can quickly infer that most firms have three to five general partners.

Within Asia, average firm sizes vary widely—from $10 million in Thailand to $67 million in Japan. The data reveal something of the underlying economics within funds of this size. Typically, the venture capital partnership or firm receives a 2% to 2.5% manage-

FIGURE 3-7 **Average Size of Venture Capital Firms**

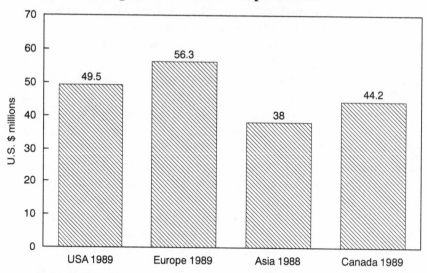

Source: Data from *Asian Venture Capital Journal, EVCA Yearbook,* and *Venture Capital Journal.*

ment fee, based on total committed capital. Thus, a $50 million fund would generate $1 to $1.25 million each year for salaries and expenses for managing the fund. While this may seem like a lot of money, it does not go all that far for partners living and doing business today in most major cities, especially London or Paris. A survey reported at the 1990 Venture Forum showed total compensation for partners in the United States ranged from a low of $212,000 in corporate and industrial funds, to $363,000 in private independent funds, and to $548,000 in funds associated with financial institutions. Office expenses, travel, and two or three junior associates with salaries of $50,000 to $75,000 a year can chew up the management fee in a hurry.

Such numbers also make it evident that there is a threshold fund size of at least $20 to $25 million, by U.S. standards at least, needed to support the quality of management talent necessary to succeed. At the other extreme, one can see the incentive to raising larger and larger megafunds. A $200+ million fund may have only two or three additional general partners but a lot more fee income to go around. By focusing on substantial LBOs, MBOs, and larger expansion financings, economies of scale come into play.

Deal Size According to Stage of Venture

The amount of capital invested is directly related to the stage of the venture at the time of the investment. Seed investments for creating a prototype, conducting beta tests, and developing a sense of the market and a business plan require considerably less capital than a company starting up with significant requirements in facilities, manpower, marketing expenditures, and materials. The former can be funded for as little as $10,000 to $100,000 and usually average under $500,000. Later-stage and LBO transactions in established ventures require substantially larger rounds of financing.

Figure 3-8 confirms a strong similarity in deal size between the United States and Europe for 1989. Rather than doling out a single lump sum upfront, investors have long practiced a "one-step-at-a-time" philosophy. The decision to invest in subsequent rounds depends on the progress made during the previous round and whether the future prospects and the valuation are likely to yield an attractive return.

The one startling exception to this pattern is Australia, as shown in Figure 3-9. Here we see an industry that looks even more like classic venture capital than did the United States' in the peak days of the 1960s and early 1980s. Australia has a decided emphasis on seed, startup, and early-stage investing. That stands in contrast to the abandonment of such early-stage companies elsewhere in the world.

Unfortunately, the news from Australia has a dark side. In August 1989, a working party established under the auspices of the Management Investment Company (MIC) Licensing Board, and under the leadership of Ralph Ward-Ambler, reported to the

FIGURE 3-8 **Average Size of Investment at Different Stages: United States versus Europe and the United Kingdom, 1989 (in $ thousands)**

	Seed	*Startup*	*Early*	*Expansion*	*LBO/MBO acquisition*
United States	$483	$655	$578	$623	$2,196
Europe and the United Kingdom	$357	$409	$404	$617	$1,882

Source: Data from Venture Economics, Inc., and EVCA.

FIGURE 3-9 **Australian Investments by Stage, 1988 (Cumulative: $144 million)**

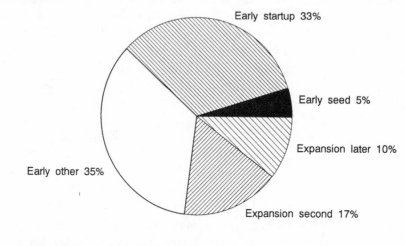

Proportion Invested by Industry

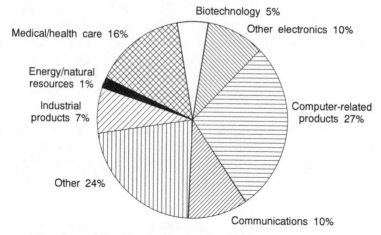

Source: Data from *Asian Venture Capital Journal.*

Minister of Commerce and Industry on the role of the young industry in the innovation process. They concluded that the MIC program had been a catalyst in the establishment of a venture capital industry in Australia; that there were structural problems associated with the program that militated against its effectiveness in the future; and that the MIC program should not be extended beyond June 30, 1991. Their primary recommendation was to create a "fund of funds" in Australia to provide capital to growing businesses.[8] The termination of the program will surely lead to a further shake-out within the Australian venture capital industry and a major reappraisal by all concerned. Those few venture firms that have managed to find a self-sustaining niche will prevail. We suspect that, as in the United Kingdom and Europe, most of the survivors will gravitate to later-stage investing. One recent example is Venture Management Associates of Australia, which has raised $40 million for a new Japan-Australia fund that will invest in existing firms with proven track records and the potential to capture world, particularly Japanese, markets. Main backers are C. Itoh and Co., the large Japanese trading house, and certain large corporations in Tokyo and Chicago. If this fund reflects the future direction of the Australian venture business, then classic venture capital is on the wane there as well.

Targeted Industry/Technology Sectors

In Chapter 2 we presented data that indicated a shift in investing preferences in the United States over the past decade. A decided taste for electronics, computer hardware, and other technology-based ventures has given way to an appetite for more diverse and less technology-based businesses. By 1989, medical and health-care–related investments in the United States attracted the largest number of investments (685) and dollars ($468.8 million). The computer-related group, though seemingly larger, was fairly evenly divided between software and hardware. (See Figure 3-10.) Communications (638), consumer-related products (424), and "other" products and services (303) ranked third, fourth, and fifth in dollars. Ten years ago, these two categories were virtually nonexistent in the portfolios of venture capital firms. In 1989, totally nontech categories attracted nearly twice as many deals and dollars as did any other category.[9] Computer hardware and systems had dropped to fifth, and electronics to seventh.

The European investing pattern has even less resemblance to the technology-based, new and early-stage company investing that was the trademark of classic venture capital prior to the mid-1980s. Fully 78% of the money invested in Europe in 1989 (see Figure 3-10) was in industrial products (8%), consumer-related products (31%), and "other" (39%). The remainder was divided among six sectors, five of them technology-based. In Europe, and as we have seen in the United States, there is a preference for larger deals by way of expansion financings: LBOs, MBOs, and MBIs in established companies. Such investments enable the deployment of larger

FIGURE 3-10 **Industry Sector Investments, Europe and USA, 1989**

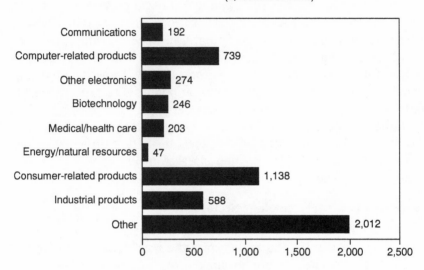

European Venture Capital, 1989
(5,439 investments)

Sector	Investments
Communications	192
Computer-related products	739
Other electronics	274
Biotechnology	246
Medical/health care	203
Energy/natural resources	47
Consumer-related products	1,138
Industrial products	588
Other	2,012

Source: Data from *EVCA Yearbook.*

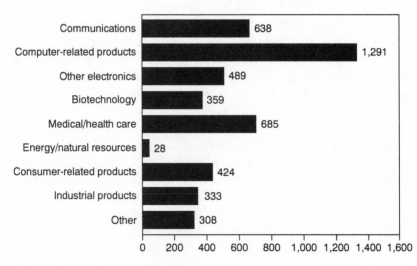

U.S. Venture Capital, 1989
(4,555 investments)

Sector	Investments
Communications	638
Computer-related products	1,291
Other electronics	489
Biotechnology	359
Medical/health care	685
Energy/natural resources	28
Consumer-related products	424
Industrial products	333
Other	308

Source: Data from Venture Economics, Inc.

sums, with less perceived risk, and a faster exit window than "classic high-tech venture deals." According to the EVCA's 1990 annual report, "the computer sector itself may have become saturated, the substantial increases recorded in the biotechnology and communications sectors are clearly indicative of growth emerging in other technology-oriented sectors."[10]

The Canadian venture-capital community also has a very weak taste for the traditional venture-capital technology areas—computer hardware, electronics, biotechnology, and communications account for just 20% combined. They too have been keen to invest in the consumer-related (17%) and "other" (46%) fields but have shown an appetite for industrial products (10%) as well.

Japan's dominant player has allocated its investments in a way that mirrors the European pattern. As of 1988, JAFCO invested only 39% of its capital in computer-related, electronics, biotech, and medical/health-related companies (the United States invested 66% in 1989 while Europe invested 20%), with consumer-related deals attracting 25%, industrial products 10%, and other areas 25%.

Part of this is due to the natural workings of the entrepreneurial process, the competitive dynamics of the birth, maturation, and death of firms. There may be no better barometer of the rise and fall of America's growth industries than the investments made by venture capitalists. Industries with the fastest growth also have the highest birth and death rates among businesses. The predominance of the "other" category reflects the new heterogeneity of the global venture-capital industry. Many new venture capital firms have focused on opportunities previously ignored by the industry and other investors. Examples of this abound in specialty retailing, waste management, environmental products and services, and computer software. What was hot ten years ago is not today, and this should be the case when the market dynamics are at work.

The overriding conclusion about global venture capital from these data is that it is not just the American venture-capital industry that has changed radically, redefining the territory and perverting classic venture-capital investing. European, Canadian, and JAFCO data paint the same picture. As in the United States, the industry looks more like merchant capital than classic venture capital.

There are two exceptions, however: Australia and Singapore. The investing preferences in each of these countries are very much the opposite of what we have seen elsewhere. There, the appetite for the traditional targets of venture capital investing in innovative, technology-based industries dominates. Both countries also are seeking to compete in location- and transportation-insensitive technologies where they can finance and nurture companies that can compete in global markets such as medical products.

New versus Follow-On Investments

A final dimension to examine is the balance of new versus follow-on investments by venture funds. A new investment is just that: the first time a venture fund puts money into a company. Follow-on investments are subsequent rounds made in the same company. Data for the United States and Europe depict very different patterns (see Figure 3-11). New financings dominate the investing activity in Europe (69%), compared with 22% in the United States. Not shown is Canada, where new financings accounted for 75% of the investing activity in 1989.

There are several possible reasons for these differences. First, the European and Canadian venture-capital industries have just completed their first decade, one of explosive growth. By necessity, they have engaged predominantly in new financings, since there was no prior base of first rounds. In sharp contrast to the staged investments and multiple rounds of the United States, single-round financing, particularly in the LBO and MBO deals, abounds. Second, because the industry is still expanding, with new money pouring in, investors are at the front end of the investment cycle. There is substantial pressure to get the money invested within two to three years after it is raised. Third, the United States in the late

FIGURE 3-11 **New versus Follow-On Number of Investments, 1989**

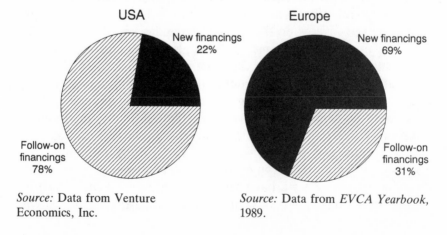

Source: Data from Venture Economics, Inc.

Source: Data from *EVCA Yearbook,* 1989.

1980s was plagued by a dormant IPO market and a very sluggish environment for harvesting. Finally, it is entirely possible that the Europeans and Canadians are simply more aggressive in their efforts to take the plunge and invest in companies for the first time. U.S. investors may have become gun-shy as a result of the turbulent 1980s.

GLOBAL VENTURE CAPITAL OR NATIONAL MERCHANT CAPITAL?

The perversion of classic venture-capital investing is not confined to the American scene. A new breed of venture capitalists has emerged globally in the last decade leaving in its wake a substantially altered, redefined, and expanded industry. But today the term "venture capital" is clearly a misnomer. It is very different from the classic U.S. venture capital. The preference for predominantly equity investments in new, young, and emerging companies, usually with innovative and technology-based products and services, is an even smaller part of worldwide venture-capital investing activity than in the United States. Rather, "merchant capital," or "business development capital" better reflects the capabilities and investing strategies of today's global venture capitalists. As a result, a global scarcity in "classic venture capital" exists both by way of money, inclination, and the skills that characterized the pioneers in American venture capital (see Chapter 9). Other factors that may account for this are the requirements of institutional investors for faster liquidity and less risk. Greater risk aversion and less patience characterize much of the merchant capital now in vogue, which suits institutional investors just fine. As a result, opportunities in startup and early-stage companies continue to outpace the willingness of venture capitalists in U.S., European, and British markets.

Global venture capital is far from homogeneous. For one thing, it is a mirage. While capital may come from all parts of the globe and while cross-border investing is markedly on the rise in Europe and North America, along with increasing involvement in Europe by foreign entities, investing is still predominantly domestic in character. Only 13.5% of the total invested by EVCA members in 1990 was invested outside the venture capitalists' home countries. Further, just 2% of all the EVCA member firms invested 75% or more outside their own country.

Industry structure differs from nation to nation. There are

more firms in the United States, but the average size of venture funds is larger in the United Kingdom and smaller in the rest of Europe. Competition and syndication patterns also differ. In the United States, the most active funds have well-developed international linkages and co-investing relationships; this is much less common in Europe.

The amount of capital flowing in and being invested varies greatly, with Europe now surpassing the United States on an annual basis. Moreover, until recently, the total pool of capital was larger in the United States, but it will be surpassed by Europe's in the early 1990s. According to a 1990 EVCA survey, members anticipated lower industry returns in the 8% to 30% range (a mid-point of 18%–19%), expecting their own funds to perform at 12% to 40% (a mid-point of 26%). Such expectations on the high end must have an all-too-familiar ring for American venture capitalists who lived through the 1980s.

Sources of capital differ substantially: banks and financial institutions dominate Europe; pension funds provide the lead role in the United States; and individuals and families are the main suppliers of capital for pools in Canada and Australia.

Finally, strategies and practices affecting when, where, and how funds are invested vary substantially as well. The typical deal size, the stage of the portfolio at which the investments are made, who manages the money, and appetites for particular industry sectors showed some commonalties among U.S., European, Canadian, and Japanese firms, but there were surprising differences in Australia and Singapore. In Europe future investment targets are the eclectic "other" category, including a wide array of businesses, buyouts and buyins; electronics and startups remain out of favor with EVCA members in the early 1990s.

IMPLICATIONS FOR THE 1990s

The aftermath of the turbulent 1980s continues to buffet the American and worldwide venture-capital industry. More financing alternatives, substitutes, and competitors of venture capital, including a continued growth in corporate venturing in the European region, are expected. In Europe, for example, the restructuring of underperforming assets, industries with potential for consolidation, and secondary purchases from owners are more the style of merchant capital, with only a smattering of new-technology startups.[11]

These developments further threaten the lackluster rates of

return many venture capitalists have achieved in recent years both in the United States and Europe. The European region may be on the brink of its own shake-out, as the parallels with the explosive growth and unsupported optimism of the United States during the 1980s are uncomfortably close. Our sense is that the track record of these funds is quite poor, other than an occasional hit produced by a peak in the unlisted securities markets in the United Kingdom and France.

One reasonable explanation for many of the changes we have discussed is that they are simply the result of the entrepreneurial process of value creation and enhancement in action. Entrepreneurs and venture investors have recognized and pursued new market opportunities in previously "plain vanilla" industries and at later stages in which there was little interest previously. (This shift probably was exacerbated by the maturation of the technology wave from the 1960s and 1970s, which was microprocessor-based.) One can infer from where the bets are being made today that venture capital investors simply do not see the potential payoffs for the risks and efforts required to find, launch, nurture, and grow technology-based companies that they saw ten and twenty years ago. Instead, they find the highest use for the capital in other forms of enterprise.

One significant strategic option that will become available in the next decade is global venture capital, both sources of capital and opportunities to invest. In America, co-investing and syndicating networks during the 1970s and 1980s beat a well-worn path between California and Massachusetts. Such linkages, if replicated on a global basis, offer promising opportunities. For one thing, Europe 1992 is a reality: with 345 million people, it is the wealthiest marketplace in the world. The size and growth potential of these national markets are too enticing to ignore. Without an entry wedge and foothold in Europe, U.S. venture-capital investors may find themselves facing entry barriers and competition that will be difficult to overcome.

There is the distinct possibility that the upside for wealth creation in the European region and the former Soviet Union in the next two decades will lead the world. To compete in the decade ahead and have a shot at the most exciting new and emerging industries and technologies of the 1990s and beyond, venture capitalists need to develop ties outside the United States. Venture capital firms that are content to stay at home will likely wake up to discover that the global village has become a global jungle.

Savvy entrepreneurs and venture capitalists already have their eyes on global markets. One very experienced international investor we know began in 1988 to sell his thirty or so companies in North America and invest in smaller private companies in Europe, in anticipation of 1992. Sometime in the near future, we will see global megafunds. The prototype already exists in Advent, the Boston-based billion-dollar-plus group of funds with more than 300 portfolio companies operating in sixteen nations worldwide.

One thing Americans need to understand is that there is pervasive privacy to the way business is done in Europe and Britain. The highly selective, elitist educational systems and cultures of Britain, France, and Germany produce networks of relationships at the top of financial, business, and government institutions that are unparalleled in the United States. And there are the bureaucratic structures of the EEC commissioners who will oversee the regulatory, banking, taxing, licensing, and other aspects of governance after 1992. Understanding and mastering this complicated maze will be a requirement for entering and doing business. Attempting to do so without a partner who has a foothold and knows the ropes is the highest risk strategy.

IN CONCLUSION: THE NEW PLAYERS

A harsh, but in many ways valid explanation for the decline and deemphasis of classic venture-capital investing may lie in the competencies and skills of the new players in the industry. Many professionals entered the business during the frenzy of the early 1980s. The business must have appeared deceptively easy to these newcomers. Many came from prestigious MBA programs followed by stints at investment banks or other financial or consulting organizations. They typically brought strong analytical and financial skills but little business-building experience. Later-stage deals and LBOs make better use of these skills and are both less punishing on the neophyte and apparently more rewarding.

The decks are stacked against classic venture capital even more in Europe, where the presence of banks as dominant institutional backers has had a direct impact on the shape of strategy and practice in venture capital investing. In the United Kingdom, for instance, a bank may have the right to insist that a company have a chief financial officer, or may object to specific candidates. This financial officer may be required to report directly to the bank's lending officer, in addition to the board of directors of the company.

Furthermore, every company in the United Kingdom is required to be audited by an acceptable accounting firm, preferably one of the major firms.

In Germany, the venture capital industry is dominated by former bank credit managers. This being the case, it is not hard to see how the industry has gravitated toward established companies, LBOs, and management buyouts and buyins, rather than startup and early-stage investing. A banker is more accustomed to analyzing income statements and balance sheets from known, existing companies. There is also a powerful motivation to avoid bad loans. Some of these bank-trained investors may develop into successful venture capitalists: the precedent exists. Yet there is a significant mismatch of their skills and attitudes and those necessary for success in classic venture capital. After all, who ever heard of a bank making a loan to a startup entrepreneur with little or no collateral and no net worth?

CHAPTER 4

Revolutionary New Industries Financed with Venture Capital

M OST AMERICANS are unaware of the profound effect that venture capital in all its forms has on how they live and work. Without the products and services of venture-capital-backed companies, life in today's society would be very different. Consider the following scenario:

It's 8:15 A.M. in Boston. Jane Cadwaller, vice president of marketing of Back Bay Denims, arrives at her office and switches on her desktop Compaq 286 personal computer. While she unlocks her desk and filing cabinets, her computer boots Microsoft DOS from her Seagate hard drive. She connects to the DEC VAX minicomputer via the 3Com local area network and reads her overnight electronic mail. She needs a hard copy of one of the messages so she prints it out on her laser printer with Adobe PostScript. While it's printing, she unpacks her GRiD laptop and removes the Dysan 3½-inch floppy disk with sales projections on a Lotus 1-2-3 worksheet that she prepared at home last night. She inserts the disk into her desktop and copies them onto its hard drive.

Jane's immediate priority is to prepare for the 10:30 A.M. meeting of the executive committee at which she will present her advertising campaign. The next two hours are going to be very hectic. The art work for her presentation has yet to arrive from the New York advertising agency, which was unable to ship it until 6:00 P.M. the night before. But that is the least of her worries—Federal Express has never let her down. However, she is worried about the sales projection exhibits for her presentation. She quickly imports the numbers from her Lotus 1-2-3 worksheet into Harvard Graphics, deftly configures the graphs, and prints them out on overhead transparencies bought from Staples. Then the designer calls from his Cellular One car phone to inform her that the spring collection of jeans is almost finished on his Sun Microsystems CAD/CAM system. He needs to know the estimated sales projections so that he can get cost quotes from their cut-and-sew shops in Hong Kong and Sri Lanka. He wants to fax the designs to them tomorrow. Jane's projections are high. She expects this collection to be a big hit because Back Bay Denim is introducing its prewashed look with denim treated with Genencor's new bioengineered enzyme.

The day is a success. On the way home, Jane stops at an automatic teller machine (ATM) connected to a Tandem fail-safe computer, drives to a Jiffy Lube for a ten-minute lube and oil change, and then visits her father, who is recovering from a heart attack. He is very fortunate. He suffered chest pains as he sat watching television at home. At once, he summoned help from the emergency unit of his local hospital by pressing the button on his Lifeline System home-hospital link. In fifteen minutes, the emergency medical technicians had him at the hospital. Speedy treatment with t-PA minimized permanent damage to his heart. Jane's last stop is at J. C. Bildner's market where she buys a packet of Trios tortellini and the sauce to go with it.

As soon as she arrives home, Jane asks her husband, John, to put three quarts of water on the stove for the tortellini. She then pours a couple of Samuel Adams beers and breaks open a bag of Smartfood cheese-flavored popcorn. As they wait for the water to boil, John lays the cutlery on their Italian dining table, which they recently bought from Domain. "What have you got planned for this evening?" John asks. "Well," Jane replies, "would you like to go to Filene's Basement to shop for some clothes? It's having a special sale of Liz Claiborne dresses that I would like to look at. Or we could watch a movie on Continental Cablevision. I have to catch an early morning flight to Chicago on Midway."

Although Jane and her husband may not realize it, every one of the named products and services in this scenario is from a company backed with venture capital—from individuals, organized funds, or corporations—at some stage of its life. And lower down in the value-added chain are other products and services from venture-capital-backed companies; for example, the 80286 chip that is the brain of Jane's computer was invented by Intel, the integrated circuit that makes all the electronics possible was invented independently at both Fairchild Semiconductor and Texas Instruments, and the ion implantation technique that is critical to manufacturing chips was pioneered at High Voltage Engineering and developed at Extrion.

Some venture-capital-backed companies create products so revolutionary that they give birth to new industries; others bring about evolutionary change in existing industries. Let's take another look at our Jane and John scenario:

The minicomputer industry was created by Ken Olsen's Digital Equipment Corporation. The personal computer industry was made possible when Ted Hoff—inspired by the architecture of DEC's PDP-8—developed Intel's microprocessor. Sales of Apple microcomputers—developed by Steve Jobs and Steve Wozniak—were turbocharged by Dan Bricklin's Visicalc spreadsheet. Subsequently, sales of the IBM PC with its DOS software from Bill Gates's Microsoft were rocketed into the stratosphere by Mitch Kapor's Lotus 1-2-3 worksheet. Miniaturization of hard-disk drives was led by Al Shugart, first at Shugart Associates and then at Seagate Technology, Inc. Fail-safe computers—crucial to on-line transaction processing—were the brainchild of James Treybig, founder of Tandem. Computer-aided design and manufacturing (CAD/CAM) was pioneered by Philippe Villers at Computervision, and powerful workstations that put CAD/CAM within reach of even the smallest manufacturing company were developed at Bill Poduska's Apollo, Scott McNealy's Sun Microsystems, and DEC. The connectivity that allows computers to communicate with one another was pioneered by Gordon Bell at DEC and by Bob Metcalfe, inventor of the local area network (LAN) protocol called Ethernet and founder of 3Com.

Of course, what made the computer revolution possible was Shockley, Bardeen, and Brattain's invention of the transistor at Bell Labs in 1947. Without doubt, the invention of the transistor was one of the most important ever. Some have called it the major invention of the century.[1] Others have even suggested that it was the most significant invention since the wheel.[2] No Nobel Prize was more deserved than the one awarded to Shockley, Bardeen, and Brattain in 1956.

Another Nobel Prize–winning discovery, the basic structure

of DNA by Francis Crick and James Watson, lies at the heart of another revolution, biotechnology, that promises as much for the improvement of mankind's well-being as semiconductors do. Genentech, which developed t-PA, the blood-clot–dissolving drug for treating heart attacks, has been the most successful of the hundreds of biotechnology companies founded since the birth of the industry in 1971. Many of them, like Genentech, were funded with venture capital.

Venture capital was vital to the firms that set the pace for the commercial development of three of our most important scientific discoveries, the programmable electronic computer, the transistor, and DNA. It is one of the crucial ingredients in the mix of scientific discovery, entrepreneurial talent, and finance that drives new industries, some powerful enough to transform society.

In this chapter, we will look at venture capital's role in fostering the semiconductor, computer, and biotechnology industries. That's not to downplay its importance to other industries. The revolution in the way packages are shipped and delivered, for example, was caused by Fred Smith's Federal Express.

SEMICONDUCTORS

Silicon Valley

When William Shockley founded his company in Stanford University's Research Park in 1955, no one knew then that he was starting an industry that was to give a whole region its name: Silicon Valley. Shockley chose Palo Alto as the site for his company partly because it was where he grew up and his mother still lived there, partly because he was aware that entrepreneurial electronics companies were hatching there, and partly because Arnold Beckman, his financial backer and founder of Beckman Instruments, had located one of his divisions in the Stanford Research Park.

One of Shockley's motivations for starting his transistor company in 1955 was his conclusion that "the most creative people were not adequately rewarded as employees in industry."[3] Shockley attracted to his transistor company the brightest and best young men, who formed the nucleus of entrepreneurial scientists and engineers that built the semiconductor industry in Silicon Valley. But they didn't make their fortunes at Shockley's company. Wealth came later when they started and built their own companies.

In 1957, eight of them left to found Fairchild Semiconductor.

Robert Noyce was one of them. According to Noyce, one of their principal reasons for leaving was that they could get equity in a startup company rather than simply working for a salary for the rest of their lives. They weren't disappointed. Seven years later, each of the eight received about $250,000 when Fairchild Semiconductor was bought out by its parent, Fairchild Instrument and Camera—not a shabby return on their original investments of $500 each.[4] But it was only the prelude to bigger returns from their next startup.

When the Shockley Eight launched the first company to focus exclusively on silicon devices (rather than those of germanium), they were financed by Sherman Fairchild. At the time he was the largest individual stockholder of IBM through stock inherited from his father who was one of IBM's founders. Sherman owned Fairchild Instrument and Camera, which set up the Shockley Eight as Fairchild Semiconductor.[5] Venture capitalist Arthur Rock helped arrange the financing.

Thus, we see a pattern emerging at the start of the semiconductor industry in Silicon Valley: a scientific breakthrough followed by commercial exploitation by entrepreneurial scientists and engineers financed with venture capital from technologically savvy, wealthy investors. We shall see how the organized venture-capital industry was crucial in the next stage.

Intel: The Fairest of the "Fairchildren"

There can be little doubt that Fairchild was the breeding ground for the technology entrepreneurs—sometimes dubbed "Fairchildren"—who built the semiconductor industry in Silicon Valley. About half the firms can trace their roots to Fairchild. It is a distinguished list of movers and shapers, among them, Intel, National Semiconductor, and Advanced Micro Devices (AMD). But the fairest of them all is Intel.

In the summer of 1959, Noyce, then director of R&D at Fairchild, invented the integrated circuit. (Jack Kilby at Texas Instruments independently discovered the same concept a few months earlier. Today, Kilby and Noyce are recognized as the co-inventors of the integrated circuit.) The importance of the integrated circuit to the development of the semiconductor industry was second only to the invention of the transistor itself. So Noyce was already a legendary figure when he and Gordon Moore resigned from Fairchild in 1968.

Noyce and Moore, with Rock as their venture capitalist,

launched their next semiconductor company, Intel. Rock as lead investor raised $2.5 million and Noyce and Moore each invested about $250,000. Through years of tireless endeavor, they multiplied their original investments of $500 in Fairchild a hundred-thousand-fold. In 1982, Moore owned 9.6% of Intel, with a market value of more than $100 million, and Noyce owned 3.6%.[6] No one deserved it more. They had been at the forefront of building a new industry. Their companies were responsible for breakthroughs that trans-formed not only the semiconductor industry but society itself.

The transistor was the basic building block for microelectron-ics. Then came the integrated circuit that made it possible to build electronic circuits out of discrete components—transistors, capac-itors, resistors—on one chip. The body, so to speak, had its com-ponents connected together with a nervous system. All it needed was a brain to give it intelligence. It was on the brain that Intel focused. First, it developed memory chips, then, almost by chance, it invented the microprocessor.

Microprocessor: The Computer on a Chip

Ted Hoff was looking for a way to simplify electronic calculators when he invented the microprocessor in 1969. Intel had been approached by a Japanese company to design chips for a proposed desktop calculator. The chips as originally conceived were very complex—much too complicated for Hoff's liking. He had a PDP-8 minicomputer—DEC's phenomenally successful minicomputer—on his desk and he wondered why calculator chips had to be so much more complicated.[7] With the PDP-8 architecture fresh in his mind, he set about designing a microprocessor, which is simply a central processing unit (CPU) on a chip.[8] Intel shipped the first commercial microprocessors in 1971. It was the beginning of an-other revolution—one that, according to Hoff himself, will last for fifty to a hundred years as more and more functions that have been performed only by human brains will be done by machines. No wonder Hoff has been acclaimed one of the most influential sci-entists of the post–World War II era.[9]

The Role of Organized Venture Capital

Rock's investment in Intel was about as perfect as any venture capitalist could wish for. Noyce and Moore were two superstars of the semiconductor industry with proven track records. The industry was still in its early-growth stage. True, U.S. sales were over a billion dollars, but the industry was still fragmented enough that the entry barriers for startup companies were not overwhelming.

Before Rock launched Intel, there had been only a handful of venture-capital-backed startups. But that was about to change. Other budding entrepreneurs were making proposals to other venture capitalists. Between 1967 and 1972, about thirty companies were started with venture capital (Figure 4-1), including such luminaries as National Semiconductor—which was started the year before Intel—and Advanced Micro Devices.

As Figure 4-1 shows, the surge in venture capital investing preceded the surge in industry sales by about four years. It would be extreme to state that the venture capital industry deserves all the credit for the success of the semiconductor industry. After all, giants such as AT&T, IBM, and Motorola also played a big role. However, it is fair to claim that venture capital accelerated the invention and commercialization of new products. Today, Intel, National Semiconductor, and Advanced Micro Devices account for sales of more than $7 billion.

FIGURE 4-1 **Semiconductor Industry: Cumulative Number of Venture Capital Investments and Industry Shipments**

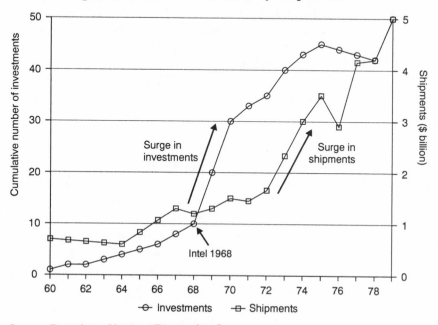

Source: Data from Venture Economics, Inc.

COMPUTERS

Throughout the 1960s and 1970s, IBM stood astride the computer marketplace like a colossus so that few people—even those familiar with the industry—are aware that venture capital was in at the birth of the commercial industry. During World War II, J. Presper Eckert, Jr., and John Maulchy were leading members of the team that developed the first general-purpose computing machine, ENIAC, at the University of Pennsylvania. Early in 1946, they had a working computer. Soon afterward, they formed Eckert-Maulchy Corporation to develop and sell UNIVAC computers, which were based on the ENIAC design, for business and government purposes.[10]

In 1948, Eckert-Maulchy began marketing its computer—six years before IBM delivered its first business computer. The response from potential customers was very positive, but actual orders were hard to come by because the company was severely hampered by lack of adequate financing. Eckert and Maulchy knew about a new form of financing for high-tech startups being pioneered by ARD in Boston.[11] But they did not get financing from ARD or any other firm in the infant venture-capital industry. Instead, they turned to American Totalizer, a Philadelphia company that made racetrack tote boards, for backing. Even so, as Eckert-Maulchy struggled to get its UNIVAC working, it was woefully short of cash. It was forced to sell out to Remington Rand, a major office equipment company, in 1950.

Another startup, Engineering Research Associates (ERA), embarked on a course similar to Eckert-Maulchy's after World War II. It grew out of a group developing electronic calculators for the navy during the war. A Washington financier, John E. Parker, seeking peacetime work for Northwest Aeronautical Corporation's St. Paul glider plant provided ERA with the plant and financing in return for half the equity.[12] Through that happenstance, Minneapolis–St. Paul grew into one of the centers of the computer industry. ERA, like Eckert-Maulchy, was acquired by Remington Rand.

The first UNIVAC I was delivered to the Census Bureau in mid-1951, three years before IBM delivered its first computer for business applications. Most observers agree that Remington Rand's UNIVAC was superior to IBM's offering. But by the end of 1956, IBM had 70% of the market. One can only muse about what might have happened if venture capital had been as abundant at the end of the 1940s as it is today. In 1957, William Norris, one of the founders of ERA and then head of what had become the Sperry Rand UNIVAC division left in disgust and took fifty engineers with him to Control Data Corporation (CDC).[13]

We'll return to CDC later, but for now we want to turn to Boston, where two other engineer-entrepreneurs were about to launch a different kind of computer company, DEC, with venture capital backing from ARD. It was the beginning of the minicomputer industry, and venture capital was there at its conception, nurtured its infancy, supported it through adolescence, and didn't abandon it when it faltered in adulthood. DEC single-handedly created the minicomputer. And as we shall see later, when it comes to personal computers, venture-capital-backed companies can claim the lion's share of the credit for the innovations that drive that segment. What's more, venture capital has played a crucial role in the developing of other segments of the computer industry, including workstations and supercomputers.

Minicomputers

In 1957, ARD's Bill Congleton visited MIT's Lincoln Laboratories. In those days, venture capitalists from ARD would from time to time be shown around MIT's labs to talk to scientists and engineers who were working on interesting technologies that might make good investments. On that particular day, Congleton was taken to see the computer research of two young engineers, Ken Olsen and Harlan Anderson, who were working at Lincoln Labs. He was impressed with what he heard and suggested that if they wanted to start a business of their own, ARD might be interested in funding it.[14]

Their first attempt at a proposal to ARD was a four-page plan. Congleton asked them to flesh it out with more details. After researching business and economics texts in the Lexington Public Library, they resubmitted a four-year business plan. It was good enough for Olsen and Anderson to be invited to make an oral proposal to ARD's board at its Boston offices. Many a would-be high-tech entrepreneur has stood before that board and faced the legendary General Doriot. "Just assume that I understand sophomore physics," he would say somewhat disarmingly early in the presentation as the technology was being explained.[15] The general's penetrating business questions—honed on generations of Harvard Business School students and spoken with a French accent—would follow later as he took the measure of the man and his idea.

Doriot used to say something like "Always consider investing in a grade A man with a grade B idea. Never invest in a grade B man with a grade A idea." He knew what he was talking about; over the years, he invested in about 150 companies and watched over them as they struggled to grow. In Olsen, he had that rare grade A man. At MIT's Lincoln Labs, Olsen was known as the man who got things done on the Whirlwind computer project, which was the fastest computer in the 1950s. Olsen had led a team that built a memory test computer in an astonishing nine months. He knew a great deal about IBM because he was MIT's liaison with 200 IBM engineers who were working on the air force's Semi-Automatic Ground Environment (SAGE) project—for which Whirlwind was the computer—with MIT. Olsen actually worked inside IBM's Poughkeepsie plant for a little more than a year. He was as familiar as anyone with IBM's design and manufacturing capabilities.

So ARD had in Olsen a grade A man, but what about the market? The ARD board was wary of computers. It is said that Congleton even counseled Olsen and Anderson not to use the word *computer* when making their presentation to ARD's board.[16] At the time, some of America's most successful corporations, RCA and GE among them, were losing money in that new industry. And according to a market study by the prestigious consulting firm Arthur D. Little, the total demand for computers of all types was $2.4 billion. Applications of computer processing, it was believed, would be limited to very large-scale computational projects.[17] Nevertheless, there was evidence of a burgeoning industry. With sales from its blossoming computer division, IBM's revenues topped $1 billion in 1957, and by 1958, 1,200 businesses and government agencies were using about 1,700 computers.

ARD decided to fund Olsen and Anderson. It invested $70,000 for what eventually turned out to be 77% of the equity of the company. It also agreed to loan the company a further $30,000 during its first year. Because ARD was so nervous about competing in the computer industry, Olsen and Anderson agreed not to build computers right away; the company's name, originally proposed as Digital Computer Corporation, became Digital Equipment Corporation.[18] DEC never again raised equity financing until it went public nine years later. When it needed more cash in 1963, ARD provided a $300,000 loan.

The majority of DEC's board seats were held by ARD staff. Board meetings were held at ARD's offices in Boston. Although

Doriot didn't have a seat on the board until 1972, he was Olsen's sounding board and adviser from the start. According to Pat Liles, himself a Harvard Business School professor and a venture capitalist, "You couldn't really say that it was ARD that made DEC such a smashing success; but it was ARD's tender, loving care that got it through a difficult childhood."[19]

"The nice thing about $70,000 is that there are so few of them, you can watch every one," Olsen says.[20] Olsen and Anderson moved into a nineteenth-century woolen mill. They furnished it with second-hand furniture. Tools were purchased from the Sears catalog. They built much of their own equipment, as cheaply as possible. Their first products were digital laboratory modules and digital systems modules. They sold $94,000 worth in their first year and made a profit at the same time—a very rare feat indeed in the annals of high-tech startups.

In 1959, they went after the market they had intended to enter all along, computers. The first PDP-1—called a "programmable data processor" to avoid the *C* word—was shipped at the end of 1960. It appeared to be an advance on DEC's line of logic modules; it was in fact a general-purpose computer about the size of a refrigerator built with semiconductor components rather than vacuum tubes and equipped with a cathode ray tube (CRT) monitor. True, it had only 4K of memory and performed just 100,000 additions per second, but at $120,000, it gave more performance for the price than anyone expected.

In 1960, the industry was dominated by huge million-dollar mainframes housed in glass-walled rooms isolated from the user, who submitted stacks of punched cards that had to be fed into the computer by special operators. The end-user often waited a day or more for the output only to find that the program had been unable to run because of an error in the punched cards.

What DEC did with the PDP-1 was revolutionary: it put the computer into the hands of the user, who could interact with it directly via a keyboard and see what was entered on a monitor. It was the beginning of a new era in computing. A new industry, minicomputers, was born.

From its beginning, DEC benefited from its ties with MIT. Its engineering atmosphere appealed to MIT engineers and scientists. DEC's products were much more friendly to scientists and engineers than IBM's number-crunching goliaths. To engineers who wanted to build things, DEC looked very inviting. It was just the kind of place that was attractive to Gordon Bell, an MIT graduate student. He joined DEC as its second computer engineer in the summer of 1960. Over the next two decades or so, he was the engineering genius who, second only to Olsen, built the minicomputer industry.

Bell—hailed as the Frank Lloyd Wright of computers by *Datamation* magazine—conceived the architecture of DEC's line of minicomputers. The company added models to its PDP line in fairly quick succession. In 1965, it introduced its PDP-8, with Bell's architecture implemented by Edson de Castro—a project leader who had proven his mettle on the PDP-5. The PDP-8 was aggressively priced at $18,000—well below anything else with comparable performance. It was an instant best-seller. More than 50,000 were sold in the next 15 years.

Propelled by the PDP-8's phenomenal success, DEC grew geometrically over two decades to become the only true challenger to IBM worldwide. The October 1986 *Fortune* hailed Olsen as America's most successful entrepreneur ever—surpassing even Henry Ford. Three decades after it introduced its first computer, the PDP-1, DEC's sales revenue was $13 billion—placing it thirtieth on the *Fortune* 500. Its net income was almost $1.1 billion, and it employed about 120,000 people at more than five hundred locations worldwide. It was the biggest employer in two states, Massachusetts and New Hampshire.

One year after it introduced the PDP-8, DEC went public at $22 per share. Olsen's share of the company was worth $7 million. ARD's $70,000 had multiplied to more than $37 million—a return rate of about 100% per year over nine years. DEC's sales were growing at a 30% to 40% rate. Not surprisingly, success of that sort attracted both entrepreneurs and venture capitalists. Other minicomputer startups began to appear. One researcher found that 170 different firms introduced minicomputers at one time or another over about two decades beginning about 1960. Of those, 108 were founded specifically to produce minicomputers.[21] The cumulative number of minicomputer startups is shown in Figure 4-2.

Perhaps the most visible of these startups was Data General. It was founded in 1968 by a group of former DEC employees led by de Castro and financed by New York venture capitalist Fred Adler. Before Adler chose to invest in Data General, he had vetted dozens of other proposals for minicomputer startups from would-be entrepreneurs. De Castro's proposal was the first to meet his criteria. It wasn't perfect. No one wanted to be president, so Adler himself acted as president for the first six months until de Castro

FIGURE 4-2 **Minicomputer Industry: Cumulative Number of Startup Companies and Industry Shipments**

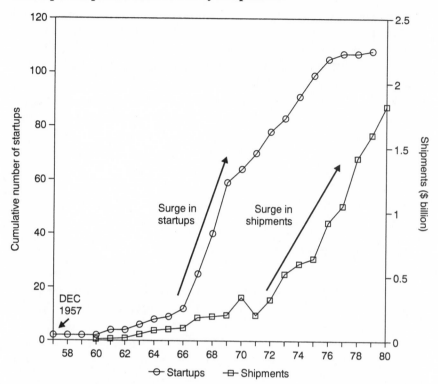

Source: Data from Venture Economics, Inc.

was convinced to take that position. Just as Doriot and his ARD staffers counseled DEC, so too Adler nurtured Data General, often on a daily basis.[22]

"Data General was the son, emphatically the son of DEC," according to Tracy Kidder in his best-seller *The Soul of a New Machine*.[23] But it was a son unloved by Olsen and his staff at DEC. Data General's Nova minicomputer was an instant success. In the first year, two hundred Novas were shipped to customers that might well have bought PDPs from DEC. Data General rapidly rocketed out of a pack of about seventy different companies manufacturing minicomputers in 1970 to be number three in the industry.

Data General was followed in 1972 by Prime Computer, another venture-capital-backed startup, with Bill Poduska—the MIT computer engineer who later founded Apollo and then Stellar (subsequently Stardent) computer—as one of the founders. And it was not just startups that benefited from venture capital: when

Wang Laboratories was growing rapidly in the late 1970s with its word processor, it borrowed money to finance its expansion from Massachusetts Capital Resource Company—a venture capital fund started at the initiative of Governor Michael Dukakis and a handful of Massachusetts pension companies. And more recently, Prime was rescued from a shotgun marriage to a decidedly hostile suitor by a venture-capital white knight, J. H. Whitney & Co.

The region of Massachusetts where those minicomputer companies were located—loosely referred to as Route 128—was the minicomputer capital of the world. As the economy grew and people prospered, engineer-entrepreneurs and the venture capitalists who backed them were heroes. Other types of venture-capital-backed computer companies sprang up. Notable among the new products were two hybrids of the minicomputer: fail-safe (or, as they are sometimes called, fault-tolerant) computers and workstations.

Fail-Safe Computers

Few things are more annoying than being told the computer is down when you are trying to make an airline reservation or withdraw cash from an ATM. In 1975, James Treybig, then marketing manager for Hewlett-Packard's minicomputers, saw the need for a new kind of computer—one that had a much higher on-line reliability. His idea was quite revolutionary. No one knew how big it was likely to be. Fortunately, Kleiner Perkins, a San Francisco venture capital firm, was intrigued enough with the idea to put up about $50,000 for Treybig to do a marketing study, with much more money to follow if the numbers were attractive. Kleiner Perkins liked the plan and invested in Treybig's company, Tandem Computer. The deal was one of the first examples of a venture capital firm incubating a would-be startup.

Treybig says that Tandem could not have happened anywhere in the world except Silicon Valley, where he was able to find capital, very supportive vendors, and people with an attitude that made Tandem succeed.[24] In its first decade, Tandem's growth was astounding, sometimes doubling from year to year. For 1989, its revenue was $1.7 billion.

Tandem did not have the new industry segment, fail-safe computers, to itself for very long. As we have already seen, a new, rapidly growing industry soon attracts other entrepreneurs and venture capitalists eager to fund them. By the beginning of the 1980s, other fledglings found venture capital investors. More than $100 million of venture capital was invested in half-a-dozen startups that included Stratus Computer, Synapse Computer, Auragen Systems, Tolerant Systems, Parallel Computers, and Sequoia Systems. Bill Foster founded Stratus. At the time, he was vice president at Data General and, before that, one of the developers of Hewlett-Packard's very successful HP 3000 minicomputer. His company is now number two in the industry, with 1990 sales of $404 million. Most of Stratus's venture-capital-backed cohorts never became viable.

Workstations

Impressive as the growth of the fail-safe segment has been, it pales in comparison with another: workstations—an industry pioneered by Poduska's venture-capital-backed Apollo. Workstations are the brightest segment of the entire computer hardware industry, with 1990 sales topping $8 billion and growing at more than 50% annually.[25]

A few years after the 1980 birth of Apollo in Chelmsford, Massachusetts, another star, Sun Microsystems, appeared on its western horizon. And Sun—true to its name—is the brightest of them all. Started in Mountain View, California, by Vinod Khosla, Andy Bechtolsheim, and Scott McNealy with venture capital in 1983, its 1991 sales reached $3.2 billion.

The promise of the workstation market together with his reputation enabled Poduska—who had left Apollo—to raise $50 million of venture capital to start his high-end graphics workstation company, Stellar, in 1985. Faced with mounting development costs and disappointing sales, it subsequently merged with Ardent, a competitor with woes similar to its own. Unfortunately, the merged company, Stardent, with Poduska as CEO and Bell—another veteran of venture-capital-backed companies—as its chief scientist, was unable to survive. The venture capital industry suffered one of its biggest financial losses when Stardent closed down in 1991.

Supercomputers

As DEC's minicomputers were creating an industry underneath IBM's business-oriented number crunchers in the 1960s, Control Data Corporation's powerful scientific computers were creating a niche above them. CDC's computers were designed by Seymour Cray, who subsequently left CDC to start his own supercomputer company, Cray Research, financed by venture capital. Cray set the pace for the supercomputer industry by building machines that outperformed all others. He is a living legend in the computer industry. In 1990, he left Cray Research and started another computer firm, Cray Computer Corporation, to build even faster supercomputers. He is not alone. A new generation of venture-capital-backed computer entrepreneurs is racing to build "machines that are powerful enough to transform science."[26] Among the contenders are Steve Chen's Supercomputing Systems—another spinoff from Cray Research; Danny Hillis's Thinking Machines with its massive parallel-processing technology that found its beginnings in Hillis's Ph.D. dissertation at MIT; and Burton Smith's processor-memory network system company, Tera Computer—an apt name for a company in a race to produce tera levels of performance (a trillion operations a second, a trillion bytes of memory, and a trillion byte per second communication rate).

Microcomputers

The first microcomputers appeared around 1974. They were almost exclusively the domain of so-called nerds who were passionate about taking computing to the masses.[27] The key to their dream was Ted Hoff's microprocessor. By 1975, hobbyists were playing with microprocessor computers—microcomputers as they were then called—that could be put together for a thousand or so dollars. Preeminent among microcomputer kits was the Altair 8800 with Intel's 8080A microprocessor. It was introduced as a $400 kit that, with the addition of peripherals costing another couple of thousand dollars, became a useful—if rather primitive—computer for anyone with the ability to program it. About two thousand were sold in 1975, mainly to engineers and scientists. In 1977, Micro Instrument and Technology Systems (MITS), which made the Altair, was acquired by Pertec—a venture-capital-backed computer-peripheral manufacturer—for $6 million.[28]

Apple Computer Two of the hobbyists who were tinkering with microcomputers were Steven Jobs and Stephan Wozniak, who had been friends since their schooldays in Silicon Valley. Wozniak was an authentic computer nerd. He had tinkered with computers from childhood. He built a computer that won first prize in a science fair. His SAT math score was a perfect 800, but after stints at the University of Colorado, De Anza College, and Berkeley, he dropped out of school and went to work for Hewlett-Packard. Jobs had an even briefer encounter with higher education: after one semester at Reed College, he left to look for a swami in India. When he and Wozniak began working on their microcomputer, Jobs was working at Atari, the leading video game company.[29]

Jobs and Wozniak's computer, the Apple I in kit form, was an instant hit with computer hobbyists. The Byte Shop—the first full-time retail computer store in the world, which had opened in Silicon Valley in December 1975—ordered 25 Apples in June 1976. The owner of The Byte Shop urged Jobs and Wozniak to put their computer board in a case because his customers wanted complete units, not just kits. When they did so, both Apple and The Byte Shop had a hot product on their hands. In the following years, The Byte Shop grew to a chain of 75 stores. "Without intending to do so, Wozniak and Jobs had launched the microcomputer by responding to consumer demand."[30]

Apple soon outgrew its manufacturing facility in Jobs's parents' garage. Their company, financed initially with $1,300 raised by selling Jobs's Volkswagen and Wozniak's calculator, needed capital for expansion. They looked to their employers for help. Wozniak proposed to his supervisor that Hewlett-Packard should produce what later became the Apple II. Perhaps not surprisingly, he was rejected. After all, he had no formal qualifications in computer design; indeed, he did not even have a college degree. At Atari, Jobs tried to convince founder Nolan Bushnell to manufacture Apples. He too was rejected.

However, on the suggestion of Bushnell and Regis McKenna, a Silicon Valley marketing ace, they contacted Don Valentine, a venture capitalist, in the fall of 1976. In those days, Jobs's appearance was a hangover from his swami days. It definitely did not project the image of Doriot's grade A man—even by Silicon Valley's casual standards. Valentine did not invest. But he did put them in touch with Mike Markkula, who had recently retired from Intel a wealthy man. Markkula saw the potential in Apple, and he knew how to raise money. He personally invested $91,000, secured a line of credit from Bank of America, put together a business plan, and raised $600,000 of venture capital. One of the investors was Rock, Intel's venture capitalist.

The Apple II was formally introduced in April 1977. Apple's sales grew rapidly from $2.5 million in 1977 to $15 million in 1978. In 1978, Dan Bricklin, a Harvard business student and former programmer at DEC, introduced the first electronic spreadsheet, Visicalc, designed for the Apple II. It could do in minutes tasks that previously had taken days. The microcomputer now had the power to liberate managers from the data guardians in the computer departments. According to one source, "Armed with Visicalc, the Apple II's sales took off, and the personal computer industry was created."[31] Apple's sales jumped to $70 million in 1979, $117 million in 1980, and $335 million in 1981. By 1982, Apple IIs were selling at the rate of more than 33,000 units a month. With 1982 sales of $583 million, Apple hit the *Fortune* 500 list. It was a record. At five years of age, it was the youngest company, ever, to join that exclusive list.

IBM's personal computers Spurred into action by Apple's success—and to a lesser extent by Tandy's and Commodore's—IBM decided to imitate the way venture-capital-backed entrepreneurial companies develop products. It set up its own personal computer startup in Boca Raton, Florida. What's more, it co-opted the talent of entrepreneurial companies by buying products from them. Abandoning its traditional philosophy of developing everything in-house, it sourced out 80% of its personal computer.[32]

Many of IBM's suppliers were venture-capital-backed companies. Even the microprocessor—the brain of the computer—was bought from Intel, despite IBM's stature as one of the largest and most innovative semiconductor manufacturers in the world. Indeed, the partnership proved so important to both companies that IBM invested in Intel. By 1983, it owned about 20% of Intel's equity.

Almost in contrast to what happened in other segments of the computer industry, venture-capital-backed companies and IBM worked together to build the personal computer market. In the early days of the industry, when demand sometimes exceeded supply, IBM was a gentle blue giant. The introduction of its microcomputer in August 1981 was greeted by Apple with a full-page advertisement run nationally that blazed "Welcome IBM!" With its entry, IBM—a household name synonymous with computers—legitimized microcomputers in the eyes of business managers, dispelling any doubts about their validity in the workplace. Indeed, it was now OK for *anyone* to have a "personal computer," as IBM named the microcomputer. IBM was flooded with orders. There were even waiting lists for IBM computers—a rising tide lifts all boats.

Software

IBM—just like Jobs at Apple—understood that software would be crucial to the success of its personal computer. It turned to a small, venture-capital-backed company, Microsoft, for its MS-DOS operating system. Bill Gates was a Harvard sophomore when he developed the BASIC-8 programming language for microcomputers. He dropped out of school to start up Microsoft. His first product, BASIC, was important to the success of Apple. When IBM chose the MS-DOS operating system, Microsoft's future was assured. With IBM's imprimatur, MS-DOS soon became the operating system of choice for non-Apple microcomputers.

Another venture-capital-backed company contributing to IBM's success was Mitch Kapor's Lotus Development Corporation, which introduced its 1-2-3 spreadsheet in January 1983. There were other spreadsheets—Visicalc being the most notable—but none of them could compete with 1-2-3. Ben Rosen, the venture capitalist who backed Lotus, was on his way to becoming the hottest personal computer pundit in the mid-1980s.

IBM-Compatible Hardware and Software

Personal computer sales topped $5.4 billion in 1982.[33] By then literally hundreds of companies were considering entering the market or had already done so. In the same week of May 1982 that DEC announced its ill-fated personal computer, four other companies introduced PCs.[34] What turned out to be the most successful of the IBM-compatible manufacturers, Compaq, was another of Rosen's investments. Founded by Rod Canion initially to make transportable PCs, it quickly added a complete range of high-performance PCs, soon breaking Apple's record for the shortest time from founding to the *Fortune* 500 list. Rosen—always a passionate promoter of the products of his portfolio companies—was now a star not just of venture capital but of the PC industry itself.

The personal computer industry grew at a torrid pace. Entrepreneurs were exploiting every niche along the value-added stream from semiconductors to retail stores. Many were backed by venture capital. Here are the names, products, and 1990 sales revenues of some notable successes to add to those we have already named: Seagate Technology (disk drives, $2.4 billion); AST (add-on boards and computers, $534 million); Tandon Corporation (drives and computers, $422 million); Adobe (software, $169 million); Novell (connectivity, $423 million); Cypress Semiconductor (microprocessors and memory chips, $199 million), Chips and Technologies (semiconductor chips, $293 million); Businessland (retail stores, $1.4 billion).

Just as some experts were fretting that venture capitalists had invested too much money in too many hard-drive companies,[35]

Conner Peripherals was started. One of its investors was Compaq. Conner's 3½-inch miniature hard drive soon became the standard for laptop personal computers—the fastest-growing segment of the industry. With 1989 sales of $705 million, it climbed into the *Fortune* 500 in just three years, breaking the record held by Compaq. (We'll have more to say about the hard-drive industry in the next chapter.)

Of course, not all the companies were successful. On the contrary, many fell by the wayside. Who remembers Osborne's computer or Eagle's computer or Ovation's software or Shugart Associates' drives or, for that matter, DEC's Rainbow? Apart from Apple, all computers not compatible with the IBM PC ended in failure.

BIOTECHNOLOGY

"Preeminence in the life sciences, abundant venture capital and an entrepreneurial spirit have combined to give the United States a commanding lead in the commercial application of new biotechnological techniques."[36] That 1984 quote succinctly explains why the United States leads the world in biotechnology, where breakthrough discoveries are driving a commercial revolution every bit as profound as those driven by semiconductors and computers. And as in the case of semiconductors and computers, "the ease with which new companies can spring into existence in the United States . . . is a powerful spur to copious innovation and, perhaps more important, its rapid exploitation."[37]

The modern biotechnology industry had its origins in university research labs in Europe and the United States during the 1950s and 1960s. The basic breakthrough was Francis Crick and James Watson's Nobel Prize–winning discovery of the structure of DNA at Cambridge University in 1953. Since then, scientists have found new tools that enable them to manipulate the genetic information of living cells. Two of the most widely used biotechnologies are recombinant DNA—commonly known as genetic engineering— and monoclonal antibody technologies.

Recombinant DNA technology emerged in the 1960s and early 1970s from the laboratories of U.S. universities such as Stanford, Harvard, MIT, University of California, Berkeley, and University of California, San Francisco. The commercial opportunities created by the critical discoveries of university scientists were not developed by large, established companies, as might have been expected, but by small entrepreneurial companies that owe their existence to the U.S. financial community's willingness to provide the risk capital.[38] Today, thousands of companies, universities, and institutes throughout the world are working in biotechnology, but the most dynamic segment by far is the U.S. startup firms created with financial backing from venture capital firms and corporate investors.[39] Between 1971 and 1987, more than 350 such firms came into being in the United States.[40] The total investment was estimated to be $1 to $2 billion. Today, that investment is measured in tens of billions.

The very existence of those biotechnology startups shows that classic venture capitalists are a patient bunch who have the stamina for long-term investments. Anyone investing in a venture started to develop genetically engineered drugs knows it will be a very long time before meaningful profits are realized. It takes eight to ten years, at the minimum, to bring a new drug from discovery to market and costs at least $75 to $100 million.[41] Some observers even put the number at more than $200 million.* Genentech, which emerged as the foremost biotechnology startup of the 1970s, illustrates the resourcefulness of entrepreneurs in raising funds in this industry.

Genentech

Genentech was a brainchild of the venture capital industry itself. Its CEO and co-founder, Robert Swanson, had been a partner in Kleiner Perkins. He decided to leave to start his own company and he hit upon the idea of forming a company to capitalize on biotechnology. By reading the scientific literature, Swanson identified the leading biotechnology scientists and contacted them.

"Everybody said I was too early—it would take ten years to turn out the first microorganism from a human hormone or maybe twenty years to have a commercial product—everybody except Herb Boyer."[42] Swanson was referring to Professor Herbert Boyer at the University of California at San Francisco who is co-inventor of the patents that, according to some observers, form the basis of the biotechnology industry. When Swanson and Boyer met at the beginning of 1976, they almost immediately agreed to become partners to explore the commercial possibilities of recombinant DNA. Boyer named their venture Genentech, an acronym for genetic engineering technology.

---

*A 1990 Tufts University study found the average cost of developing a new drug was $231 million for a major pharmaceutical company.

Swanson resigned from Kleiner Perkins. Financing himself with his savings, he and Boyer produced a business plan with the expectation that Genentech could develop commercial products faster than almost anyone believed was feasible. They proposed to tap into the scientific talent of the California university system to develop targeted drugs for treating humans.

Swanson returned to Kleiner Perkins a few months later—this time as a supplicant with the Genentech business plan in hand—and at the end of his first meeting had a commitment of $100,000 in return for 25% of the equity. That seed money allowed Swanson and Boyer to start their company. With the business under way, Kleiner Perkins put together another round of venture capital nine months later. That second round raised $850,000 for another 25% of the equity. Then just seven months later, Genentech announced its first success, a genetically engineered human brain hormone, somatosin. According to Swanson, they shrank ten years of development into seven months. The venture capitalists willingly put in a third round of money, but this time they got only 8.6% of the equity in return for $950,000. In just sixteen months, the value of Genentech had shot up from $400,000 to $11,000,000.

Genentech rapidly built on its early successes and, in 1980, went public. By then, the infant biotechnology industry—long on promise but short on performance—had captured the imagination of public investors. Genentech's IPO was a spectacular success, raising $36 million for 12% of the company. Investors valued the company at $300 million—not bad for a four-year-old company in an industry awash in a sea of red ink.

Biotechnology companies have insatiable appetites for money to fuel their R&D programs. Because of the long gestation period and FDA approval process for new genetically engineered products, especially prescription drugs, they have a burn rate that cannot be financed by internally generated cash flow. Genentech was extremely resourceful in raising money not only from venture capital funds and an IPO but also through R&D partnerships and strategic partnerships with well-heeled corporations and a large Euro convertible bond issue. In 1990, with annual sales at $400 million and profit of $44 million, Genentech sold 60% of its equity to the Swiss pharmaceutical giant Roche Holdings for $2.1 billion. Genentech's financing history is a pattern that is being repeated by other successful firms. More and more tiny biotechnology companies are getting financing from pharmaceutical giants. The world's drug companies established strategic alliances with 167 biotechnology firms in 1990, compared with only 37 in 1986.[43]

Since being acquired, Genentech itself has become a source of venture capital. It is investing some of its $700 million cash hoard in startups aimed at marrying Genentech's technology to new approaches to developing synthetic chemical drugs.

San Diego's Biotech Industry

San Diego is one of the leading centers of biotechnology in the world. Just like Route 128 with minicomputer startups and Silicon Valley with semiconductor startups, San Diego has the right mix of scientists, engineers, entrepreneurs, and financing to hatch and nurture biotechnology fledglings. The rise of San Diego's biotechnology industry gives important insights into how a region builds a high-tech industry.

According to a longitudinal study by Daryl Mitton—a pioneering entrepreneurship professor at San Diego State University—the right mix in San Diego was research institutions that attracted world-class scientists, a city government that provided considerable incentives for companies to locate in San Diego, universities that actively fostered biotechnology entrepreneurs, and venture capital.[44] Mitton's research was the source on which we base this account of San Diego's biotechnology industry.

Prior to the late 1950s, San Diego's economy was primarily dependent on the military and retirees. Then, in 1956, General Dynamics established a research laboratory overlooking the Pacific on 300 acres donated by the city of San Diego. Within a few years, 250 leading scientists and engineers were working there in a campus-like atmosphere. By the mid-1970s, it employed 3,000 people. In 1960, the state opened the University of California at San Diego (UCSD) on a campus adjacent to that laboratory. From the beginning, UCSD was successful in attracting excellent research faculty. In 1961, the Scripp's Clinic and Research Foundation established its Research Institute nearby. In 1963, the Salk Institute of Biological Studies opened in the same vicinity. And in 1976, the La Jolla Cancer Research Foundation was set up. In the 1970s and 1980s, those research institutions and others that followed were fertile sources of biotechnologists.

San Diego's commercial biotechnology industry began when Calbiochem located there in 1971. It chose San Diego rather than Los Angeles because of its concentration of biotechnology research, affordably priced real estate near the research institutions, and an attractive life-style. Like many pioneers, Calbiochem has had a checkered history. The firm has been bought and sold, and key people have come and gone. Former employees have started three biotechnology firms in San Diego.

A very important milestone occurred in 1978 when two UCSD scientists, Ivor Royston and Howard Birndorf, founded Hybritech to develop products based on monoclonal antibody technology. Their initial funding of $300,000 came from Kleiner Perkins Caufield & Byers—the same venture capital firm, but now with a longer name, that had bet on Genentech—who also helped them recruit an experienced CEO, Ted Greene. Like Genentech, Hybritech financed its growth with follow-on rounds of venture capital, R&D partnerships, corporate strategic partners, and an IPO. In 1976, the company was sold to Eli Lilly for about $500 million. As Mitton put it, Hybritech was the first San Diego firm to make it big.

Not only was Hybritech a role model for would-be entrepreneurs from other institutions, it produced its own entrepreneurs who left to form their own companies. Approximately 90 biotechnology companies had set up shop in San Diego from 1971 to 1991. About 37% of them can trace their roots to other local biotechnology companies; a dozen or more were direct descendants of Hybritech. About 51% trace their roots to research institutions, with UCSD being the progenitor of 34 companies and Scripp's Clinic and Research Foundation 24 companies. And the remaining 12% were firms that moved to San Diego. In terms of the numbers, San Diego ranks fifth as a biotechnology center, behind the San Francisco Bay area with 160 companies, the New York tristate area with 134, Boston with 114, and Washington, DC, with 107.[45]

Venture capital was an important factor in the spawning of this industry. Hybritech itself invested $2 million in Gen-Probe, which was founded in 1983 by Birndorf. In 1988, Gen-Probe, by then successful, invested $1 million in its spinoff, Genta. A year later, Gen-Probe was acquired by a Japanese pharmaceutical company for $111 million. In 1986, Greene left Hybritech with his CFO, Tim Wollaeger, to form Biovest Partners, a venture capital fund specializing in seed-stage biotechnology companies. Within two years, they had funded five firms in the San Diego area and one in San Francisco.

All sources of capital for every biotechnology company that opened in San Diego through 1990 were researched very meticulously by Mitton. What he observed is probably quite representative of biotechnology industry funding elsewhere. A total of $1.372 billion was raised from a variety of sources (Figure 4-3). Most of the funding was risk capital of one kind or another. Twenty-eight percent came from formal venture capital and institutional private placements, with another 20% from public offerings. The largest source of capital—35% of total funding—was corporate strategic partners. This is a very important source for growing biotechnology companies because big firms, especially global pharmaceutical concerns, not only have very deep pockets but also provide strategic support with product testing, regulation compliance, marketing, and distribution. Thirty San Diego biotechnology companies have at least one formal agreement with a corporate strategic partner. More than half have agreements with more than one corporate partner. Of the $482 million from corporate partners, 45% came from America, 29% from Japan, and 26% from Europe.

Biotechnology Today

In 1991, there were more than 1,200 biotechnology companies in the United States.[46] Their products span a whole range of industries, including therapeutic drugs, diagnostic testing, agriculture, textiles,

FIGURE 4-3 **Sources of Capital for San Diego Biotechnology Companies**

Source of financing	Capital ($ million)	Percentage of total
Corporate strategic partners	482.0	35.1
Venture capital and other institutional private placement	386.1	28.1
Public offerings	278.7	20.3
R&D partnerships	140.0	10.2
Debt	68.0	5.0
Founder/angel financing	10.5	0.8
SBIR grants	6.7	0.5
Total	1,372.0	100.0

Source: D. G. Mitton "Tracking the Trends in Designer Genes," in N. Churchill, ed., *Frontiers of Entrepreneurship Research 1991* (Wellesley, MA; Center for Entrepreneurial Studies, Babson College, 1991).

and food manufacturing. Of course, not all of them were backed by venture capital, but there can be no doubt about venture capital's pivotal role in the commercialization of biotechnology. Just look at the leading companies in 1989 (see Figure 4-4). Venture capital was the key source of funding for many of them. Genentech, the most famous of the venture-capital-backed biotechnology start-ups, dominates the list with 42% of the total sales of the companies on the list and twice the profits of its nearest rival. And when the sales of Genencor, its joint venture with Corning, are added in, Genentech accounts for half the sales of the companies listed in Figure 4-4. (Genentech and Corning sold their interest in January 1991.)

For an industry that has received so much investment, biotechnology still remains short on performance and long on promise. The numbers in Figure 4-4 speak for themselves. The total revenues of all ten firms didn't quite amount to $1 billion in 1989. On top of that, they had combined losses of more than $33 million and spent more than $411 million on R&D. With such a high R&D burn rate, it's no wonder that the 1989 annual sales of all biotechnology companies added together amounted to only a fraction of the total money invested in all those companies up to that date. A meaningful return on the investment is still a long way off.

Biotechnology stands in stark contrast to the personal computer industry, which is about the same age. Personal computers

FIGURE 4-4 **Leading Biotechnology Companies, 1989**

Company	Sales ($ millions)	Profit ($ millions)	R&D ($ millions)
Genentech	400.5	44.0	156.9
Amgen	152.2	19.1	62.5
Life Technologies	134.2	13.2	11.3
Genencor International	70.0	n.a.	25.0
Genetics Institute	43.6	(28.7)	n.a.
Biogen	40.9	3.2	n.a.
Chiron	35.5	(21.6)	46.1
Centocor	27.6	0.1	45.4
CETUS	25.2	(49.9)	49.4
Genzyme	23.8	(13.0)	15.0
Total	953.5	(33.6)	411.6

Source: "Enzyme-Eaten Jeans," Forbes, October 29, 1990.

are a $90+ billion industry versus about $3 to $4 billion for bio-technology companies. The sales of the leading half-dozen venture-capital-backed personal computer companies are measured in billions of dollars, while the leading biotechnology companies are measured, at most, in hundreds of millions. And whereas the most recent star of the personal computer industry, Conner Peripherals, crashed through the billion-dollar annual sales level when it was four years old, the superstar of biotechnology, Genentech, will be a fifteen-year-old veteran, maybe older, before it has its first billion-dollar year.

Nonetheless, venture capital is still flowing into biotech firms with promising new technologies. For instance, according to some experts, the next drug revolution will be so-called antisense compounds. The first antisense company, Gilead Sciences, was started with venture capital less than four years ago. It was soon followed by other startups. Gilead Sciences, Genta, Isis Pharmaceuticals, and Triplex were able to garner $30 million of venture capital.[47] That shows how classic venture capitalists are willing to bet on new technologies with the promise of revolutionizing industries, even when the payoff is uncertain and far in the future.

LESSONS FROM THE CREATION OF NEW INDUSTRIES

Let's take stock of the lessons to be learned from the formation and growth of new high-tech industries. What we have been looking at in this chapter are the kind of entrepreneurs whom Joseph Schumpeter—the famous Moravian economist—wrote about in 1912 when he was explaining how industrial revolutions suddenly increased the standard of living of a few industrialized nations.[48] (When the first industrial revolution began in Great Britain about 1760, no nation enjoyed a standard of living equal to that of Imperial Rome two thousand years earlier. But from 1870 to 1979, for example, the standard of living of sixteen nations jumped sevenfold, on average.[49]) Schumpeter reasoned that entrepreneurs deserved the credit for the industrial revolution—those men and women with the imagination and drive to destroy the existing economic order by creating enterprises that develop new products, introduce new methods of production, exploit untapped natural resources, and organize in different ways.[50]

What are the crucial ingredients that facilitate high-tech entrepreneurship in the United States? It seems to us that they stem from (1) technical discoveries that open the window of opportunity;

(2) men and women with the vision to spot those opportunities, with the creativity to transform that vision into products, and with the determination to start and build companies to commercialize those products; and (3) resources—primarily risk capital—to fund and nurture those companies.

The United States has developed its incredible high-tech industries in a laissez-faire way with neither the benefit nor the hindrance of a government directing industrial policy. Perhaps that is what is unique about the U.S. system: the government has provided many of the opportunities by funding R&D but given enterprise free rein to decide which technologies are worth pursuing as commercial ventures.

General Doriot's creation of the first high-tech venture-capital fund at the end of World War II was, in itself, a great entrepreneurial decision. ARD was what Schumpeter had in mind when he wrote about new types of organization that transform economies. Venture capital became the financing of choice—perhaps the only form of financing—for the visionary high-tech entrepreneurs such as Olsen, Noyce, Jobs, and Swanson. Small wonder that U.S. venture capital is the envy of the industrial world. According to Jiro Tokyama, dean of the Nomura School of Advanced Management in Japan and a highly influential economist, "The entrepreneurial firms and the venture capital are the great advantages you [Americans] have."[51]

Keeping the Elephants Agile

Besides their important role in creating new industries in the United States, venture-capital-backed companies also serve the economy well by goading giant firms—categorized as elephants by David Birch[52]—to stay agile. Listen to IBM's CEO, John Akers: "The fact that we're losing market share makes me goddamn mad. . . . The tension level is not high enough . . . the business is in crisis."[53] Nowhere is IBM's loss more painful than in personal computers, where its market share is remorselessly depleted by new products developed at lightning speed by nimble venture-capital-backed companies, many of whom didn't even exist when IBM introduced its first microcomputer in 1981 and coined the term "personal computer." Ten years later, IBM-compatible PCs outsold IBM's own brand better than four to one in the United States.

Akers seems to be echoing, more than a quarter of a century later, what his illustrious predecessor, Thomas J. Watson, Jr., wrote in 1964 out of frustration that CDC had introduced a computer more powerful than anything available from IBM. CDC's laboratories, he pointed out, had "only 34 people including the janitor. Of these, 14 are engineers and 4 are programmers, and only one person has a Ph.D. . . . Contrasting this with our own vast development activities, I fail to understand why we have lost our industry leadership by letting someone else introduce the world's most powerful computer."[54]

Perhaps that says what small high-tech entrepreneurial companies do best of all: unencumbered by large bureaucracies, they have new products on the market while large companies still have them in the planning stage. The best venture capitalists know how to nurture those kinds of companies. They know how to attract the brightest and best people, how to foster a climate that enables them to be creative, and how to motivate them with a meaningful share of the ownership of the business. In short, the best venture capitalists know how to add value beyond money to their portfolio companies.

CHAPTER 5

Venture Capital Investing Strategies: The Case of Capital Market Myopia*

IN THEIR SEMINAL STUDY of venture capital investing in the Winchester hard-disk–drive industry, our colleagues William A. Sahlman and Howard H. Stevenson of the Harvard Business School analyzed a phenomenon they call "capital market myopia," a situation in which capital markets ignore the logical implications of their individual investment decisions. Viewed in isolation, each decision seems to make sense. When taken together, however, they are a prescription for disaster. Capital market myopia, according to Sahlman and Stevenson, leads to overfunding of industries and unsustainable levels of valuation in the stock market.

We have included a condensed version of their pioneering work because of its powerful insights, its lessons for the industry, and its wider implications for today's buffeted and bruised venture capitalists. Their logic and analysis, when applied to the Winchester hard-disk–drive industry, brought forth some stunning revelations. Following their provocative discussion, we will provide a postscript and some reflections on subsequent developments in the hard-disk–drive industry, including a possible exception to the myopia rule.

*The authors wish to express their appreciation to Professors Sahlman and Stevenson for their cooperation and support in making possible the inclusion of their pioneering work "Capital Market Myopia," and their helpful comments on drafts of our postscript to the chapter.

One of the secrets of success is to invest on favorable terms, at low company valuations. Like the surfer in search of the perfect wave, venture capitalists are on an eternal quest for the imperfect market. Bill Egan of Burr, Egan & Deleage put it simply: "What we are looking for is to make bets in a non-auction market. Period. The more players there are for a deal, the less we like it." As we shall see in this chapter, finding the imperfect market is one thing; keeping it to yourself is another.

Capital Market Myopia*

We argue that capital market participants should have seen the "myopia" problem coming. They should have known that valuation levels were absurd. The data necessary to anticipate the problem were readily available before the industry shake-out began and stock prices collapsed. We offer some simple lessons to help investors and entrepreneurs avoid charter membership into the greater fool club.

From 1977 to 1984, professional venture-capital firms invested almost $400 million in 43 different manufacturers of Winchester disk drives. The majority of that capital was invested in the two years, 1983 and 1984, when $270 million was invested in approximately 51 distinct financing rounds, including 21 startup or early-stage investments.[1]

During this same period, the public capital markets were also a large supplier of funds to the disk-drive industry. The total amount of money raised in public offerings of common stocks for participants in the industry was over $800 million. During the middle part of 1983, the capital markets assigned a value in excess of $5 billion to 12 publicly traded, venture-capital-backed hard-disk–drive manufacturers. The strong market valuation of these companies paralleled the boom in other high-technology stocks and rising valuation levels in the stock market in general.

The industry served by these companies was experiencing explosive growth by any measure. In 1978, total sales of hard-disk drives to the original equipment manufacturer (OEM) market were

*Pages 126 to 142 are adapted from William A. Sahlman and Howard H. Stevenson, "Capital Market Myopia," 288-055. Boston: Harvard Business School, 1987. Versions of this paper were published in John A. Hornaday et al., eds., *Frontiers of Entrepreneurship Research* (Wellesley, MA: Center for Entrepreneurial Studies, Babson College) and *Journal of Business Venturing,* vol. 1, no. 1 (Winter 1986), pp. 7–30.

only $27 million. By 1983, total sales were approximately $1.3 billion. Projected sales in 1984 were almost $2.4 billion, an 84% increase. By 1987, sales were expected to reach $4.5 billion.[2]

Given these sanguine projections for the industry, the exuberance in the venture capital community and stock market seems somewhat plausible. However, by the end of 1984, the value assigned to those same 12 manufacturers of disk drives had declined from a height of $5.4 billion to only $1.4 billion. Further, the fundamentals for almost every participant had deteriorated badly, particularly in late 1984. Losses began to appear, and sales even declined for some companies. One company, Seagate, had revenues in each of the first two quarters of 1984 of approximately $100 million only to have total revenues in the third quarter fall to the $50 million level. For all 12 companies, aggregate net income in the quarter ended September 30, 1984, was only $2.3 million, down from an average of $24.2 million in the previous three quarters.

Capital market myopia leads to overfunding of industries and unsustainable levels of valuation in the stock market. While we use the Winchester disk-drive industry to elucidate the phenomenon, capital market myopia has arisen in many other industries many times in the past. No doubt, it will occur in the future.

THE WINCHESTER DISK-DRIVE INDUSTRY (1973–1983)

Winchester disk drives are high-speed data-storage devices for computers. The technology was first introduced in 1973 by IBM. After IBM, a number of independent firms introduced competitive products based on the same basic technology. New entrants included Memorex, CDC, and Storage Technology.

For the most part, these disk drives were designed for use with mainframe computer systems and later minicomputers. The drives were expensive relative to alternative data-storage technologies like magnetic tape or floppy-disk drives. However, performance of Winchester disk drives was far superior to these less expensive media.

As had always been the case in the computer industry, there was an inexorable increase in the performance of machines combined with a decline in cost. This statement was true of the computers; it was also true of peripherals such as disk drives. In 1973, the cost of 10 megabytes of hard-disk capacity was almost $40,000: by 1983, the same 10 megabytes cost one-tenth as much. Equally important, as mini- and microcomputers increased in power, so too did data-storage requirements. Hard-disk drives were tailor-made to meet these needs.

By the late 1970s, many analysts predicted an especially bright future for suppliers of hard-disk drives to the OEM marketplace. One prominent analyst, Jim Porter of *DISK/TREND Reports,* predicted in 1979 that total sales of hard-disk drives to the OEM market would be almost $700 million by 1983, up from only $27 million for all of 1978. The following year, Porter was forced to revise upward his forecast: $1.1 billion in 1983 and $1.5 billion in 1984. The pattern of rising expectations is evident in the 76.5% projected compound annual growth rate in sales for the period 1978–1987.

These projections did not go unnoticed in the industry. A number of executives in firms active in the data-storage industry decided to go after a share of the OEM market. Typical were some executives at Memorex, one of the early entrants into the Winchester disk-drive industry. William Schroeder, a product planning manager, and Al Wilson, a disk-drive project manager at Memorex with 27 years of disk-drive engineering experience, left Memorex in 1978 to form Priam Computer Corporation to produce high-performance, 14-inch disk drives for the small business computer market. Priam's drives would incorporate the same basic technology as had been used by IBM in its initial product in the area but would be much less expensive to manufacture.

Priam was able to garner capital funding from some of the leading venture capital firms. The venture capital community was attracted to the industry's explosive growth prospects. Moreover, the quality of the entrepreneurial team at a startup like Priam was very high.

Priam, to illustrate, started essentially from scratch in 1978. Early work centered on designing a 14-inch, 34-megabyte Winchester drive for sale to OEMs. Before production could begin, however, competing firms announced plans to introduce competitive 8-inch products. Priam was forced to start a parallel development effort for an 8-inch line of drives. Finally, Priam, like other startups, had to design a complete manufacturing system in an industry in which quality control was absolutely essential.

Many other startups joined Priam in entering the market. Each new entrant learned something from previous entrants in terms of how to attack particular industry problems such as manufacturing. Each used the best available technology. Each newcomer also benefited from new information about the nature of the market and could thus tailor its plans to the needs of the OEM industry.

As the industry evolved, there were many dramatic shifts in the marketplace. One of the most important was the move toward smaller-dimension disk drives, first from 14-inch to 8-inch and later to the 5 1/4-inch size. Projections called for the 5 1/4-inch segment to grow at the fastest rate.

Finding equity capital to fund startups in the industry was relatively easy. The industry growth prospects were excellent. The entrepreneurs were extremely well qualified. Some, like Alan Shugart, had already been involved with successful ventures. Others, like Vertex Peripherals, a late 1981 startup focusing on the 5 1/4-inch disk-drive segment, had top executives who cumulatively had more than 100 years of disk-drive industry experience.

Equally important, the late 1970s and early 1980s were characterized by a sharp increase in the level of funds available for venture capital investment. From an almost imperceptible $10 million in new capital committed to the venture capital industry in 1975, $1.3 billion was committed in 1981.

The period from the mid-1970s to the early 1980s was also a period of robust stock-market performance. The stocks of smaller companies, including many high-technology companies, had been stellar performers from 1975 to 1981. Higher prices for stocks and greater venture capital activity also were a contributing factor in the reemergence of the new issues market. From a low in 1975, in which four companies with a net worth of under $5 million raised $16 million, 306 small companies raised $1.7 billion in 1981 alone.

With respect to the disk-drive industry per se, the ebullience of the IPO markets was an important factor in the development of the industry. First, a number of firms began to raise capital through the public market rather than continue reliance on venture capital funding. Seagate, for example, raised $26 million net in September 1981, having only introduced its first product in July 1980. The value assigned to Seagate after that offering was $185 million, over 18 times greater than the preceding twelve months' sales. Tandon, Cipher Data, and Onyx + IMI (then called Dorado Systems) also raised money in the IPO market on favorable terms during 1981. In fact, Tandon actually raised money twice in 1981, $17 million in February and $53 million in November.

The fact that the IPO market was receptive to disk-drive companies was very important in several dimensions. First, the IPOs revealed how intensely profitable investments in disk-drive companies could be. The venture capitalists in Seagate had paid $1 million for 17% of the company. Their share of Seagate's total post-IPO market value was worth almost $32 million.

The second reason why an attractive IPO market was important was that the venture capitalists were able to see a way in which they could convert illiquid letter stock holdings into liquid holdings of registered common stock.

The final and obvious reason why the hot IPO market was important in shaping the industry was that the participants in the industry were able to raise large amounts of equity capital on attractive terms.

WHAT HAPPENED?

To summarize, the period from 1977 to 1983 was one in which a number of factors contributed to a massive infusion of capital—from venture capitalists and from the capital markets—into the Winchester disk-drive industry. The product market was very attractive. There was an ample supply of management talent. There was also an ample supply of risk capital available on attractive terms, particularly from the public capital market.

The confluence of these factors produced a remarkable chapter in American business history. Seagate went from a standing start in 1979 to revenues in the year ended December 31, 1983, of $223 million, with net income of more than $30 million. A number of the other participants showed similarly striking records through 1983.

The total industry grew at a remarkable rate during the period from 1979 to 1983. To illustrate, total disk-storage industry revenues rose from $3.5 billion in 1978 to slightly over $9 billion in 1983. The OEM segment of the industry increased from $473 million to $1.9 billion over the same period. Projections called for 1987 revenues of $22.6 billion for the entire disk-drive industry.

The spectacular performance of the industry and of the companies was reflected in the stock market. The highest valuations were attained in mid-1983. The aggregate market value of the 12 public companies during 1983, measuring each at the high for the year, was $5.4 billion.[3] This figure can be compared to total sales for the year for these companies of $1.2 billion and total net income of $100 million. Sales and net income for the previous year were $587 and $48 million, respectively.

To put the valuation figures in perspective, the mid-1983 total market value of Burroughs, DEC, Honeywell, NCR, and Sperry was only $12.8 billion on 1983 sales and net income of $22.2 and $1.1 billion, respectively.

Equally revealing is a comparison of the lofty valuation figures for the disk-drive companies with those accorded a broad mix of companies at about the same time. For example, at the end of 1982, for $5.5 billion an investor could have purchased a portfolio comprised of the following 10 companies: Commerce Clearing House, PaineWebber, SCOA Industries, Tucson Electric, Cray Research, Potlatch, Emhart, ALCO Standard, Belco, and Norton Simon. In 1982, these companies generated $11.8 billion in sales and $546 million in net income.

Finally, when making these valuation comparisons, it is important to note that a large percentage of the income generated by the hard-disk–drive companies came from interest income on excess cash raised in the IPO market. Specifically, in 1983, the 12 disk-drive companies actually had net interest expense in that year.

To summarize, the industry has benefited substantially from the chain of success:

> →Projected growth
>   ↓
> Valuation increase
>   ↓
> Access to capital
>   ↓
> New technical and human resources available
>   ↓
> Technological and manufacturing innovation
>   ↓
> Price reductions
>   ↓
> New uses of disk drives
>   ↓
> └─Projected growth

However, while the industry as a whole and individual companies made tremendous strides in fundamental operating performance during this period, many companies ran into difficulties. The sources of problems were many but fell into a few broad categories: technology, manufacturing, market development, customer base, competition, and finance.

In the technology area, the fundamental fact of life in the hard-disk–drive industry was that disk drives were complicated products to design and manufacture. Moreover, there are many different possible ways to design them. As new firms entered the market, more ambitious standards were set for all competitors in terms of product performance. However, in order to achieve these ambitious goals, new related technology in areas such as platter media would have to be developed. Some companies, such as Evotek, were never able to create the product envisioned in their business plans because media suppliers were never able to supply them.

Further, the OEM marketplace to which the disk drives were directed was not an easy market to sell. Several issues arose. First, while the total industry was experiencing explosive growth, it was not always clear who the winners would be. Many of the OEMs were not very solid in terms of financial health or market penetration. When the computer industry began a shake-out in late 1983 and 1984, many of these companies folded, including Eagle, Franklin, and Osborne.

To make matters worse, many in the OEM marketplace had fallen into the log-linear extrapolation trap. That is, projections called for a continuation of very high growth rates. However, in 1983, there was a significant downturn in the rate of growth of computer sales when compared to projections. Companies whose plans were based on the more optimistic projections experienced great difficulty. They were caught on the horns of the classic growth-industry dilemma. If they did not staff, build, and finance for growth, they could never achieve it. If they prepared for growth and it did not arrive on schedule, they were faced with the painful and often permanently damaging need to scale back people and plant and give great disappointment to the financial backers.

The greatest single industrywide problem that arose in 1983 and 1984 was the increased intensity of competition. Any industry with more than 70 companies vying for a share of the market is an industry in which margins are difficult to sustain. Price cutting to get "designed-in" was rampant. Prices dropped more rapidly than anyone had predicted. Margins fell sharply.

The competitive battle took place on dimensions other than price as well. Firms already in the marketplace were buffeted with demands from OEMs for better products. There was essentially no customer loyalty in this kind of market, except that enforced by the nature of the product and the "design-in" phenomenon. The competitive battles made continued expenditures on R&D a necessity. But continued R&D increased the rate at which cash was consumed (the burn rate) without any assured return. Often, companies geared up to meet high growth rates but then had to scale back when the market did not develop as fast as expected.

All of these factors combined to put intense pressure on the financial resources of the companies in the industry. Companies that had raised capital in the markets were better able to weather the storm. For private companies, the problem was more serious. They were dependent on the venture capital and banking industries to supply necessary capital.

However, few problems are tougher for venture capitalists or bankers than deciding whether to put more money into a situation that develops more slowly than anticipated. It always seems that the next $1 million is all the company needs, but history shows this is a fallacy.

In this regard, the marked slowdown in the IPO market in late 1983 and the tremendous decline in the prices of some of the leading disk-drive firms from mid-1983 to late 1984 caused especially troublesome problems. Basically, the public capital markets were no longer a viable source of funds for the disk-drive industry. One firm, Miniscribe, that went public in November of 1983 had to scale back the number of shares being offered from 3 to 2 million and the price from $15.00 to $11.50. Nor were the public capital markets available to some of the firms that supplied the drive manufacturers or used their products.

The venture capital market also experienced a significant decline in available funds in 1984. First, the amount of new capital committed declined to $4.2 billion from $4.5 billion in 1983. Second, more money had to be set aside for investment in expansion-stage financing for portfolio companies, given slow progress of those companies and the less attractive IPO market. By mid-1984, valuations in the venture capital market were down by more than 40%. This decline in valuation levels mirrored a decline in the level of the Venture 100 Index of 43% from June 1983 to June 1984 and 24% from December 1983 to June 1984.

COULD THE PROBLEMS HAVE BEEN PREDICTED?

It is always tempting to rely upon ex post facto analysis in order to demonstrate one's brilliance. In the case of the hard-disk–drive industry, however, much of what has happened was predictable. The year 1982 was critical in the industry. Almost two-thirds of the venture capital investments were made in 1982–1984. Twenty-one of twenty-six issues of common stock associated with disk-drive companies occurred in that same period. The question for a priori prediction is what could have been known and what should have been known. In order to address these questions, we have looked at the critical bets that were being placed and at the sources of information that were readily available at the time.

Identification of Critical Bets

In studying this industry in 1982, five critical bets were identifiable as determining economic success in the business. These five bets were in disk-drive technology, customer development, market maturation, manufacturing technology, and in the future requirements for research and development. In order to have a successful company, as distinguished from a profitable short-term investment, all five bets had to have favorable outcomes. The questions raised in the analysis were relatively simple. We shall examine the bets in turn.

Technology Two issues were clearly important in the technological evolution: Would other computer-systems components be developed that could utilize the projected power of the new hard disks being designed? Would the parts that make up the disk drive be available on a basis of timeliness, cost, and technical performance that would allow assembly of the finished project? These two bets were in many ways independent.

The second technological issue meant that the manufacturers of the hard drives themselves were basing their economic future on the emergence of qualified, reliable suppliers of critical components, including heads, platters, motors, and controls. In many cases, these supplier firms were also new and untested, and their specifications were elements of their own ambitious business plans. Thus an emerging company had to bet both that others saw the same technical solutions and that these suppliers would deliver on time and on budget. Many contemporary comments were made regarding the lack of judgment on the part of competitors in such bets. Unfortunately, the name of the money-raising game became having the "highest spec" product, so that for the latest disk-drive entrant, the basis of initial competition became integrating all possible state-of-the-art advancements.

Customer development As noted previously, two types of customers were emerging: the conservatives and the adventuresome. In many cases, the conservatives were the customers who had established markets, marketing, and production facilities. Their primary concern became on-time delivery without the 30% "dead on arrival" factor that characterized many drive manufacturers. The other players in the computer-systems market soon emerged as the major market for "the innovators." These customers were in a specifications war themselves and wished to be armed with the most advanced weapons. They were quick with the purchase order since that often guaranteed a place at the front of the delivery line if shortages materialized. Unfortunately, these same firms were often slow with payments for any other than evaluation samples. They, too, were dependent on the disk-drive manufacturers.

Ultimately, then, success for drive manufacturers hinged either on breaking into the credibility circle to become a supplier to a major OEM (e.g., Digital Equipment or Hewlett-Packard) or else making the right bet on which of the hundreds of houses that had hung out the systems integrator shingle were going to survive. Market credibility and financial strength had to be the sine qua non of customer selection. Unfortunately for the newly emerging disk-drive firm, breaking into the credibility circle was time-consuming and costly and did not necessarily take advantage of the technical breakthroughs that had motivated formation of the venture in the first place. Basing a strategy on the emerging computer firms exposed the new disk-drive firm to the risks associated with being a link in a chain of new ventures. At best, it could be part of the success. At worst, it could be exposed to one of three critical sources of failure—financial default of a major customer; technological usurpation by another supplier with better, faster, or cheaper specifications; or missing a crucial deadline for a customer within the credibility circle.

Market maturation A new venture in the disk-drive industry was subject to the normal forces of market maturity. The computer industry had exhibited the same pattern repeatedly: technology-based competition evolved into service-based competition, which evolved into price competition. The rapidity of new product development in the field left some with the hope that the competition would remain technology based. However, it soon became clear that OEM customers looked to the disk-drive suppliers as unenthusiastic allies in price-based battles. Even worse, the possibility was present from the start that the competitive battles would take place in both the technological *and* the price arenas, particularly given the intense competitive war being waged in the OEM computer market.

A second feature was also present regarding the pattern of

industry structure. Many of the drive customers were knowledgeable about both technology and manufacturing. There was a significant threat of forward integration on the part of the major
OEM accounts. The product had many characteristics that would
encourage such integration: it was expensive, critical to long-term
performance, shared many operations in scope with other manufacturing steps, and could be sold to others without impinging on
the proprietary technology at the core of the business. Furthermore, the industry was faced with certain knowledge that many of
the critical steps in the manufacturing process were of interest to
formidable competitors offshore in Japan, Korea, and Singapore.
In this regard, it is interesting to note that in mid-1983 there were
63 active suppliers of disk drives to the OEM market. Of these,
17 had both OEM sales *and* captive sales, and there were already
21 Japanese and European companies active in the OEM market.

Manufacturing technology The most critical assumption in many
cases was that the product could be produced at a price that would
yield profits. In many cases, manufacturing cost assumptions were
based on straight-line projection of rapid cost decreases. Such
projections were based upon experience with storage media that
heretofore had large electronic components. The question was:
Could such experience be translated to the highly significant electromechanical component in the hard-disk drives?

Future research and development The final critical bet as to the
success of the companies being funded was with respect to research
and development activities. In many cases, companies were founded
around a basic technological idea that had its origins at previous
employers. For many of the companies, the first two or three years
were devoted to perfecting the application of the idea and to
"ramping up the manufacturing." Few companies could afford the
luxury of pursuing a second-generation product while the first
generation was as yet unproduced. However, it was clear from the
continuing stream of product announcements and new company
formations that the rate of progress of the technology would continue unabated. The successful company, at a minimum, would
have to be prepared for a sequence of technological breakthroughs,
not just increased integration.

In sum, there were five key areas of uncertainty confronting
entrants into the disk-drive industry and their financial backers. A

truly successful venture would only result from simultaneous positive outcomes on all five bets.

What Could Be Known?

The above analysis was based on data in the public domain. Information was readily available on the market, the technology, and competition. The manner of new entrants' arrival made data readily accessible. Finally, the financial data available made a count of new competitors and their prospective capabilities relatively easy to assess.

Information available The fact of rapid growth in the hard-disk industry had made this an industry of interest to the providers of data. Market data were collected by such organizations as Dataquest, IDC, Venture Development Corporation, and DISK/TREND, Inc. These organizations provided extensive analyses of the market and the technology, including lists of existing and potential competitors. Technological data were readily available through a variety of industry and nonindustry sources, with magazines for general readership such as *High Technology* providing extensive overviews. *Computer Systems News* and *Mini-Micro Systems* published entire issues profiling the markets, technology, and competitors.

New entrant announcements Almost every issue of the major trade publications had announcements of new products and new companies. The battle for financing became a battle of public relations experts as new firms announced product capabilities as a preemptive strategy and as a device to gain financial market recognition. These announcements often included technical specifications, estimated development dates, customer letters of intent, and other data of great use in analysis of the bets outlined previously.

Financial data By December 1982, at least seven firms in the industry had made 12 public offerings of securities. Thus, considerable financial data were available directly from the public record. Even more valuable were the data collected by Venture Economics. This firm tracks all investments by venture capital firms. It was possible to identify the 89 placements that had been made in 43 different companies. The amount of money available and the number of independent technological new ventures was readily apparent. Data such as those collected by Venture Economics are interesting from a historical perspective; they are critical in assessing the future course of an industry.

It is also interesting to note that venture capitalists had a potentially invaluable source of data—the torrent of business plans for entrants or participants in the disk-drive and related (supplier, OEM) markets. Venture capitalists also often had simultaneous investments in one or more participants in the technological chain ranging from suppliers to drive manufacturers to computer-systems builders.

Valuation economics   Some simple calculations in mid-1983 would have revealed the absurdity of valuation levels attained by the industry participants. To illustrate, if one assumes that Porter's OEM sales forecasts for 1983 to 1987 were correct—that industry sales would grow at 15% per year for the next five years (1988 to 1992) and 10% per year for the following 20 years, that net margins would be 10%, and that net fixed assets would be 80% of sales— then the free cash flows generated by the industry can be calculated. In turn, these cash flows can be discounted to the present and compared with the valuation levels assigned in the public markets. Assuming a terminal value in year 30 equal to net book value, the present values of the projected cash flows at different discount rates are listed below:

Discount rate	Present value
10%	$5.3 billion
12%	$2.5 billion
18%	$0

The reader can assess the reasonableness of these assumptions but should keep in mind two factors: (1) the profitability assumption is very generous considering the existence of more than 70 competitors, and (2) the values calculated above pertain to the entire OEM disk-drive industry, not just the 12 companies assigned a value of $5.4 billion in mid-1983.

These data, taken as a whole, indicated the extreme risk in the bets being placed. They suggested that while the individual bets might have a reasonable probability of paying off, rational analysis clearly revealed that there was an extremely low probability for any individual firm to succeed, considering that favorable outcomes on all bets were a prerequisite for success. A profitable strategy would have been to sell short a portfolio comprised of the stocks of *all* public disk-drive companies knowing full well that a few companies would prosper, while most valuations would collapse under the weight of ruinous competition.

Despite these conditions, as late as the fall of 1983, venture capitalists and stock market investors continued to pour money into the disk-drive industry.

IMPLICATIONS

Instead of the chain of success identified previously, there was a chain of failure:

→Risks in innovation materialized
↓
Caused customer disappointments fostering conservative stances or
↓
Exposed customer financial weaknesses or
↓
Exposed supplier financial weaknesses
↓
Increased competitive pressure to find the winners
↓
Changed basis of competition to price
↓
Lowered margins
↓
Affected capital availability and reduced expenditures on future development
↓
Caused more risk of innovation to materialize

The implications of this chain for the industry are obvious. It is interesting to note the important role of the capital markets in the chain. The availability of external capital served as one of the major precipitating elements both for the growth and for the downward spiral. Moreover, problems in the supply of capital affected disk-drive users and disk-drive suppliers, exacerbating the financial woes of the disk-drive manufacturers themselves.

When the data are examined, it seems clear that those in the private and public capital markets had the best vantage point to anticipate:

- the emergence of numerous well-financed competitors;
- the existence of multiple competing technologies;
- the absolute requirement for continuing R&D expenditures; and
- the need for external capital to fund working capital, plant, and equipment that could not be generated internally during periods of rapid growth.[4]

The professional investors did not serve the function of policing the capital markets. In fact, they continued to pour money into the industry well after the game should have been finished.

This capital market myopia may prove to be costly for both early and later players. It may prove costly from a national policy point of view as well. Initiatives may well be abandoned that might have provided the bases for improved national competitiveness. The industry has been sufficiently decimated to open the doors to foreign competition without credible threat of competitive retaliation. Moreover, the havoc wreaked in the capital markets may make it far harder for companies to raise money on acceptable terms in the future.

It is clear that massive industry restructuring will occur. Some major mergers have already been announced. Failures are being announced weekly. The returns to investors will be positive if and only if they can avoid becoming as myopically pessimistic as they were myopically optimistic. In late 1984, some of the public disk-drive companies were trading at prices below net working capital per share.

LESSONS TO BE LEARNED

There are several lessons that we believe can be learned by careful examination of the disk-drive experience in the period under study.

Taking the Broad View of the Industry Is the Key to Profitable Investment. The investment mania visited on the hard-disk–drive industry involved inherent assumptions about long-run industry size and profitability and about the future growth, profitability, and access to capital for each individual company. These assumptions, had they been stated explicitly, would not have been acceptable to the rational investor. Certainly valuations arise that cannot be justified under any circumstances. These are the times for the manager to raise money from the public capital markets. Those managers who took advantage of unsustainable valuation levels now have a chance to survive the shake-out.

Growth Is Not Equivalent to Profitability. The high growth rate in the industry made it the focus of considerable managerial, investor, and technological attention. The industry attracted so many resources that the growth had high probability of being unprofitable. Excesses in the capital market turned an opportunity into a disaster.

Profits for Some Are Not Equivalent to a Good Business. Many players made high profits by investing in the hard-disk–drive business, including the investment bankers and certain of the venture capital groups that invested early enough to catch the wave of euphoria in the stock market and still sell under Rule 144. Many others rode the cycle up and down without liquidity. For many buyers of disk-drive stocks in 1983, losses were massive. Short-term successes of some gave the illusion of long-term profitability for all. Investors should not be fooled by such inevitably ephemeral successes.

Market Instability Can Be All Bad News. Very rapid change often creates entrepreneurial opportunity; it also creates risk. Analysis of the hard-disk–drive industry reveals the dark side of rapid technological evolution and of customer instability. Early players are often preempted by changes in technology and in customer needs. Early birds are not always winners in product markets, but latecomers are almost always losers.

Recognizing the Chain. One of the more important lessons to be learned from the tale of the disk-drive industry is that all players—entrepreneurs, venture capitalists, investment bankers, industry analysts, and investors—must recognize the chains involved in such a process. First, there was a technological chain, a series of bets on technological advances in disk-drive components, disk-drive designs, and end-user designs. Then, there was a financial chain, a series of related bets on the internal financial health of each player in the technological chain and on the nature of access to capital in the private and public markets. The likelihood that *any* player in the disk-drive industry would prosper without a serious setback because of a weak link was effectively zero. Indeed, weaknesses in the chain were created by *exactly the same people* whose financial success depends on an unbroken series of favorable outcomes.

SUMMARY

The process of industry analysis described here can be applied in many settings. All industry participants must focus first on the prospects for the industry. How large will it be? How profitable will it be? What will the path to maturity look like? Then, analysis of the prospects for individual players can be assessed. Ultimately, the effects of decisions at the individual company level *must be reconciled* with the aggregate industry view. Had this process been applied in the Winchester disk-drive industry, the carnage would have been far less severe.

The lessons from the disk-drive industry appear to have broad applicability in other industries ranging from biotechnology to integrated software to pizza parlors to theaters. People who invest both their money and their sweat can benefit substantially from the kind of financial, strategic, and competitive analysis that has been outlined here.

In this information age, a great deal of timely, relevant data are available. Wise investors accept consensus conclusion at their peril. Good decision making requires independent judgment. In essence, capital market myopia is a treatable disease.*

POSTSCRIPT: THE IMPOSSIBILITY THEOREM

Extending their classical rational-analytical approach Sahlman and Stevenson subsequently developed what they call "the impossibility theorem" of venture capital investing. Considering the pattern that had occurred in hard-disk drives, they wondered how such a phenomenon might play itself out on a broader scale. They established that the target internal rate of return (IRR) for venture-capital industry investments in the early and mid-1980s was 25% to 50% per year and that the investment horizon was seven years. From this, they calculated the amount of value that must be created at any point in time for investors to achieve the target rate of return. They further assumed that venture capitalists are likely to end up owning 30% of the companies in which they invest and could thus calculate the implied value of the companies. Given the amount of capital committed to the industry during the previous seven years, their calculations revealed a staggering requirement, shown in the table below:[5]

Rate of return	*Required total value of portfolio companies, 1988*
@ 25%	$188.8 billion
@ 35%	$261.9 billion
@ 50%	$422.5 billion

Sahlman went on to demonstrate that the venture capital industry must create companies with very large market values for investors to achieve their required rate of return. For example, compared

---

*While DISK/TREND, Inc., and Venture Economics graciously supplied data for this paper, responsibility resides with the authors for the analysis and conclusions.

to the total market value of all 4,506 NASDAQ-traded stocks as of 1988, the value of the venture-capital-backed companies would, at 25% IRR, equate to 49.2%; at 35% IRR, to 68.2%; and at 50% IRR, to 110% of the NASDAQ total value! One perceives the source of their term: "impossibility theorem."

The aftermath of the carnage in the hard-disk–drive industry continued into 1989. Priam was one of the stars of 1983. With sales of $60 million, it raised $70 million in the hot IPO market of June 1983 for a market capitalization of $260 million. The stock soared to a high of $23 a share and then fell to $1 as the competitive consequences of market myopia took effect. In the fall of 1989, the company filed for bankruptcy. Many of the original 43 companies experienced a similar fate. These losses were both unprecedented and shocking. The warnings of Sahlman and Stevenson were more prophetic than anyone had imagined. An entire industry had fallen victim to "the greater fool theory" or "sheep following sheep," as some derisively call it. To make matters worse, the mounting evidence of declining rates of return in the venture capital industry as the 1980s progressed was another resounding confirmation of "the impossibility theorem" and the reality that myopia was not confined to the hard-disk–drive industry.

EXCEPTION TO THE MYOPIA RULE

As we have said, we consider "Capital Market Myopia" a seminal work. Its analysis yielded some useful warning signals for investors and entrepreneurs alike. Having said that, we also maintain that it is flawed by an overreliance on its rational-analytical elegance. If such an analysis and its conclusions were applied by entrepreneurs and investors—not to mention policymakers—as the principal determinant of whether to launch a new company, most, we contend, would end up "throwing away the baby and keeping the stork," to paraphrase Mae West.

What is missing from this classical rational-analytical application of financial economics to the venture-capital investing process? We contend that the most critical ingredient in the birth of extraordinary new companies and industries is the visionary leadership, imagination, ingenuity, and creative capacity of the founding entrepreneur and team. Truly great companies and industries have such leaders. In addition, classical rational-analytical models are usually too limited to foresee and predict accurately the future impact of the highly dynamic entrepreneurial process, especially its relentless, stubborn, resilient, zealous capacity to learn, to adapt, to grow, to improve, and to create anew. This is why classic venture capital has always been the "art of the exception," rather than the art of the average.

Furthermore, consider the following contradiction of the impossibility theorem: Just as the disaster of the hard-disk–drive industry was becoming apparent to even the most starry-eyed, a new entrant to this gutted industry had the temerity to test the waters. From June through December of 1985, that company had total startup expenses of $160,000, all spent on research and development, as one would expect. In June 1986, it sold 8,797,650 shares of convertible preferred stock ($.68 a share) to one of its major customers for $6 million. By year-end 1986, the company had lost more than $4.3 million and had no sales. In August 1987, as if capital market myopia were on the march again, the company sold $27.5 million of series B preferred stock at a price of $4.34 a share to a group including venture capital investors The Centennial Funds, Prudential Venture Partners, and John Hancock Venture Capital. Had myopia turned to madness? Clearly, the hard-disk–drive carnage was at this time far from ended.

In the next three years, this company and its fortunes exploded just as fast as the hard-disk–drive industry had imploded. The company's results for 1987, 1988, and 1989 were in complete defiance of the rest of the ill-starred industry. The company's sales in its first year of shipping its new 3 1/2-inch Winchester disk drives were $133.2 million, followed by $256.6 million in 1988 and $704.9 million in 1989. Conner Peripherals had defied the laws of the marketplace, if not gravity. Besides its major customer, Compaq Computer, it was also a supplier to such OEMs as DEC, Toshiba Corporation, Zenith Data Systems, Inc., AST Research, Dell Computer Corporation, GRiD Systems Corporation, NEC, Sharp, and Sun Microsystems, Inc. By the end of 1990, sales were running at an annualized rate of over $1.5 billion. Others, such as Toshiba, were announcing new products in the next cycle of the technology wave with the 2 1/2-inch micro-hard-disk drives. The Houdinis of the hard-disk–drive industry had not become claustrophobic after all. How could this be? Since the carnage was far from over, why would someone invest now?

The Art of the Exceptional

What did Conner and its backers know about the industry that others had missed? Extraordinarily successful new ventures like

Conner Peripherals have always been the art of the exceptional. Investments that turn out so remarkably often look like a real mess early on or in the middle. Federal Express's million-dollar-a-month loss for twenty-nine months is a classic example; many investors abandoned the FedEx ship too early. Creative intuition invariably plays a major role in the judgment calls required by such complex bets as these. Overreliance on classic financial and economic analyses of industry structure may mask or obscure some of the best opportunities. We are not saying that such analyses should not be done but that it may erroneously infer precision and accuracy that belie the dynamics and realities of a rapidly changing marketplace and cannot take into account the superior learning abilities of the best entrepreneurs. It may also guarantee that you follow the myopia rule but fail to see the exception in its midst. To paraphrase General Doriot: "I have never yet met an MBA who cannot analyze a company to the point where it is clearly not worth investing in."

Conner and his associates had a quite different vision and more creative grasp of the opportunities and the competitive advantages that were possible than could be derived from classic financial analysis alone. They also had a different sense of the timing to pursue such opportunities. Given the earlier mayhem, they recognized that there were advantages to being a later entrant. Many earlier competitors were either drowning or under water when Conner came to the scene, and there were few entrants. The OEMs had begun to sort out the two or three stable and dependable suppliers of disk drives. Too many had been burned by their earlier strategy of forcing disk-drive manufacturers into cutthroat competition; the result had been that a lot of drives either failed to perform or could not be delivered on time. Conner recognized that the OEM market was moving to a new stage, and he proceeded according to that knowledge.

We agree with Sahlman and Stevenson that overcrowding such as occurred in the hard-disk–drive industry could have been foreseen, from an investor's perspective at least, with careful analysis of the industry data available at the time. But this foresight might not have been possible far enough in advance to make a difference. The problem stems from inadequate lead times and highly imperfect information. We liken this process of awareness and decision making to the takeoff of a small airplane. You have to attain lift-off velocity by the time you are at the halfway point of the runway in order to abort the takeoff with enough runway left to come to a safe stop. Once aloft, if the engine fails before reaching at least one thousand feet, there is no turning back. The safest survival route is straight ahead to as soft an emergency landing as possible. A new company passes through a similar series of points of no return when it gets off the ground. Even with the customary staged capital commitments to minimize the risk and to preserve the option to continue or abandon, there is tremendous momentum in a company. If you ease off the throttle every time unsettling news about R&D or a new product is announced, you will never get off the ground. That is what risk and uncertainty are all about. Just because competitors exist does not mean they will survive.

There are a multitude of decision points in a hard-disk–drive startup, and the various lead times required in the hard-disk–drive industry only complicate matters. These might look something like this:

Critical task	Months to complete
Develop concept and business plan; raise seed money	3–9 months
Conduct R&D to develop and test prototype and get ready for full manufacturing	6–18 months
Raise startup funding at tail end of R&D proof	2–6 months
Obtain orders, build facility, go to manufacturing, ship product, establish marketplace proof of performance	6–12 months
Total elapsed time	17–45 months

Even if all goes as planned—and it rarely ever does—it will still take another one to three years or more before it is clear who the industry market leaders are. And in technology wars, there is always the risk of a competitor blindsiding the industry with a breakthrough. Security measures and secrecy in such companies rival and surpass those of the Manhattan Project.

Still another factor could supersede the wisdom derived from the industry analysis done by Sahlman and Stevenson: human ego. It is hard to imagine highly confident and competitive entrepreneurs and their backers stepping away from an attractive new market just because they recognize that other challengers will be likewise drawn to the arena. Fierce competitors relish challenge. Such mindsets can have a powerful and, unfortunately, perverse effect on company strategy.

Finally, looking back on the industry, it is easy to overlook how consumers benefited from this competition. The cost of hard-disk drives today is a fraction of what it was even five or six years ago. There is a second side benefit as well. The success of Conner Peripherals, and other new companies, derives from the experiences of their founders and executives at Priam and Seagate during the trying days when capital market myopia was on the rampage. The company's family tree is revealing. Founder and chairman Finis F. Conner was vice chairman and co-founder of Seagate Technology, Inc., a manufacturer of rigid magnetic disk drives. William Schroeder was a co-founder of Priam Computer Corporation. John P. Squires, senior vice president of engineering was a co-founder of Co-Data Memory Corporation before it merged with Conner in 1986. C. Scott Holt, the vice president of marketing, had been vice president of sales and marketing at Seagate. Carl W. Neun, vice president of finance, had held various positions at Shugart Associates. In the case of Conner Peripherals, this learning curve helped to prevent what would have appeared to the less knowledgeable as yet another capital market myopia accident waiting to happen. What might appear on the surface to some as great risk can yield in time to renewed opportunity as savvy entrepreneurs recognize how industry changes can open up successful entry strategies. There will still be pitfalls, but the rewards of being right can outweigh the risks of being wrong, as Conner Peripherals proved.

CONCLUSION

The implications for the venture capital industry are apparent. How can we encourage and foster the entrepreneurial value creation process without grasping defeat from the jaws of victory, as was done in so many hard-disk–drive deals? One answer lies in the market response already well under way. The decline in returns and the industry shake-out have led to a new sobriety and caution against a repeat of the myopia malaise. The largest single improvement was recognition of the need to temper investing strategies with industry and competitor analysis, such as we have seen here, in order to map more carefully both the opportunities and mine fields. Meeting part of this need is a new West Coast company, Venture One. By pooling information in Venture One's proprietary database, its backers, a cooperating group of leading Bay Area venture-capital funds, are attempting to track specifically information about simultaneous investing decisions that can lead to overcrowding. Such sharing was common in the good old days of classic venture-capital investing and seems to be in favor again, at least with some, as the lessons of capital market myopia have sunk in.

If Conner Peripherals is a model of how to compete in an industry that had a very unattractive industry structure, it nonetheless faces a major challenge: how to sustain its competitive advantage in the 1990s. The risk of rapid technological obsolescence is still present; Conner will need at least to keep pace. Compared to the early 1980s, however, the industry is considerably less hostile and competitive. And Conner's relative bargaining power now, given its size and importance to its major customer and partner Compaq Computer, is a far cry from the cowboy days of 1981 to 1985.

Finally, we can also reach a quite opposite conclusion from Sahlman and Stevenson's: we should be extremely grateful that the hard-disk–drive phenomenon could happen! Indeed, isn't it a powerful example of what our colleague Michael Porter would describe as the single most important factor in a nation's ability to achieve world-class competitiveness—fierce, vigorous domestic competition in the industry sector? After all, we have seen the birth and growth of a multibillion-dollar industry, the diffusion of hard-disk technology to microcomputers and desktop computers, dramatic consumer benefits per dollar of purchases, and a wiser breed of entrepreneurs and investors alike. If these market forces work well, we would expect to see significant and functional adjustments within the hard-disk drive and venture capital industries. We would expect to see fewer competitors and lower rates of return to investors. In Chapter 6, we will witness these market forces at work as we examine how venture capital funds have performed over the past decade.

What is the alternative to what we have seen in the hard-disk–drive industry? One view in vogue among some economists and policymakers is a predisposition toward a centralized authority to ensure that such carnage does not happen again. Imagine that a National Industrial Policy Board was formed back in 1981. It decided that a tandem of IBM and AT&T should head up America's efforts in hard-disk–drive technology and that small startup companies and their venture capital backers were simply a waste of national resources. Does anyone seriously believe that market development, price-performance characteristics, and technological advances would be anywhere close to what we have today if IBM and AT&T had been in charge?

CHAPTER 6

Performance of Venture Capital Funds: Rates of Return

IN 1982, an economist at the National Science Foundation characterized venture capital as an industry "shrouded in empirical secrecy and an aura of beliefs."[1] This was especially true when it came to rates of return, which, according to industry folklore, ranged from 30% to 50% and even higher. A 1984 congressional survey found that independent private venture capital firms expected a minimum annualized rate of return on individual investments that ranged from 75% for seed-stage financing to about 35% per year for bridge financing. The same study found independent private venture-capital firms experienced a 31% annual net capital appreciation rate over the period 1982–1984. The report went on to conclude that "the persistence of above average rates of return on venture capital investments suggests that capital markets may be under-allocating funds to risky, entrepreneurial investments."[2] In the mid-1980s, it was reported that limited partners were expecting returns of 40% to 60%, and some were hoping for 75%[3]—high enough to arouse even the sleepiest pension fund manager. There was, however, an astonishing paucity of reliable information to support such expectations. As one pension fund manager told us in 1985, "Depending on whose [rates of return] we believe, we should have anywhere from as little as 5% to as much as 50% of our portfolio in venture capital."

In 1985–1986, in response to the need for valid and reliable data on the actual returns from venture capital funds, we helped Venture Economics start its returns database. By 1989, the database contained information on 42% of all the funds formed from 1970 through 1987 and on 65% of the capital under management. That sample of 197 funds represented the universe remarkably well, with 3% seed-stage, 16% early-stage, 74% balanced, and 7% late-stage investments.

Venture Economics' first publication of the actual returns on those funds caused a stir. The figures—to put it mildly—were disappointing. Since 1980, overall returns had briefly peaked above 30% in 1983—the year of the IPO frenzy—and then slid relentlessly to the single digits by 1988. A *Wall Street Journal* headline said it all, "Recent Venture Funds Perform Poorly As Unrealistic Expectations Wear Off."[4]

In this chapter, we will look at historical rates of return to see if there was ever any justification for those anticipated returns of 30% to 50%. Then we will examine the actual returns in the 1980s. We will explain why those returns were so poor—perhaps hitting an all-time low—at the end of the decade. We will end with a discussion of what has to happen if they are to recover in the 1990s.

HISTORICAL RETURNS

The industry abounds with anecdotes and hearsay. For example, everyone knows about ARD's investment in DEC. Even if the amount invested varies from $60,000 to $70,000 and the amount returned in about twelve years varies from $500 million to $600 million, depending on who is speaking,[5] the annualized rate of return of 130% or thereabouts is the stuff legends are made of. But what is the reality? Figure 6-1 lists the rates of return cited in the scholarly literature. Even with as spectacular an investment as DEC in its portfolio, ARD's annualized rate of return for the twenty years from 1946 to 1966 was only 14%.[6] In 1966, of course, the value of its investment in DEC was still growing. By the late 1970s, when DEC had been harvested and ARD had become part of Textron, ARD's annualized rate of return fell into the single digits.[7]

Two of the best-known private venture-capital firms are Bessemer Securities and Hambrecht & Quist. According to Poindexter, Bessemer reported a 17% compound rate of return for the period from 1967 to 1974, and Hambrecht & Quist, a 15% compound rate of return over several years through 1972.[8]

Most tests on venture capital profitability have used small samples of publicly held SBICs. A study of 14 public venture-

FIGURE 6-1 **Venture Capital: Compound Annual Rates of Return**

14%   American Research and Development (1946–1966)[1]

14%   92 venture capital firms[2]

    13%   59 venture capital firms managing one-third of the venture capital pool

    12%   29 public venture-capital firms (mainly SBICs, 1961–1973)

    17%   Bessemer Securities (1967–1974)

    15%   Hambrecht & Quist (few years through 1972)

11%   14 public venture-capital firms (primarily SBICs)[3]

23%   110 actual investments in portfolio companies (gross return before annual management fee)[4]

27%   11 public venture-capital firms (based on stock prices, 1974–1979)[5]

16%   Public venture-capital firms (based on stock prices, 1959–1985)[6]

24%   Simulation of hypothetical venture-capital investments[7]

15%   Simulation of 100 funds[8]

---

[1]W. Rotch, "The Pattern of Success in Venture Capital Financing," *Financial Analysis Journal* (September–October 1966), pp. 141–147.

[2]J. B. Poindexter, "The Efficiency of Financial Markets: The Venture Capital Case," Ph.D. diss., New York University, 1976.

[3]R. B. Faucett, "The Management of Venture Capital Investment Companies," MBA thesis, MIT, 1971.

[4]J. P. Hoban, "Characteristics of Venture Capital Investing," Ph.D. diss., University of Utah, 1976.

[5]J. D. Martin and W. P. Petty, "An Analysis of the Performance of Publicly Traded Venture Capital Companies," *Journal of Financial and Quantitative Analysis,* vol. 18, no. 3 (1983), pp. 401–410.

[6]R. G. Ibbotson and G. P. Brinson, *Investment Markets* (New York: McGraw-Hill, 1987), 99–100.

[7]W. A. Wells, "Venture Capital Decision-Making," Ph.D. diss., Carnegie-Mellon University, 1974.

[8]H. H. Stevenson, D. F. Muzyka, and J. A. Timmons, "Venture Capital in a New Era: A Simulation of the Impact of the Changes in Investment Patterns," in R. Ronstadt et al., eds., *Frontiers of Entrepreneurship Research 1986* (Wellesley, MA: Center for Entrepreneurial Studies, Babson College, 1986), pp. 380–403.

---

capital firms found the rate of return to average 11%.[9] Hoban constructed a portfolio composed of 110 actual venture-capital investments made by four different venture-capital firms in 50 different companies from 1960 to 1968.[10] The four venture-capital firms were a publicly held SBIC, a private partnership, a private corporation owned by a wealthy family, and a subsidiary of a large bank-holding company. He found the gross (before management fees and income taxes) annualized rate of return of the portfolio to be 22.9% through the end of 1975. Poindexter gathered data from 29 publicly held firms consisting of 26 SBICs and three companies investing in venture capital. The geometric mean of the annual rate of return for the 29 firms for the period 1961 to 1973 was 11.6%. Over the same period, Poindexter found that the annualized rate of return of the Standard & Poor's 500 was 7.1%.[11] It is worth noting that the rate of return for the sample of venture capital firms depended strongly on the calendar period over which they were computed: it was 10.7% for the period 1961 to 1966, 31% for 1967 to 1971, and 1.2% for 1972 to 1973.

Martin and Petty computed the compound rate of return on the publicly traded stock of 11 publicly traded venture-capital firms (of which all but two were in Poindexter's sample) for each of the six years from 1974 to 1979.[12] The average rate of return was 27%. Unfortunately, this was not the actual rate of return on the firms' venture capital investments. The two rates should not be compared because there may be little or no relationship between their values at any one time. For example, Arthur D. Little, former chairman of Narragansett Capital Corporation, which was in both Poindexter's and Martin and Petty's samples, stated that in the mid-1970s Narragansett's share price fell to 80% below the book value of the assets in its portfolio.[13]

A study by First Chicago Investment Advisors used a methodology similar to Martin and Petty's to study the rates of return of public venture-capital companies from 1959 through 1985. The compound annual rate of return over the 26-year period was 16%.[14]

It is not easy to obtain the data needed to calculate the actual rates of return of venture capital investments—not even for publicly held funds such as Poindexter's sample of 29. It is necessary to dig into the financial statements in annual reports and 10Ks to get operating expenses, interest expenses, income dividends, capital gains dividends, operating income, interest income, net assets, long-term debt, and net worth. Those numbers must be adjusted to allow for additional public offerings and stock splits. The reliability of the net asset figure may be questionable because most of the value resides in a fund's portfolio. The value of that portfolio is an estimate of the current market value of the companies in the portfolio, and most of those companies are private.

Poindexter surveyed 270 venture capital firms that managed the bulk of the domestic venture-capital pool. He estimated that the 59 respondents who supplied rate-of-return data managed one-third of the domestic pool of venture capital. They were asked to estimate their firms' compound rates of return since inception. The mean of the estimated rates of return was 13.3%, with a range from 35% to −40%.[15]

A number of models have simulated the rates of return of venture capital firms. Wells studied the decision-making process of venture capitalists.[16] He asked them to estimate the rates of return they expected from 17 investments. From their estimates, he constructed a hypothetical venture-capital firm that drew its ventures from the distribution of estimated rates of return. The simulated portfolio for his hypothetical venture-capital firm produced a compound rate of return of 24%.

Stevenson, Muzyka, and Timmons used a Monte Carlo simulation model that was developed with published data on venture-capital fund performance and interviews with fund managers.[17] Their simulation of the returns of 100 funds showed an average return of 15% with a range from 10% to 35% and one fund returning greater than 35%. A potential flaw in their model was the assumption that there was zero correlation among investments for both the investment partnership and the investment domain as a whole.

Summary

Our survey of returns is from scholarly research published in the academic literature as opposed to anecdotal accounts in the business press. It shows that rather than the folklore figure of 30% to 50%, actual venture-capital returns have most often been in the teens, with occasional periods in the 20% to 30% range and rare spikes above 30%.

PERFORMANCE IN THE 1980s

As this book has reported, the inflow of U.S. venture capital dried to a mere trickle by the mid-1970s. A common complaint by entrepreneurs at that time was that there was not enough venture capital available. It was an investor's market. Then, at the end of the 1970s, the floodgates opened, and the United States was awash with venture capital; the situation of the mid-1970s was suddenly reversed, and according to some observers, by the early 1980s, there was too much capital chasing too few good deals. It had become an investee's market. What effect did this change have on the rates of return? Again, we look at the results of a study of the performance of the venture capital funds in the Venture Economics database.

Method

As noted in Chapter 1, venture capital partnerships are composed of limited partners and general partners. The limited partners provide the money, and the general partners provide the management. Venture capitalists in one venture capital firm may be general partners in several partnerships under the management umbrella of that firm. Some of the older venture capital firms manage half-a-dozen or so partnerships. In return, the general partners receive an annual management fee and a share of any profit that the partnership makes. The annual management fee is usually 2% to 3% of the paid-in capital, and the general partners' share of the profit is usually 20%; the other 80% goes to the limited partners. Partnerships generally have a ten-year life, which can often be extended.

When a new partnership is formed, the money committed to it is paid in several installments (takedowns) over the first two or three years. The general partners send reports and financial statements to the limited partners, usually quarterly. From those financial statements, limited partners can calculate their share of the book or "residual" value of the partnership. The residual value consists of any uninvested capital and the estimate of the partnership's share of the value of portfolio companies in which the partnership has invested. When a company in the partnership's portfolio goes public, the limited partners may receive their share of the stock in that company, although the venture capital partnership often holds back stock for a period before distributing it. That eventual disbursement is usually valued at the offering price per share of the public offering, although when a stock carries restrictions on its sale, its price is often discounted by 20% to 30%. In addition to stock, there may be other disbursements such as cash dividends.

Traditionally, venture capital partnerships do not disseminate information from which it is possible to determine their performance, specifically their rates of return. However, limited partners have information on takedowns, disbursements, and residuals from which internal rates of return (IRRs) can be computed.

Computations of IRRs

There is no standard industrywide method for computing the financial returns of venture capital funds. Increasingly, limited partners compute their IRRs based on their cash-on-cash returns, plus their share of the residual value of the venture capital fund's holdings of cash and investments in portfolio companies that have yet to be distributed to the limited partners.

The algorithm for computing IRRs is fairly simple in principle. The residual, the disbursements, and the takedowns are each reduced to their present value on the date of the first takedown. A disbursement of D dollars has a present value of $D/(1 + IRR/100)^t$, where IRR is the annualized internal rate of return, and t is the time in years from the date of the first takedown to the date of the disbursement. The present values of a takedown of T dollars and a residual of R dollars can be computed the same way. Then, by iteration, the value of IRR is computed at the end of each calendar quarter by finding its value when the present value of the takedowns equals the present value of all the disbursements plus the present value of the residual.

Limitations

In practice, it is not quite that simple. First, there are limitations in some of the data sets. Some pension funds record the actual dates of transactions; others record them at the end of the month in which they occur. To put them all on the same basis, transactions are computed as if they occurred on the last day of the month.

Second, although it is easy to construct an algorithm that computes the limited partners' share of a residual, it is difficult to compute it reliably without knowing the intricate details of the partnership agreement, specifically when and how the general partners' share of the profit is recognized. In principle, general partners do not get any share of the profit until the limited partners have received all the money that they paid into the fund. After that, the profit is split, usually on a 20/80 basis. However, once the residual plus disbursements exceed the sum of the takedowns, the fund is making a profit on paper. Most funds then recognize the unrealized profit that is in the residual. When that point is reached, the general partners hold back their anticipated share of future profits from subsequent disbursements to the limited partners.

The following simplifying method is used to compute the limited partners' residual value: (1) when the sum of the distributions is less than the sum of the takedowns (paid-in capital), the

total value of the fund's residual is multiplied by the limited partners' percentage ownership of the fund; and (2) when the sum of
the distributions exceeds the sum of the takedowns, the total value
of the fund's residual is multiplied by the limited partners' percentage ownership of the fund multiplied by the limited partners'
percentage of the allocation of the profits.

A third limitation is the reliability of the valuation of the
residuals. Most funds have valuation committees that estimate the
value of their portfolios of investments in companies that have no
publicly traded stock. Thus, the value of the residual is a somewhat
subjective judgment of each fund's valuation committee. This problem is mitigated to some extent by the existence of many different
funds, and there is no reason to believe that there is any overall
bias, either high or low, by the valuation committees.

Before we present the actual rates of return, we should point
out that the venture capital industry has been debating the issue
of how portfolios should be valued. An ad hoc committee of the
National Venture Capital Association charged with developing
guidelines proposed a standard valuation method in 1990.[18] It also
recommended that, while data should be collected during the first
few years of a fund's life, no rates of return should be compiled
until the end of the third year. Venture Economics, which compiled
the returns presented in the next section, goes even further: in its
annual *Investment Benchmarks Report*, it only includes returns of
funds with at least four years of operating history.

Annualized Rates of Return

The annualized rates of return for all the funds in the database are
presented in Figure 6-2. This figure shows the capital weighted
average, median, and top quartile of the IRRs by calendar year
for all funds formed from 1969 through 1985. The median IRR
peaked in 1982 at 27%. The capital weighted average also peaked
in 1982 at 32%. The top quartile* peaked one year later at 44%.
These overall returns are in line with what we learned from our
historical survey of the scholarly literature: overall returns from
venture capital are typically below 20% with only brief spikes above
30%. However, the top-quartile funds perform much better, with
returns above 20% in nine out of sixteen years, above 30% in four
of those years, and above 40% one year.

---

*The top-quartile return is the point where 25% of the returns of a group are
higher and 75% are lower.

FIGURE 6-2 **Overall Rates of Return (Mature funds ≥ five years old)**

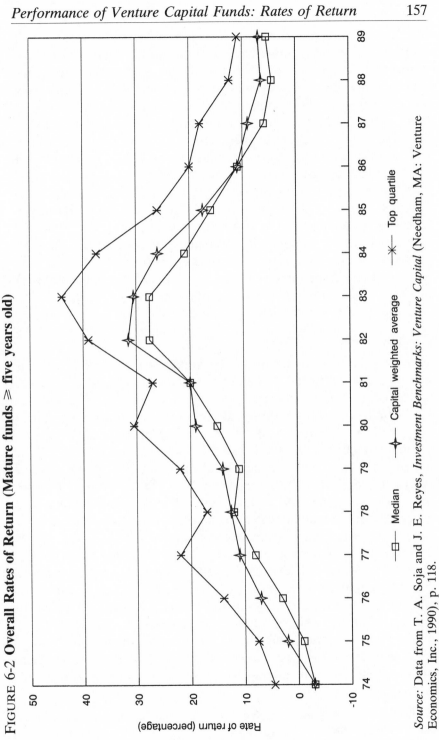

—□— Median   —✦— Capital weighted average   —✳— Top quartile

Source: Data from T. A. Soja and J. E. Reyes, *Investment Benchmarks: Venture Capital* (Needham, MA: Venture Economics, Inc., 1990), p. 118.

The information presented in Figure 6-2 must be viewed with caution because it agglomerates the IRRs of all funds at least five years old in a given year regardless of the age of the funds. This is potentially misleading because it is expected that as funds grow older, their portfolio companies move closer to being harvested (e.g., initial public offerings, mergers, and so forth) or have actually been harvested. Thus, it is likely that the rate of return of a fund will increase with age, all other things being equal. Of course, all other things are not equal. One important factor is the calendar date, which can have a major effect on IRRs; for example, as Figure 6-2 shows, IRRs peaked in 1982–1983. The year when a fund was started also can have a major effect. A new fund typically invests its money in portfolio companies during the first three to four years of its life. Hence, for example, funds started in 1978 had portfolio companies that went public in the hot 1983 IPO market. Thus, three temporal factors have to be separated: the year a fund was started, its age, and calendar year.

Calendar Date

The funds were grouped in annual vintages according to year in which they were started.* The median IRRs of each group of funds by calendar year started are presented in Figure 6-3. The 1977 to 1979 vintage, which comprises seven funds, performed spectacularly, with a median rate of return peaking at 35% in 1983, then gradually declining to 24% by 1989. Funds formed after 1979 did not perform as well. For example, at the end of 1985, the average returns of the 1981, 1982, 1983, and 1984 vintages were all lower than 10%, with the 1984 vintage being slightly negative. By 1989, every post–1979 vintage was returning less than 10%, and, what's worse, all post–1980 vintages were below 5%.

The median returns in Figure 6-3 demonstrate the dramatic effect of the frenzied IPO market of 1983, when 121 venture-capital-backed companies went public, usually with spectacular offerings. Valuations of venture capital portfolios skyrocketed. Price-to-earnings ratios of 40 to 60 for venture-capital-backed IPOs were common.[19] Some were much higher. At the height of the feeding frenzy, for example, Stratus Computer went public with an offering price of almost 200 times its annualized earnings. Other companies had

---

*In the context of the venture capital industry, vintage has the same meaning as cohort, which is the term demographers use for people born in the same year who pass through life's cycles together.

FIGURE 6-3 **Median Rates of Return by Calendar Year**

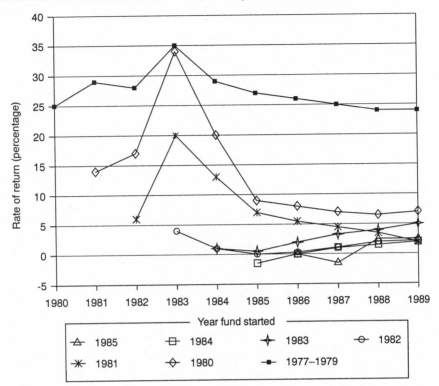

Source: Data from T. A. Soja and J. E. Reyes, *Investment Benchmarks: Venture Capital* (Needham, MA: Venture Economics, Inc. 1990).

no trouble going public even though they had lost money every quarter since they were founded. This confirmed what Poindexter and others had noted: hot IPO markets are by far the most important cause of peaks in venture capital returns.[20]

Age of Funds

The IRRs of the funds grouped according to their starting dates were plotted against the ages of the funds (see Figure 6-4). The figure shows that, at age five, the earlier a fund was started, the higher its rate of return.

As a fund gets older, the value of its portfolio is expected to increase as the companies it has invested in grow in value. The frequency distribution of each of the groups of three- and five-year-old funds is shown in Figure 6-5. It shows that the median of

FIGURE 6-4 **Median Rates of Return by Age of Fund**

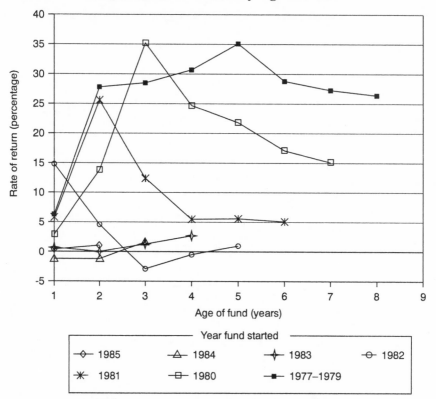

Source: Data from T. A. Soja and J. E. Reyes, *Investment Benchmarks: Venture Capital* (Needham, MA: Venture Economics, Inc. 1990).

the distribution is higher for the older funds than for the younger ones (25% versus 13%).*

Type of Fund

According to finance theory, early-stage funds should outperform later-stage and balanced funds because of their greater risk. Clearly, investments in high-technology companies that have yet to develop products and markets are a lot chancier than investments in a management buyout of a low-technology company with mature products and developed markets. This appears to be true in prac-

---

*The frequency distributions should be viewed with caution because they are not controlled for the starting date of the funds. For example, the starting date of three-year-old funds could be any year from 1978 to 1982.

FIGURE 6-5 **Distribution of Returns for All Three- and Five-Year-Old Funds (Funds started 1978 through 1982)**

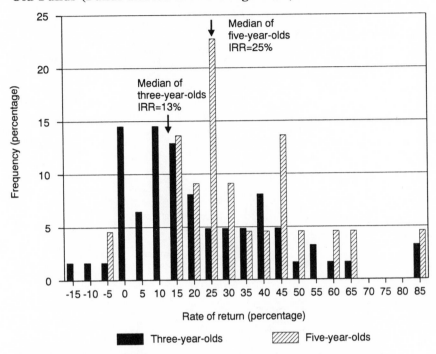

Source: Data from W. D. Bygrave et al., "Early Rates of Return on 131 Venture Capital Funds Started 1978–1984," *Journal of Business Venturing*, vol. 4, no. 2 (1989), pp. 93–106.

tice: early-stage funds yielded somewhat higher returns than did later-stage and balanced funds (see Figure 6-6). Later-stage funds had the lowest returns.

Size of Fund

Both small funds (less than $25 million) and big funds (more than $100 million) produced higher returns than did midsized funds ($25 million to $49.9 million). This is probably because the key to successful venture capital is knowledge. And a fund's knowledge depends on its resources, especially its professionals. Small funds have limited resources, so they take a narrow focus. They tend to specialize in a few niches in which they are experts (e.g., early-stage computer companies). Big funds have more abundant professional resources, so they are able to be successful with a broader focus. Midsized funds, on the other hand, may have investment

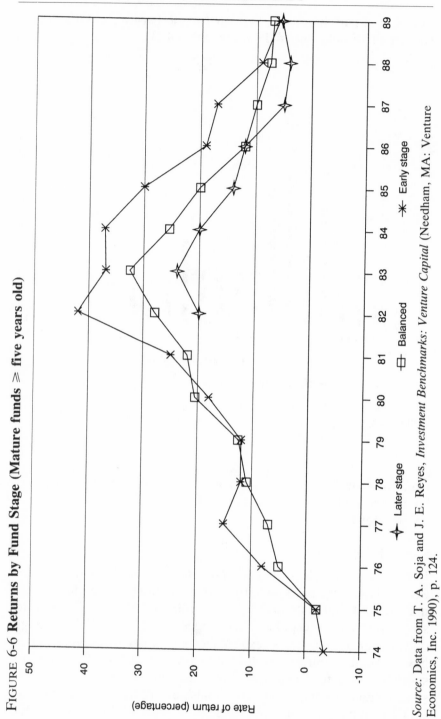

FIGURE 6-6 **Returns by Fund Stage (Mature funds ≥ five years old)**

Source: Data from T. A. Soja and J. E. Reyes, *Investment Benchmarks: Venture Capital* (Needham, MA: Venture Economics, Inc. 1990), p. 124.

strategies too broad for their resources. This outcome is what Porter's competitive strategy framework predicts: midsized funds have the lowest returns (see Figure 6-7).

FROM ECSTASY TO AGONY

The early 1980s were glorious days for venture capital. Returns climbed steeply to heights not seen since the late 1960s, the previous glory era. But the euphoria was short-lived. After reaching their lofty peak in 1983, returns began a downward slide that continued through the end of the decade. When compared to the performance of the stock markets in recent years, venture capital returns have been well below risk-adjusted expectations since 1983. *Forbes* summed it up this way:

> Even the top performers are hurting. Take Boston-based TA Associates, one of the most successful of the large firms, with over $400 million under management. The 41% average return it has enjoyed over the past 11 years masks the fact that money invested in 1983 has returned less than a passbook 5.5%.
>
> "It used to be hard not to make money," TA Associates general partner P. Andrews McLane says ruefully. "It's definitely not as easy now."[21]

Many factors contributed to the declining returns. As we have noted, some observers said it was too much money chasing too few deals. Others said it was too much money chasing too many bad deals. Without question, there was a shortage of quality deals to invest in. Complicating that problem was a shortage of experienced venture capitalists to seek out deals, evaluate them, invest in them, and oversee the investments. Then, when it was time to start harvesting the quality deals that had grown into successful companies, investors had lost their appetites for IPOs. Stock flotations were impossible for most venture-capital-backed companies. Or if they were possible, valuations were down. Let's look at these factors in more detail.

Availability of Capital and Deals

In the 1980s, institutions, especially pension funds, supplied more and more capital to venture capital funds. There was concern that the flood of money would lower returns. As a 1988 *Business Week*

FIGURE 6-7 **Returns by Fund Size (Mature funds ≥ five years old)**

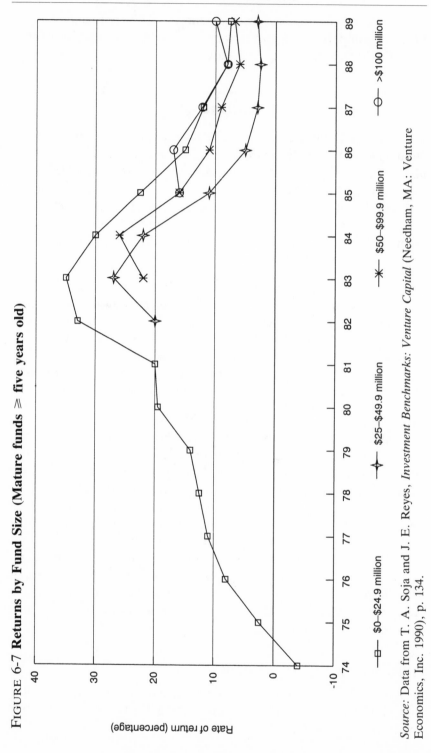

Source: Data from T. A. Soja and J. E. Reyes, *Investment Benchmarks: Venture Capital* (Needham, MA: Venture Economics, Inc. 1990), p. 134.

article reported:

> [Venture capitalists] spent years cajoling pension funds to invest part of their $3 trillion kitty in startups. Now the funds are complying—with a vengeance. They're "preparing to unleash hundreds of millions of dollars on venture capitalists who already have too much money," frets Don Valentine, a general partner of Sequoia Capital in Menlo Park, California. Many other veteran venture capitalists share his worry that the flood of venture capital will force prices of fledgling companies higher while lowering returns for most investors.[22]

That sentiment had been expressed earlier at the National Venture Capital Association annual meeting in May 1987, when William Hambrecht, another leader of the venture capital industry, commented that what was happening in the industry at that time was "Economics 101." There were too many dollars coming into the industry, and competition for deals was pushing returns down.[23]

Availability of Venture Capitalists

In 1978, there was no shortage of applicants wanting to enter the venture capital profession. What was in short supply, however, was venture capitalists with ten or more years of experience.[24] The number of professionals in the industry increased from 597 in 1977 to 1,494 in 1983—a 150% increase. The capital under their management increased from $2.5 billion to $12 billion—a 380% increase. And the average capital per professional increased from $4.2 million to $8.1 million—a 93% increase.[25]

In other words, for the industry as a whole, venture capitalists were managing more money but were less experienced in 1983 than in 1977. Of 61 new partnerships* formed in the period from 1977 to 1982, the level of the general partners' experience was only 5.2 years.[26] And that level dropped further in 1983.

Harvest

The most decisive determinant of the returns on venture capital investments is the health of the IPO market. When the IPO market is buoyant, it's comparatively easy to float new issues of venture-capital-backed companies at high valuations. This causes venture capital returns to rise, because, as we shall see in the next chapter, IPOs, on average, provide the most bountiful harvest of venture capital investments.

*New partnerships are new venture capital funds raised by new firms. In contrast, follow-on partnerships are new venture capital funds raised by existing firms.

CHAPTER 7

Harvesting the Investments

J UST LIKE FARMERS, venture capitalists seed, tend, and feed portfolio companies in the hopes of reaping a bountiful harvest. A few harvests fail miserably, a few succeed gloriously, while most fall in between. The most magnificent harvest of all, initial public offerings, will be examined in detail in this chapter. We will look at the IPO market for venture-capital-backed companies in the 1980s and show that since 1984 there has been a drought. We will argue that the IPO drought is the main cause for the unsatisfactory returns on venture capital since 1983.

TYPES OF HARVEST

When venture capitalists invest in portfolio companies, they do so in expectation that those investments will yield substantial returns in a few years. By far the most common way of attaining those gains is through IPOs.

The gains realized through IPOs were almost five times greater than the next most profitable methods, according to a study of how 26 venture capital funds exited 442 investments from 1970 to 1982.[1] That study found that 30% of the exits were through IPOs, 23% acquisitions, 6% company buybacks, 9% secondary sales, 6% liquidations, and 26% write-offs. Gains were produced by IPOs (1.95* times investment), acquisitions (0.40 times), company buy-

*(amount returned − amount invested)/amount invested

167

backs (0.37 times), and secondary sales (0.41 times). Losses were suffered in liquidations (-0.34 times investment) and write-offs (-0.37 times)

Relatively few of the companies in those venture capital firms' portfolios produced large gains; almost a third lost money, and another third either broke even or produced only nominal gains. Almost 50% of the final total value of a portfolio came from only 6.8% of all its investments, and 75% of the final value came from only 15.7%, according to an analysis of 383 investments that were harvested by 13 venture capital funds from 1969 to 1985. In contrast, money was lost on 34.5% of the investments.[2]

The average holding period of those 383 investments was about four years, which varied little according to the exit route. When the gains and losses are sorted according to the stage of the company at the time of the investment, we see that early-stage investments yielded proportionately more big winners (amount returned ≥ 5 times the investment) and total losers than either expansions or LBOs/acquisitions (Figure 7-1). This is what finance theory predicts. It's interesting that the ratio of big winners (≥ 5 times) to other winners-mediocrities-partial losers to total losers was almost exactly 2:6:2, which is a rule of thumb for a successful venture-capital portfolio.

Figure 7-1 **Gains and Losses by Stage of Initial Investment**

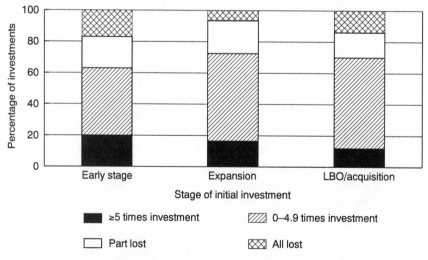

Source: Data from R. Khoylian, *Venture Capital Performance* (Needham, MA: Venture Economics, Inc., 1988), p. 9.

Sevin Rosen Management Company, one of the hottest venture capital funds throughout the 1980s, is a textbook example of the 2-6-2 rule. According to Ben Rosen, his firm invested in 36 companies. Eight went public, 8 went bankrupt, and 20 were still in incubation at the beginning of 1988.[3] Sevin Rosen's two funds, both specializing in early-stage computer and semiconductor companies, earned several hundred million dollars on an investment of $85 million.[4] Among its winners were Lotus Development, Compaq Computer, and Silicon Graphics; among its losers were Osborne Computer, Synapse Computer, and Enmasse Computer.

Its $2.5 million investment in Compaq was worth $40 million at the IPO, and its $2.1 million bet on Lotus was worth $70 million at the IPO. The $400,000 it invested in Osborne, however, was a total loss. Since only two of its investments were worth $110 million at the time of the IPO (and much more subsequently), it shows that a fund needs a few spectacular winners if it is to make high returns on its entire portfolio.

IPOs: THE GOLDEN HARVEST

A healthy IPO market gives the venture capital industry its vitality. Without IPOs the venture-capital investment process would not be viable. When venture-capital-backed companies go public, the returns are sometimes spectacular. Returns of 50 times the first round of venture capital—or even more—have occasionally been realized. Examples of impressive returns of venture-capital-backed IPOs during the past decade include Apple, with a 235 times return, Lotus 63 times, and Compaq 38 times. It is heady stuff for investors. But what are the returns overall? Do some industries have higher returns than others? How does time (both calendar and elapsed) affect them? How do the returns for different rounds of venture capital compare? And what are the returns to the public stockholders who buy stock at the IPO?

THE REALITIES OF IPO RETURNS

To answer these questions, we will now look at the returns from venture-capital-backed companies that had IPOs over the decade 1979 to 1988. They were in four high-technology industries, all of them major forces in the entrepreneurial revolution.[5]

Of the 77 companies in the data set, 31 were classified as computer hardware companies, 18 as computer software, 18 as communications, and 10 as biotechnology. One company had an IPO in 1979, 2 in 1980, 4 in 1981, 4 in 1982, 13 in 1983, 9 in 1984, 7 in 1985, 15 in 1986, 21 in 1987, and 1 in 1988. The average price per share for each round of venture capital was $2.16 ($0.09 minimum; $10.50 maximum) for the first, $3.79 ($0.13 minimum; $13.01 maximum) for the second, and $5.35 ($0.93 minimum; $13.50 maximum) for the third. The average price of the IPO was $12.66 ($5.00 minimum; $30.00 maximum) (Figure 7-2). The median age of the companies at the time of their IPOs was 48 months; the median time from the first round of venture capital to the IPO was 34 months. The median time from founding to first round was 10 months; the first to the second round was 14 months; the second to third round was 11 months; and third to IPO was 17 months.

Times Return

The return on the venture capital at the IPO was 22.5 times for the first round, 10.0 times for the second round, and 3.7 times for the third round. The times returns* at one, two, three, and four years after the IPO are listed in Figure 7-3.

First Round   The times return for the first round is graphed quarterly in Figure 7-4. The trend shows a steady rise from 22.5 at the IPO to 61.7 at the end of the seventeenth quarter. The fluctuations

FIGURE 7-2 **Adjusted Price per Share by Round**

	1st Round	*2d Round*	*3d Round*	*IPO*
Price/Share	$ 2.16	$ 3.79	$ 5.35	$12.66
Minimum	0.09	0.13	0.93	5.00
Maximum	10.50	13.01	13.50	30.00

FIGURE 7-3 **Yearly Times Return by Round of Venture Capital**

Round	*IPO*	*Year 1*	*Year 2*	*Year 3*	*Year 4*
First	22.5	42.1	40.8	39.2	61.7
Second	10.0	13.9	20.2	21.6	38.1
Third	3.7	5.4	5.0	6.3	13.5

*Times return = amount returned/amount invested.

FIGURE 7-4 **Quarterly Times Return by Round of Venture Capital**

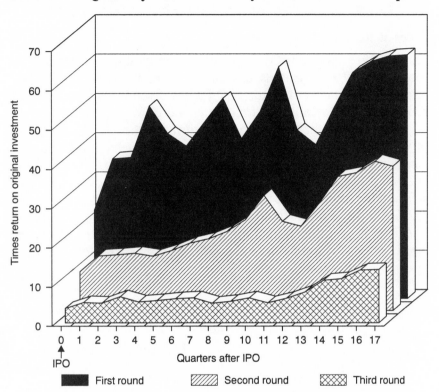

in the trend line are due primarily to companies dropping out of the data set as more time elapses after the IPO (the data set drops from 71 at the IPO to 24 at quarter 17). The performance of a stock is followed quarterly after the IPO because venture capital funds typically sell none, or very little, of their stock in portfolio companies at the time of the initial offering. The timing and the quantity of the post-IPO sales are restricted by agreements with IPO underwriters and by SEC Rule 144, which governs the sale of unregistered stock. In some cases, venture capital funds wait to sell the stock because they expect its value to rise. Hence, in some cases it may be years after an IPO before a venture capital fund sells its investment in a portfolio company.

Second and Third Rounds The times return for the second and third rounds of venture capital are also shown in Figure 7-4. As finance theory predicts, the highest returns were earned on the first round, because it was the most risky, and the lowest returns were earned on the third round because it was the least risky.

Rates of Return

At the time of the IPO, the average compound annual rate of return for 77 first rounds of venture capital was 220%; by the seventeenth quarter after the IPO (about seven years after the first round of venture capital), it had declined to 57%.

To see what happened to the returns on the first three rounds of venture capital, a subset of 36 companies, each of which had at least three rounds of venture capital, was examined. The returns on rounds 1, 2, and 3 for those companies are shown in Figure 7-5. At the time of the IPO, the return on the first round was 192%; on the second round, 163%; and on the third round, 208%. Because those three rounds of venture capital were held for different lengths of time before the IPO, we found that four quarters

FIGURE 7-5 **IRR by Round of Venture Capital**

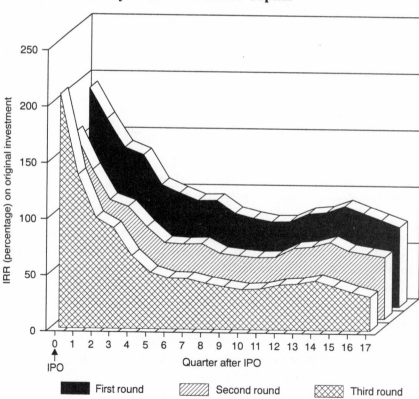

after the IPO the returns were 107%, 80%, and 65%; eight quarters, 82%, 57%, and 41%; 12 quarters, 82%, 62%, and 43%; and 17 quarters, 71%, 55%, and 30%. Again, this is because risk decreases with each successive round of venture capital.

Length of Time from First Round to the IPO

According to industry gurus, the more successful venture capital companies do not rush to harvest their investments. Rather, as we will discuss in Chapter 9, they patiently build value in their portfolio companies before they take them public. We were able to look for that effect by comparing the investment performance of companies as a function of the length of time from the first venture-capital investment to the IPO. We divided the companies into two groups of equal size: those for which the elapsed time from first venture capital to IPO was shorter than 34 months, and those for which it was longer than 34 months. The difference was striking (see Figure 7-6). At the IPO, those taking more than 34 months to go public earned 31.3 times the first round of venture capital versus 13.4

FIGURE 7-6 **Effect of Time from First Round to IPO on Times Return**

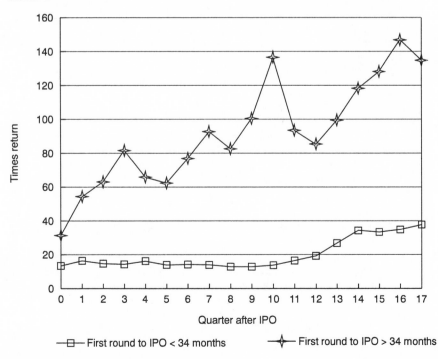

Quarter after IPO

——☐—— First round to IPO < 34 months   ——✦—— First round to IPO > 34 months

times for those taking less than 34 months. By the end of the third year after the IPO, the returns were 85.2 times versus 19.2 times. Thus, it appears that not only do companies that take longer to go public have a higher initial times return at the IPO, the times return grows at a faster rate in the following four years.

To examine the effect of the length of time that the venture capital had been invested before the IPO, we compared the rates of return of the two groups (Figure 7-7). For the first five quarters after the IPO, the group that went public in less than 34 months had the higher rate of return; thereafter, it was lower. At the IPO, the "less than 34 months" group had an annual rate of return of 287% on the first round of venture capital versus 158% for the "more than 34 months" group. However, two years after the IPO, the situation was reversed: the "more than 34 months" group had a return of 97% versus 69% for the "less than 34 months" group. And four years after the IPO, the IRRs were 84% and 49%. Thus, long-term rates of return are much better for venture capital invested in companies that take longer to go public.

FIGURE 7-7 **Effect of Time from First Round to IPO on IRR**

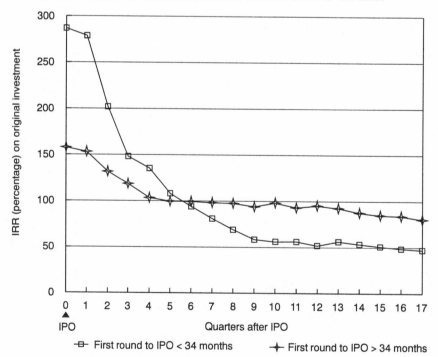

Number of Rounds of Venture Capital

Another gauge of the importance of building value in a portfolio company is the number of rounds of venture capital before the IPO. Those companies with three or more rounds had a 25.3 times return on the first round of venture capital at the IPO compared with 11.9 times for those companies with only one round. It appears that it pays to build value in a portfolio company before going public.

Proportion of Insider Sales at IPO

We theorized that the less stock insiders (venture capitalists and management) sold at the IPO, the better the subsequent performance of the investment, because insiders have the best information for predicting future performance. We divided the IPOs into one group where less than 10% of the IPO stock was sold by insiders and a second group where more than 10% was sold by insiders. There was no statistical difference between the times returns of the two groups at the IPO or in any of the subsequent 17 quarters.

Of the 24 companies where insiders sold less than 10% of the IPO stock, 14 (58.3%) were unprofitable at the time of the IPO. In contrast, of the 47 companies where insiders sold more than 10%, only 4 (8.5%) were losing money. That might explain why there was no overall difference between the performance of the two groups. In the group where insiders sell less than 10% at the IPO, losing companies with insiders who dare not sell because it sends a negative signal to potential investors balance out very successful companies with investors who choose not to sell because they think they are holding an investment with a bright future.

Profitability Immediately before IPO

The companies were separated according to whether they were profitable in the quarter that preceded their IPOs. At the IPO and for each of 17 quarters thereafter, the times return on the first round of venture capital was higher for those companies that were profitable at the time of the IPO than for those with a loss just before they went public (Figure 7-8). The difference between the times returns for profitable and unprofitable companies averaged over the 17 quarters after the IPO was significant. Thus, profitability immediately prior to an IPO may be useful for predicting a stock's performance after an IPO.

FIGURE 7-8 **Times Return by Earnings Immediately before IPO**

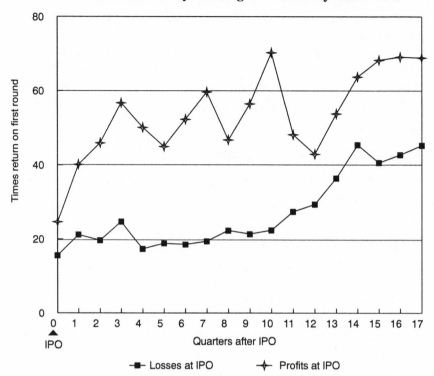

Type of Industry

The highest returns at the IPO were for computer hardware companies—31.7 times for the first round of venture capital—followed by software at 27.0 times; communications at 11.2 times; and biotechnology at 8.8 times. The explanation for these differences is probably to be found in the financial performance of these companies immediately before they went public (Figure 7-9). Computer software and hardware companies had substantially higher sales than did communications and biotechnology companies. Furthermore, software companies were quite profitable at the time of the IPO and hardware companies were at breakeven, whereas data communications and biotechnology companies were losing money. In their early years, biotechnology companies had extremely high losses—65 cents lost for every $1 of revenue—because of the long research, development, and test period before their products come to market. In contrast, computer software and hardware companies brought their products to market much faster. At the time of their

FIGURE 7-9 **Annual Sales and Net Income Overall and by Industry Segment**

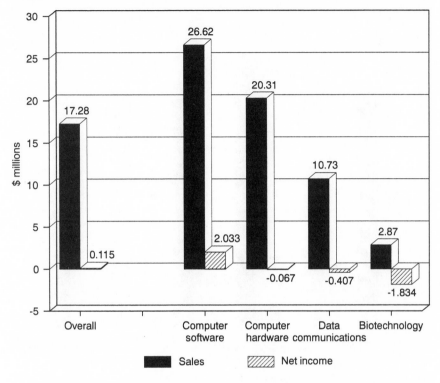

IPOs, biotechnology companies were long on promise but short on performance, while computer companies were already delivering the goods—to both customers and investors. For instance, 77% of the computer hardware companies and 100% of the software companies were profitable when they went public, but only 20% of the biotechnology companies were profitable. This is reflected in the ownership of the companies: after the IPO, management and inside directors still owned 32% of computer software companies but only 17.5% of biotechnology companies (Figure 7-10), even though computer software companies had raised only 12% less money ($26.4 million versus $30.1 million) from investors (Figure 7-11). Put another way, software companies gave up proportionately much less equity to outside investors to raise their capital.

IPO Returns versus Expectations for Venture Capitalists

According to industry wisdom, venture capitalists financing seed and startup high-technology companies are looking for compound

Figure 7-10 **Management and Inside Director Ownership before and after IPO**

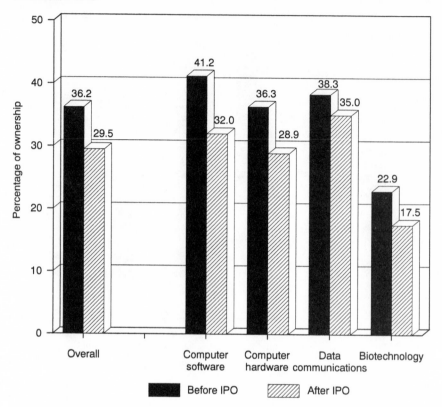

annual returns of 50% or more. For second-stage financings, they tend to look for 30% to 40%, while third-round investors may expect returns of 25% to 30%.[6] A rule of thumb is a return in five years of 7 times on the first venture capital (a compound rate of return of 48%).

The overall returns of the venture-capital-backed IPOs in our sample appear to be in line with industry wisdom. The companies were in emerging technologies. The median time from their founding to receiving their first venture capital was ten months. Thus, early-stage high-technology companies predominated in our sample. Five years after the first venture capital was invested, the average rate of return on the first round was 73%; on the second round, 54%; and on the third round, 33%. Seven years after the first round of venture capital was invested, its rate of return was

FIGURE 7-11 **Total Investment Raised before and at IPO**

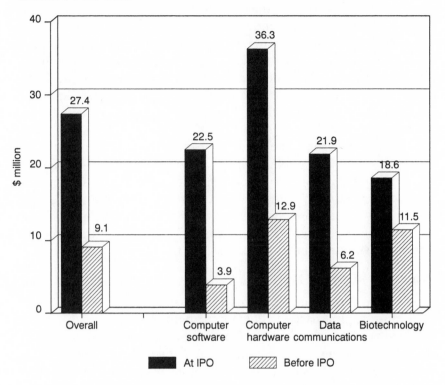

57%. Thus, the returns on our sample were on the high end of industry expectations.

If the venture capitalists sold their stock at the time of the IPO or soon after, their rate of return was very much higher than if they held on to it and sold it long term. The median rate of return on the first round of venture capital was 136% at the IPO. But they did not sell much of their holdings at the IPO—management and investors in our sample sold only 6.4% of their holdings at the IPO. Although a "rate-of-return-maximizer" would have sold as much as possible of the stock at the IPO or soon after, in practice, that was not feasible. Management and original investors still owned 72.2% of the stock after the IPO. They had to sell slowly for two reasons: SEC rules restrict the sale of unregistered stock, and, in any case, flooding the market would depress the price. Their forbearance is less startling when one realizes that, while the rate of return fell in the years after the IPO, the times return on the first round of venture capital increased from 22.5 times at the IPO to 62.0 times after 17 quarters. Thus, the total value of the investment continued to increase.

The median times return on the first round of venture capital at the IPO was 7.5, but the mean was 22.5. The mean was much higher than the median because the distribution was skewed. Some of the times returns in our sample were greater than 100, and one (Apple) was greater than 200. Those numbers are in line with the findings of others.[7]

By any measure, the returns on venture capital invested in companies that went public over the period 1979 to 1988 more than met venture capitalists' expectations. Yet, as we saw in Chapter 6, the overall returns of the funds started in the 1980s have fallen far short. The explanation lies in the IPO market. The public lost interest in speculative IPOs because—in sharp contrast to the returns of venture capital investors—theirs were dismal.

Returns to Buyers of IPOs

How well did ordinary investors fare if they bought stocks of all 77 venture-capital-backed IPOs in our data set? Figure 7-12 shows they did well for the first year or so, but if they held on to the stock, they began to lose money after two years. The median compound annual rate of return 17 quarters after the IPO was −6%, 58% of the stocks had negative returns, 23% had returns below −20%, and only 19% had returns above 20%. Public investors did better in IPOs of profitable companies that did not rush to go public than in those of losing companies that did, but, of course, the higher the quality of an IPO, the less likely that outsiders can buy it. They got the message: beware of venture-capital-backed IPOs. After 1983, many of those IPOs turned out to be terrible investments. Some IPOs, such as Victor Technologies and Priam went bankrupt, and investors lost everything. Consequently, while holders of S&P 500 and Dow Jones stocks were enjoying record-breaking gains, public holders of venture-capital-backed high-tech stocks in our data set were enduring losses, on average.

IPO Gap

Because public investors have little appetite for speculative IPOs, many venture-capital-backed companies have been unable to go public. Hence, venture capital funds have been unable to reap their expected harvests. Some companies have postponed their IPOs,

FIGURE 7-12 **IRR on Stock Bought at IPO Price**

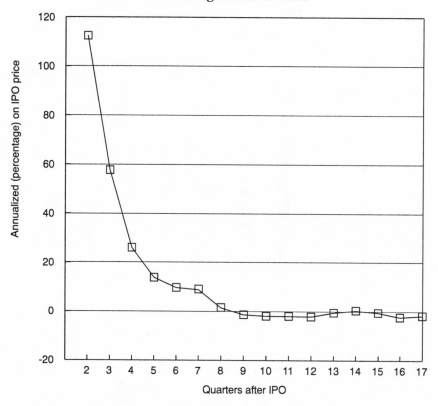

others—usually, but not always, the less promising ones—have been acquired by other companies. Figure 7-13 says it all. The number of venture-capital-backed IPOs has declined since 1986, and acquisitions as a percentage of all acquisitions and IPOs have risen from 29% in 1983 to 78% in 1989. Since returns on acquisitions are not nearly as lucrative as those on IPOs, it's not surprising that the overall returns on venture capital have declined.

The number of IPOs has been declining during a decade when the number of venture-backed companies has increased dramatically. If 20% to 30% of a fund's companies subsequently have IPOs, its returns are respectable. We know how many companies receive venture capital for the first time in any calendar year. Assuming that companies go public four years after they receive their first venture capital, we can estimate how many IPOs of venture-backed companies are needed each year to produce acceptable returns for the venture capital industry. Our computations

FIGURE 7-13 **Number of IPOs and Acquisitions of Venture-Capital-Backed Companies**

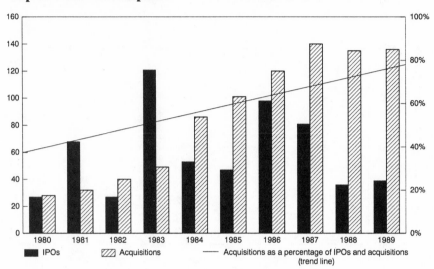

show a total shortfall of at least 200 venture-capital-backed IPOs from 1984 to 1989 (Figure 7-14). The average annual deficiency was at least 33.5—a severe deficit given that actual IPOs average only 59 per year. It's possible that a hot IPO market could close that gap, but it would have to be white hot, since the cumulative gap since 1984 is between 200 and 500 IPOs. We should remember that in the 1980s, the highest number of venture-capital-backed

FIGURE 7-14 **Estimated Gap in Venture-Capital-Backed IPOs, 1984–1989**

	Total	Average per year
Actual number of companies that received a first round of venture capital, 1980–1985	2,776	462.6
Actual number of venture-capital-backed IPOs, 1984–1989	354	59.0
Estimated IPO gap, 1984–1989, if (20% of venture-capital-backed companies have IPOs)	− 201	− 33.5
Estimated IPO gap, 1984–1989, if (30% of venture-capital-backed companies have IPOs)	− 479	− 79.8

IPOs in any one year was 121, in 1983, the next highest being 98, in 1986. The average for the decade 1980 to 1989 was 60.

There is no doubt that a healthy IPO market is crucial for the long-term prosperity of the venture capital industry. Since 1983, unfortunately, the IPO market's ability to float new issues of venture-capital-backed companies has not kept pace with the rate of creation of such companies. According to some observers, it is a fundamental structural problem because stock markets cannot absorb enough new issues to produce the returns that venture capitalists expect. Making assumptions similar to those in this section, Sahlman, for example, argued that venture capital funds would have owned 50% of the total market value of all NASDAQ stocks if their returns had been 25%, 68% if their returns had been 35%, and 110% if their returns had been 50%.[8] Clearly, that was impossible. By 1988, leading venture capitalists seem to have realized the ramifications of this for the industry as a whole.

IMPLICATIONS

As the evidence in this chapter makes clear, the IPO market is very uncertain—perhaps too uncertain to be relied upon as the main harvest route for venture capital investments. Traditionally, IPOs have yielded a harvest much more bountiful than mergers. But we should remember that, in general, only the cream of the crop goes public, whereas mergers include everything from companies in distress to huge successes. Giant companies buying venture-capital-backed companies for strategic purposes often value them higher than the IPO market would. That became very apparent in the biotech industry in the 1980s; consider, for example, Eli Lilly's purchase of Hybritech, which we discussed in Chapter 4. It's nothing new. In 1969, Xerox bought Scientific Data Systems, an eight-year-old venture-capital-backed minicomputer company with $100 million annual sales and $10 million net income, for almost $1 billion, an astronomical sum, even in that year's super hot IPO market.[9] But perhaps what is new in the 1990s is the recognition by venture capitalists and entrepreneurs alike that merging a company with a large strategic partner may be a more viable harvest objective than a public stock offering. That has important implications for how a startup company is developed.

CHAPTER 8

Syndicating Investments and Venture Capital Networks

U NCERTAINTY dominates the venture capital industry—especially that portion investing in early-stage, highly innovative companies. It's a very risky business. Success comes from having good information and the experience to use it to make decisions wisely. It has been said that 100 decision makers control the U.S. venture-capital industry.[1] These are very experienced venture capitalists with extensive networks through which they gather and disseminate information on entrepreneurs, technologies, innovations, markets, investors, and the other ingredients essential for success in selecting and investing in high-potential deals. Understanding what it takes for venture capitalists to rise to the top requires a knowledge of their networks and their experience.

Arthur Rock is one of the top venture capitalists. His backing of Intel illustrates the power of his network. When Robert Noyce needed money to start Intel in 1968, he turned to Rock for help. According to venture capital folklore, Rock got on the phone and lined up $2.5 million in thirty minutes.[2]

How could Rock raise so much money so quickly? Because of his reputation for picking winners such as Fairchild and SDS, other investors trust his judgment of would-be entrepreneurs and their ideas for high-technology startups. Despite his predilection for keeping a low profile—there is no name on the door of his office in San Francisco's financial district—he is well known within the powerful, concentrated network of top venture capitalists.

185

Today, there are about 650 venture capital firms throughout the United States. Every major metropolitan area has them. But the distribution is not uniform. Venture capitalists are concentrated in a few major areas. In 1988, two-thirds of the total pool of venture capital was managed by venture capital firms located in just three states: California (26%), New York (25%), and Massachusetts (15%). Add two more states, Connecticut and New Jersey, and three-quarters of the pool is in the Northeast and California (Figure 8-1).[3] Within those regions, venture capital firms are clustered in Silicon Valley, San Francisco, Los Angeles, Boston, and New York City. There are, for instance, about 120 venture capital firms in the Silicon Valley–San Francisco region, about 75 in greater Boston, and about 125 just in New York City. That's almost half the firms in the country.

In some places, venture capital firms are next door neighbors. In one location, 3000 Sand Hill Road in Menlo Park just off the Stanford University Campus, they are literally on top of one another in a complex of four buildings set in beautifully kept lawns planted with trees, shrubs, and flowers next to a parking lot filled with Mercedes, Jaguars, and BMWs. Thirty plus venture capital firms have headquarters or branch offices in those four buildings.

FIGURE 8-1 **Capital under Management by State, 1988**

	Capital ($ billion)	Percentage of total
California	8.12	26
New York	7.85	25
Massachusetts	4.82	15
Connecticut	1.79	6
Illinois	1.61	5
Texas	1.06	3
New Jersey	0.90	3
Minnesota	0.61	2
Maryland	0.50	2
Pennsylvania	0.46	<2
Ohio	0.46	<2
Washington	0.42	<2
Colorado	0.33	<2

Source: Venture Capital Journal (March 1989), p. 16. (Since reporting these numbers, the *Venture Capital Journal* has not reported total capital under management by state.)

They control more than $3 billion of venture capital, 10% of the total U.S. pool. And nearby in three more buildings are seven more firms with another $750 million under their management. One Stanford University sociologist, Everett Rogers, famous for his research on the diffusion of innovations and social networks, and a colleague, wrote about 3000 Sand Hill Road:

> The concentration of high-technology financiers is functional for the venture capitalists as well as for the entrepreneur. A venture banker can have a lunch with a friendly competitor and pick up useful information about a particular entrepreneur whose business plan he is considering. Such handy networks can work against a potential entrepreneur—if rejected by one venture capitalist, the whole community knows immediately. Such "pack investing" works against the ideal free market forces. There is much subjectivity in investment decisions; one venture capitalist's instincts may be wrong, and thus may influence the others.
>
> Venture capitalists commonly invest in groups of two to five ("pack investing"). There is a great deal of cronyism among venture capital firms and one venture capitalist would be considered greedy to hog an especially attractive investment. The venture capital community in Silicon Valley is like a country club. Everyone knows everyone else, news and gossip travel quickly within the group, and most of the activities of club members remain hidden from most of the public.[4]

When Rogers and Larsen wrote that, there were fifteen venture capital firms at 3000 Sand Hill Road. Five years later, their number had doubled. Clearly, the firms think there are benefits to working cheek by jowl. We will now look at one of those benefits: syndicating—the polite name for "pack investing."

SYNDICATED INVESTMENTS

From 1982 to 1984, the National Science Foundation (NSF) sponsored a research project to investigate the process of investing in highly innovative technological ventures.[5] In that NSF study, we and Venture Economics developed a database of 1,501 portfolio companies that had received a first round of venture capital over the period 1967 through 1982. The majority of those companies had received their first venture capital between 1978 and 1982, a period of unprecedented growth in the industry. For each company in that database, we knew the location, industry segment, technology, degree of innovativeness, stage of development, amount of money raised in its first round of venture capital, and the names of the venture capital firms that participated in its first-round syndication.

By looking at the syndications, we were able to study the co-investing networks of venture capital firms, especially how those networks varied according to the degree of uncertainty of their deals. At the time of our study, finance theory said that venture capitalists syndicated deals to spread financial risk. However, from discussions with high-tech venture capitalists, we learned that another important reason for syndicating deals was to share information. Hence, we wanted to learn about the relative importance of risk spreading versus information sharing as the reason for syndicating investments.

Top Venture Capital Firms

Four hundred sixty-four different venture-capital firms had invested in at least one of 1,501 companies in our database. Out of those 464 firms—essentially all the firms in the United States at the time—the group that had invested most frequently were classified as the top 61. Those top 61 firms were then broken into three groups: (1) 21 firms that invested mainly in highly innovative technology companies, (2) 21 firms that invested mainly in low-technology companies, and (3) 19 firms that did not show any particular preference for either type of company. Here are some examples from the three groups: Kleiner Perkins Caufield & Byers was classified as a top 21 high-tech firm; Narragansett Capital as a top 21 low-tech firm; and Hambrecht & Quist as a top 19 firm with no particular preference. The remaining 403 venture capital firms were lumped together as one group.

Concentration and Influence of the Top 61

The top 61 firms managed 57% of the 1982 pool of venture capital. They were concentrated geographically, with 38 of them in three states: California, Massachusetts, and New York. Their sphere of influence was extensive: three out of every four portfolio companies in our database had at least one of the top 61 as an investor. That influence was spread evenly among high-tech and low-tech companies, with approximately three-quarters of each type having at least one of the top 61 as an investor. The top 21 high-tech specialists were invested in almost 45% of all high-tech companies. Similarly, the top 21 low-tech specialists were invested in about

45% of all low-tech companies. When the top 19 firms with no particular specialization were added to either the top 21 high-tech or the top 21 low-tech firms, the resulting two groups of top 40 firms were invested in about two-thirds of all high-tech companies and about two-thirds of all low-tech companies.

Structure of Co-Investing Networks

The structure of the co-investment networks of the top venture-capital firms reveals striking differences between the syndication habits of high- and low-tech venture-capital firms. The co-invest-ment linkages among the members of the top 21 high-tech are revealed in Figure 8-2. The area of each circle in the figure is proportional to the total funds managed by the top 21 high-tech firms in a given state. Each joint investment by a pair of venture capital firms is represented by one line.

Figure 8-2 clearly shows the high-tech oases on the two coasts. It also shows how the top 21 high-tech firms are connected intra-state and interstate. Almost all connections are either within the Boston–New Jersey and the Los Angeles–San Francisco coastal corridors or between them. The networks of the top low-tech firms are quite different (see Figure 8-3). There is not nearly as much overall connectedness. Moreover, there are no dominant coastal corridors. And the Midwest and Texas are prominent.

Connectedness

The connectedness[6] of a network is the number of pairs of firms with one or more actual co-investments as a percentage of the maximum number of all possible pairs.[7] If the connectedness is 100%, every firm has co-invested one or more times with every other firm in the network.

The connectedness of all 464 venture-capital firms was only 2.3%, but it increased as the types of firms were narrowed down. The connectedness of the top 21 high-tech firms with top 21 low-tech firms was 7%. For the top 61 firms as a group, it was 22%; for the top 21 low-tech firms, it was 22%; for the top 21 high-tech firms, it was 37%; and for the 9 California top 21 high-tech firms, it was 69%.

Strength of Connections

The number of times that a pair of firms co-invests together is an indication of the strength of their mutual connection. The 9 top 21 high-tech firms headquartered in California behaved quite differ-

Figure 8-2 Joint Investments by Pairs of Top 21 High-Tech Firms

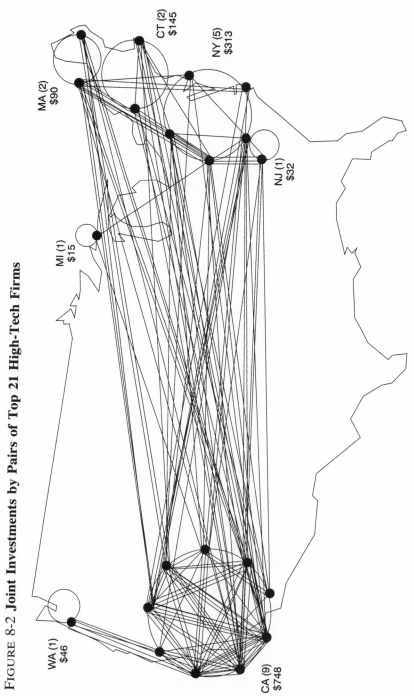

CT (2) $145

NY (5) $313

MA (2) $90

NJ (1) $32

MI (1) $15

WA (1) $46

CA (9) $748

Note: $ million of funds.

FIGURE 8-3 **Joint Investments by Pairs of Top 21 Low-Tech Firms**

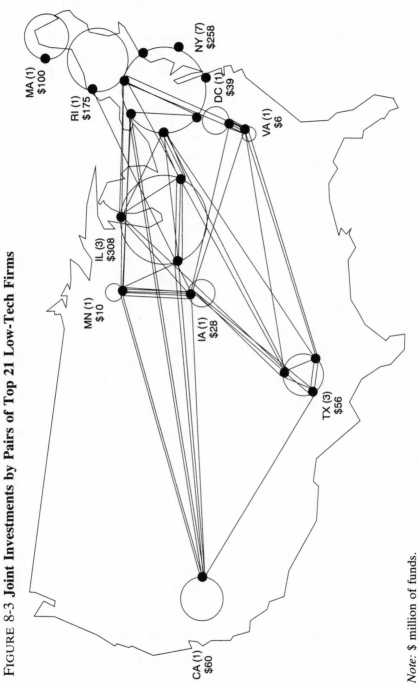

Note: $ million of funds.

ently from the 10 top 21 high-tech firms headquartered in Massachusetts, Connecticut, New York, and New Jersey. The California
firms were about twice as likely to co-invest among themselves as
with out-of-state top 21 high-tech firms. In contrast, the 10 northeastern firms had no more propensity to co-invest among themselves than with out-of-state firms.

We believe that the California firms favored each other as
syndication partners because of concentration. At the time of our
study, those 9 firms managed a whopping 71% of the total pool of
venture capital under management by California firms of all types,
whereas the 10 northeastern firms managed only 27% of the total
pool of venture capital in the Northeast. The greater concentration
of top 21 high-tech firms in California made them more aware of
competition among themselves for prospective companies to invest
in. As Rogers and Larsen commented, they could not afford to be
hogs; instead, they shared the deal flow—but, of course, not
equally. As in all social systems, there was a hierarchy.

Centrality and Hierarchy

Connectedness does not measure the strength of a connection
between two firms, nor how well a firm is bonded to a network,
nor the position of a firm in the hierarchy. Sociologists determine
those factors by measuring centrality, which, in the context of
venture capital, measures the relative importance of firms in the
network.[8]

When the top 21 high-tech venture-capital firms were ordered
according to their centrality, the top 7 were all headquartered in
California; the highest northeastern firm was ranked eighth. At the
bottom were a Washington state firm and a Michigan firm—the
only members of the top 21 high-tech group not in California or
the Northeast. In other words, those California firms had the best
access to information because they had the strongest bonds with
other firms. However, it should be stressed that the network was
a good potential source of deals for all the firms, because even the
least central firm was connected to every other firm by at least two
links.

Co-investments between the Top 61 and the Other 403 Firms

When the size of the firms was taken into consideration, the top
61 firms showed no more propensity to co-invest among themselves
than with the other 403 firms. We think this was because the other
403 firms were on average much smaller, so they fed their larger

deals to the top 61 not only to find deep-pocketed co-investors but also to gain access to the inner circle.

Tightly and Loosely Coupled Systems

The co-investment network of venture capitalist firms may be regarded as a coupled system. The overall industry is a loosely coupled system. But the coupling of the top 21 high-tech firms, especially of those in California, is quite tight. What implications does this have? Herbert Simon discusses the coupling of organizational systems.[9] According to him, if all possible pairs in a network are coupled, and if the two firms constituting a pair influence each other, then the network is tightly coupled. In that kind of system, an external influence can affect the entire system because information can flow through many channels. This may make the behavior of members of a tightly coupled system more uniform. For example, it may explain the herdlike behavior of high-tech venture capitalists when they stampede into or out of a new industry segment. It may explain the lemminglike behavior that we saw in Chapter 5, when venture capitalists continued to invest in the Winchester disk-drive industry long after it should have been apparent that the potential rewards did not justify the investments.

A loosely coupled system such as the venture capital industry as a whole has some advantages in interacting with its environment. Tightly coupled subsystems may respond quite dramatically to external forces, but their actions have little effect on other subsystems with whom they are weakly coupled. Hence, the industry benefits from the specialization of different groups because its overall health is not threatened in the short run by a downturn in the fortunes of one group. For instance, the high-technology companies favored by the top 21 high-tech firms for investments did not fare well in the second half of the 1980s, but the low-technology companies (e.g., leveraged buyouts and specialty retailers) of the sort in which the top 21 low-tech firms invest were prospering at that time. So, despite the ups and downs of the two groups, the venture capital industry as a whole was stable during that period.

A loosely coupled system may have advantages when it comes to survival, but as Karl Weick points out, it has the disadvantage of slow communication across the whole system.[10] But although the strong ties of a tightly coupled system speed communications, the information that is spread may not have as much value as that exchanged as a result of weak ties. As Mark Granovetter discovered, the information shared by members of a clique has a sameness or redundancy about it, whereas information gathered from persons in a different social set who are tied weakly to the clique is new.[11] Granovetter reasons that an innovation can reach a greater number of people when it is passed over weak lines rather than strong ones. Of course, venture capitalists have ties to many individuals besides other venture capitalists, so they are able to gather new information from different sources. Furthermore, most pairs of venture capital firms were weakly tied; there were direct links between only 2.3% of all the possible pairs among the 464 venture capital firms. Thus, there were plenty of weakly tied firms that were potential sources of information fresh to the network. This may be another explanation of why the top 61 venture-capital firms invested proportionately at least as much with firms outside their group as with firms inside it.

Information Sharing versus Risk Spreading

By comparing the extent of the co-investing in various types of portfolio companies (low tech versus high tech, early stage versus late stage, consumer versus computer) and looking at the total amount invested, it was possible to make some inferences about the relative importance of information sharing and risk spreading as reasons for syndicating deals. Our basic propositions were that (1) the more uncertain a deal, the greater the need to share information; (2) there was more uncertainty associated with high-tech than with low-tech companies, with early-stage than with late-stage companies, and with computer than with consumer companies; and (3) the larger the total investment, the larger the number of co-investors, if the uncertainty was the same.

This is what we found by examining the first-round investments in our database. There was more co-investing in high-tech than in low-tech companies, even though the average investment per company was 30% less in high-tech companies. There was more co-investing in early-stage than in late-stage companies, even though the average amount invested per early-stage company was 40% less. And there was far more co-investing in computer than in consumer companies, even though the average amount invested in computer companies was slightly less. Thus, we inferred that an important reason for co-investing was to share information to reduce uncertainty. It certainly seemed to be as important as the spreading of financial risk—perhaps more so.

The innovativeness and technology of the portfolio companies were crucial in explaining networking among venture capital firms.

Networking was prominent among venture capital firms investing in high-technology companies where business was uncertain and required sophisticated technical knowledge. In contrast, networking was less important among those firms investing in low-technology companies where business was less uncertain and required no great technical knowledge. Hence, the need to share expertise and thereby reduce uncertainty was greater for high-tech venture capital firms.

For both the top 21 high-tech firms and the top 21 low-tech firms, the size of a firm in terms of the pool of funds that it managed had no effect on its degree of co-investing. Among both groups, big firms shared investments in the same proportion as small firms, even though the big firms had deeper pockets and therefore less need to share financial risk with other firms. That again was evidence that sharing expertise was more important than spreading financial risk as a reason for co-investing.

PROFESSIONALS IN VENTURE CAPITAL NETWORKS

So far we have only looked at the networks of venture capital firms among themselves. Now we will look at the other professionals with whom they are connected. Successful venture capitalists are experts not only in picking winners out of the flock of fledgling companies but also in nurturing and building those companies. An important part of the nurturing process is the network of professional contacts such as accountants, lawyers, bankers, underwriters, entrepreneurs, managers, and consultants that they bring to the companies they invest in. Ned Heizer, the prominent Chicago venture capitalist, said this about seeing that his portfolio companies were organized and staffed properly:

> See to it that they have the right auditing firm—not only the right auditing firm but the right guy from the right auditing firm; that they have the right commercial bank, the right lawyer. See to it that they have all the professionals that they should have. We can do it much better than they can do it themselves. We have the contacts and know-how. Most entrepreneurs don't have the foggiest notion how to get the best bank or the best auditor—but we do. . . . The same is true of law firms and banks. . . . We can get good operating executives with our contacts—this is an invaluable resource.[12]

Let us look at the lawyers, accountants, and underwriters of venture-capital-backed high-technology companies that made initial

public offerings between 1979 and 1988—the same set of companies
that we looked at in Chapter 7. And just as we did in Chapter 7,
we will look at the performance of the funds and see how it was
related to their venture capitalists and underwriters.

Venture Capital Firms

Ninety-one different venture-capital firms held a total of 164 seats
on the boards of directors of our sample of 77 companies. From
that group of 91, we identified the 20 firms that held the most seats
(we called them the top 20 high-tech firms).* The top 20 high-tech
firms held 84 seats on the boards of 51 different companies, 66%
of our sample. Figure 8-4 lists the top 14 high-tech venture capital
firms.

Lead Underwriters

The lead underwriters in 52 of the IPOs—68% of the sample—
were one or more of only four investment banks—the so-called
four horsemen. One of the four horsemen, Alex. Brown, was lead
underwriter in 25% of all the IPOs. The most frequent lead underwriters are listed in Figure 8-5.[13]

FIGURE 8-4 **Number of Board Seats by Venture Capital Firm**

Firm	Number of seats
Hambrecht & Quist Venture Partners	9
Greylock Management Corporation	6
TA Associates	6
Kleiner Perkins Caufield & Byers	5
Oak Investment Partners	5
Sevin Rosen Management Company	5
Mayfield Fund	4
Merrill, Pickard, Andersen & Eyre	4
Sequoia Capital	4
Sutter Hill Ventures	4
Technology Venture Investors	4
Vanguard Associates	4
Venrock Associates	4
Welsh, Carson, Anderson & Stowe	4

*This group of firms is not the same as the top 21 referred to earlier in this
chapter. Nevertheless, almost all the firms on this top 20 list were members of
either the top 21 group specializing in high-tech or the top 19 group with no
specialization.

FIGURE 8-5 **Frequency as Lead Underwriter**

Underwriter	Number of IPOs
Alex. Brown & Sons	19
Robertson, Colman & Stephens	18
Hambrecht & Quist Incorporated	17
L. F. Rothschild, Unterberg, Towbin	14
Morgan Stanley & Co. Incorporated	11
Goldman, Sachs & Co.	9
Kidder, Peabody & Co. Incorporated	6
Montgomery Securities	6
Shearson Lehman Brothers Inc.	6

FIGURE 8-6 **Frequency as Auditor**

Accounting firm	Number of IPOs
Arthur Young	16
Coopers & Lybrand	12
Arthur Andersen	10
Peat Marwick Mitchell	10
Deloitte, Haskins, & Sells	8
Ernst & Whinney	8
Touche Ross	6
Price Waterhouse	4
Others	3

Accounting Firms

The Big 8 (now the Big 6) accounting firms were the auditors for 96% of the 77 IPOs (Figure 8-6). When Arthur Young's clients were combined with Ernst & Whinney's, the merged firm, Ernst & Young, audited 31% of the IPOs. Five accounting firms were auditors for 73% of the IPOs. The fact that Arthur Young is at the top of the list is a tribute to the firm's attention to entrepreneurs. For instance, with *Inc. Magazine,* the firm sponsors the nationwide "Entrepreneur of the Year" contest. Many of the contestants are venture-capital-backed companies. Furthermore, Ernst & Young's San Jose office has many famous Silicon Valley companies as clients. According to Dan Garner, the firm's senior partner for entrepreneurial services, it is the auditor for many of the portfolio companies of Kleiner Perkins Caufield & Byers, which is one of the most successful high-tech venture-capital firms. It's another example of the value of networks.

Law Firms

Law firms were not nearly as concentrated as accounting firms in the 77 IPOs. Nevertheless, four law firms were involved in 38% of the IPOs. They were Wilson, Sonsini, Goodrich; Cooley, Godward, Castro; Brobeck, Phledger, & Harrison; and Gaston Snow & Ely Bartlett.

PERFORMANCE

We wanted to see if there was a correlation between the performance of venture-capital-backed companies and their outside professionals. We were especially interested in their venture capital firms and lead underwriters. There are claims by both practitioners and researchers that those two groups of outside professionals make a difference to a company's performance. Our sample was not big enough to see if individual accounting firms and law firms made a difference to performance, nor are we aware of any conceptual reason—other than malfeasance—that would cause a difference.

We categorized the IPOs into two groups according to their venture capital firm: one group of 46 companies with at least one of the top 20 high-tech venture capital firms on their boards, and a second group of 25 with no top 20 on their boards. As stated in Chapter 7, performance was measured by the times return earned in the first round on venture capital at the time of the IPO and afterward. Companies with top 20 venture-capital firms performed significantly better at their IPOs than those with no top 20 on the board, and they continued to perform noticeably better for each of the seventeen quarters after their IPOs (Figure 8-7).

We then broke the IPOs into two groups according to whether they had one of the four horsemen as a lead underwriter. Companies with one or more of the four horsemen as a lead underwriter performed significantly better than those without at the IPO and for each of seventeen successive quarters after the IPO (Figure 8-8).

Eighty percent of the companies with top 20 venture capitalists on their boards had at least one of the four horsemen as a lead underwriter, whereas only 46% of companies without a top 20 venture capitalist had one of the four horsemen as a lead under-writer. Some links between lead underwriters and venture capital firms are obvious when a venture capital firm and an underwriter are affiliates (for instance, a company with Hambrecht & Quist

FIGURE 8-7 **Returns by Venture Capital Firm**

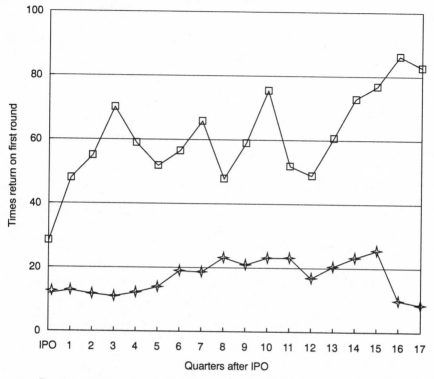

—◻— Top 20 high-tech venture-capital firms   —✦—No top 20 high-tech venture-capital firms

Venture Partners on its board is expected to have Hambrecht & Quist Incorporated as its lead underwriter). However, even when we excluded companies whose venture capital firm was affiliated with one of its lead underwriters, 76% of them had both a top 20 venture capitalist on the board and one of the four horsemen as lead underwriter.

Considering that there were at least 400 venture capital firms in 1979 increasing to more than 600 in 1988, it's remarkable that just 20 of them had board seats on two-thirds of venture-capital-backed high-tech companies that went public. What's more, companies with top 20 representation on their boards produced a much better return for their investors than those with no top 20. And CEOs of high-tech companies perceived that the top 20 high-tech firms added value but other venture-capital firms did not.[14]

Companies whose IPOs were handled by the top 4 lead underwriters produced very superior returns. Furthermore, 80% of

Figure 8-8 **Returns by Lead Underwriter**

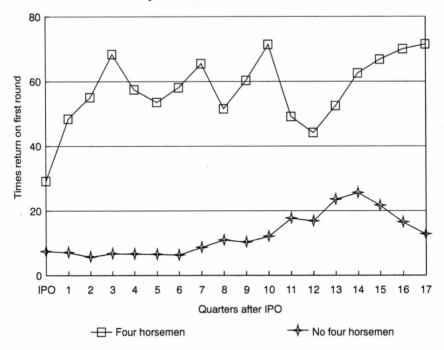

those IPOs had top 20 venture-capital firms on their boards. We were unable to separate the effect of the top 20 venture-capital firms from that of the four horsemen because our sample was too small. Nevertheless, the group of top 20–four horsemen IPOs performed significantly better than the rest of the IPOs.

What are the possible explanations for the top 20–four horsemen effect? It has been proposed that the presence of venture capital in an IPO indicates a higher degree of financial sophistication in dealing with underwriters and recognizing the realities of the market for new issues.[15] Furthermore, according to CEOs of high-tech companies, financial and investor matters are two areas where the venture capitalists on their boards are most helpful.[16] That help almost certainly includes the choice of an underwriter. For instance, two-thirds of IPOs with venture capital backing were managed by prestigious underwriters, while somewhat fewer than half of IPOs without venture capital backing were.[17]

Our findings go even further. They seem to indicate that top 20 venture capitalists may have influenced their companies in selecting not just a prestigious underwriter but one of our top 4. If that inference is correct, then selection of an underwriter may have been one of the most important value-added services of top 20 venture-capital firms because the top 20–four horsemen group produced the highest returns. It has not escaped our notice that the top 4 underwriters per se might have added no more value than already existed in a company. After all, companies with superior value are better able to attract top underwriters.[18] Likewise, top 20 venture-capital firms may have added no more value than already existed, because companies with superior potential are most likely to have top venture-capital firms on their boards. Those caveats notwithstanding, we think the superior performance of the top 20–four horsemen group of companies is evidence of the value of the professional networks of the top venture-capital firms—in this case their contacts with leading underwriters. In general, it's the more experienced venture capitalists who have the best networks.

EXPERIENCE OF VENTURE CAPITALISTS

In 1984, one entrepreneur with venture capitalists on his board made the following comment about inexperienced venture capitalists:

> Venture capital firms tend to hire very bright guys out of graduate schools in their late twenties, smart as hell, and hard working. . . . Every venture guy thinks he is a strategist. . . . So many of them have been educated in the two or three top business schools that they all think alike—not necessarily correctly, but alike.[19]

The most prominent of those two or three top business schools was Harvard. In 1982, 21% of the 451 venture capitalists listed in *Who's Who of Venture Capital* had at least one degree, either graduate or undergraduate, from Harvard University.

Beginning around 1980, the supply of venture capital outpaced the number of good deals in which it could be invested. Furthermore, the experience of the professionals who evaluated those deals and made investment decisions began to decline. Additionally, each professional had more money to manage than ever before. Under those conditions, on average, (1) the quality of the deals that venture capitalists invested in declined, and (2) venture capitalists invested money on less favorable terms. The stage was set for the decline in the performance of venture capital funds that began in the mid-1980s and continued through the remainder of the decade, as we saw so clearly in Chapter 6.

EXPERIENCE AND PERFORMANCE

What is the relationship between the experience level of a venture capitalist firm and the performance of its funds? If conventional wisdom is correct, the more experienced the general partners, the greater a fund's return. As yet no one has measured the performance of venture capital funds as a function of the years of experience of their general partners. A reasonable surrogate for experience is the number of funds that a given venture-capital firm has successfully raised, because, in general, the longer a venture capital firm has been in existence, the greater the number of its follow-on funds. (Of course, a few new funds are raised by experienced venture capitalists starting new firms.)

As we see in Figure 8-9, for most of the years from 1975 through 1989, follow-on funds have outperformed new funds. That finding supports the notion that venture capital firms with more experience outperform those with less. The investment community appears to recognize this—64% of the total pool of independent, private venture capital in 1988 and 56% in 1990 went to firms with one or more senior partners who had at least 10 years' experience. Only 6% of the capital raised went to funds in which the senior partner had less than three years' experience (Figure 8-10). What's more, the more experienced funds were able to raise much larger amounts of money: funds with at least two general partners with 10 or more years' experience raised an average of $70.2 million per fund, but those with no partner with more than five years' experience raised only $11.6 million per fund.[20]

IMPLICATIONS FOR VENTURE CAPITALISTS

Venture capital is an information-intensive business. In a business of that sort, venture capitalists become experts by specializing in niches, not by being generalists. They can learn from how outstanding performers such as Sevin Rosen built their portfolios. Ben Rosen focused on the personal computer industry while his partner L. J. Sevin concentrated on semiconductor and network technologies. As Ben Rosen said: "I've had a love affair with PCs from the beginning." That is how Rosen and Sevin became "two of the best venture capitalists in the world," according to Fred

FIGURE 8-9 **Returns by Experience (for mature funds ≥ 5 years old)**

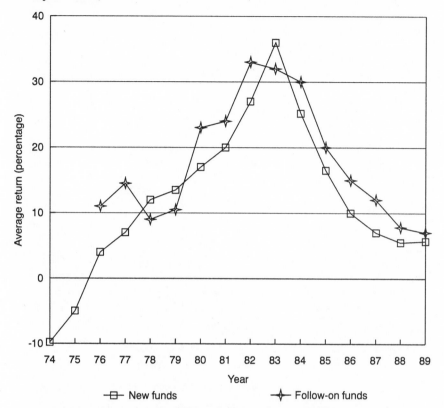

Source: Data from T. A. Soja and J. E. Reyes, *Investment Benchmarks: Venture Capital* (Needham, MA: Venture Economics, Inc., 1990), p. 142.

Adler, himself one of the leading venture capitalists.[21] Perhaps the best advice comes from William Hambrecht: "Firms should identify a unique strategy and stick with it."[22] Through specialization, firms develop the expertise that makes them valuable members of the information network.

It is vital to be well connected to other venture-capital firms. They are important sources of information and investment opportunities. For high-tech venture-capital firms, the California group is central in the network, so links to them are valuable. However, communications in a tightly coupled system are swift but potentially redundant; to ensure a supply of fresh information, members should have as many links as possible to other organizations and individuals besides venture capitalists.

FIGURE 8-10 **Venture Capital Raised in 1990**

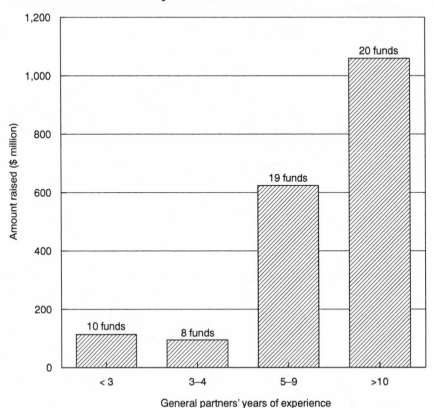

General partners' years of experience

Source: J. G. F. Bonnazio, "Venture Fund Commitments Decline to $1.8 Billion," *Venture Capital Journal* (March 1991), p. 19.

IMPLICATIONS FOR INVESTORS IN VENTURE CAPITAL FUNDS

In the 1980s, institutional investors, especially pension funds, supplied more and more capital to venture capital firms. There was concern that the flood of money would lower returns. Money from public pension funds also began to flow in, after many states changed their laws to allow those funds to make venture capital investments. In 1988, for example, the California state teachers' pension plan embarked on a three-year program to invest up to $400 million in venture capital partnerships. The chief investment officer of that $24 billion fund, Thomas E. Flanigan, assumed that returns on his venture capital investments would average 18% to 20% annually.[23] Our research suggests that an averages player, such as a pension fund manager, can expect higher returns from a portfolio of funds managed by the top firms rather than a portfolio managed by newer, less-experienced firms.

IMPLICATIONS FOR ENTREPRENEURS

When an entrepreneur submits a proposal for venture capital, it should assume that news will spread fast. Thus, it should not use a "bird-shot" approach; rather, it should select its targets with "rifle" precision. The proposal should be submitted to a few firms that are known to specialize in the type of product or service that the entrepreneur is planning to make. Entrepreneurs should be concerned about more than the price of the deal. When top 61 firms invest in a portfolio company, they bring information, contacts, and deep pockets to the companies in which they invest. Those factors are significant in nurturing a growing company.

Business plans that are referred to venture capital firms have a much better chance of being funded than plans that come in cold from entrepreneurs. The probability of a venture capital firm investing in a deal is highest for proposals from venture capital firms that have previously referred deals to them. According to one study, that probability is ten times greater than for a proposal that comes from a cold call.[24]

Once an entrepreneur is turned down by a venture capitalist, the chances of getting funded drop considerably. According to one study, entrepreneurs who were denied venture capital tried again every 19 months, on average, but were successful only every 32 months. Also, companies denied follow-on financing by previously invested venture capitalists had their chances of obtaining other venture capital reduced by 74%.[25]

We have not overlooked the effect of venture capitalists' networks on the cost of capital to the companies in which they invest. Venture capital is not a market in which the cost of capital is broadcast daily. However, through their extensive networks, venture capitalists—the leading ones in particular—are likely to have good information about the market rate being offered by other firms. In contrast, an entrepreneur has little ability to get information on the market price of a deal. A would-be entrepreneur should seek information from other sources such as bankers, lawyers, consultants, publications, and so forth. If the terms offered by one venture capitalist are not acceptable, an entrepreneur should shop for better terms. But if the entrepreneur has negotiated skillfully with the first venture firm, it is reasonable to assume that its terms will be close to the industry market rate.

Once a proposal is in the hands of one of the top 61, news of its existence will spread quickly. If it is turned down by one firm, other firms will soon find out. It is especially applicable to proposals for funding of highly innovative technology companies that are submitted to a member of the top 21 high-tech group. We know a would-be entrepreneur employed by a Route 128 high-tech company who went to California for five days to seek venture capital for his planned startup. Before he returned home, his employer had heard about his trip from a venture capitalist located in Boston.

IMPLICATIONS FOR POLICYMAKERS

Venture capitalists watch over a small but significant part of the nation's resources. Their money comes increasingly from all sectors of society as pension funds supply proportionately more and more of the total pool of venture capital. And they invest that money in portfolio companies that can become very important in a region's economic growth. As William Baumol and others have pointed out, innovative entrepreneurship of the kind that venture capital supports is a major driving force in economic growth.[26] A phrase in vogue with U.S. politicians in the mid-1980s was "bicoastal regions of prosperity." This was just before the Massachusetts Miracle turned into a mirage and Silicon Valley's prosperity began to wane. Policymakers might muse on the possibility of a relationship between that bicoastal prosperity and the locations of the top high- and low-tech venture capital firms (see Figures 8-2 and 8-3). We will discuss it further in Chapter 10.

CHAPTER 9

Venture Capital: More Than Money

VENTURE CAPITALISTS do far more than passively invest their money; in theory, at least, they also add value by being actively involved in the success of the enterprises in which they invest. At a recent industry conference, veteran California venture capitalist Brent Rider was challenged about whether the active role of the venture capitalist actually makes a difference. His response was emphatic: "Value-added often provides the margin of success over failure."

We explore this subject by examining the venture-capital investing process in detail. We will argue that classic venture-capital investing is at its best when the suppliers and users of capital work in partnership. In such instances, entrepreneurs rave about the guidance, contacts, know-how, and support of their backers. These forms of proactive involvement, it is said, differentiate venture capital investors from the passive money managers and investors. We have found, however, that there is also a dark side to involvement; venture capitalists can actually detract value and hinder a firm's progress.

In our study conducted for the National Science Foundation,[1] we sought to analyze the flows of venture capital and the investing process. Among other things, we had found that most of the capital put into the most innovative technology companies came from a small but active cadre of investors. In fact, just 5% of the 464 firms in our sample accounted for one-quarter of the funds invested in highly innovative technology companies by venture capitalists between 1967 and 1982. It was here we discovered the NBI company of Boulder, Colorado, and Burton McMurtry, its lead investor. Was this a special case, or was there more to it? We conducted in-depth interviews with 51 venture capital firms, including the most active 21, and presidents of 40 of the companies these investors had backed in order to learn what they did that was different and how.

We were struck by one phenomenon that stood out in a number of companies: plaudits from entrepreneurs for their venture capital backers' contributions to their companies' success. How generalizable was this value-adding phenomenon? Our inquiries led to further studies of larger samples that have shed light on whether and how venture capitalists add value. They do. The story of NBI and its lead investor, Burton McMurtry, is prototypical.

NBI AND ITS VENTURE CAPITALIST

At the time of our original study, NBI was one of the most successful firms in the word processing and office automation industry. Launched in 1973, the company reached sales of $167,000 in the first year. Tom Kavanagh and two partners joined the firm to propel its growth, Kavanagh becoming president. By 1982, after three rounds of venture capital and public offerings, NBI sales exceeded $100 million, and its growth continued. Kavanagh had gained significant value-added from his venture capital partners. He summarized the crux of it: "It is far more important *whose* money you get than how much you get or how much you pay for it." Such personal chemistry between the venture capitalist and the management team enables the value-added process to work. Its importance cannot be overemphasized.

At NBI, investor involvement was described as "complete immersion, but never any meddling." Particularly in the early stages, a venture partner, usually as a member of the board, was involved one or two days a month in person and as much as several hours a week on the phone. Doing what? The investors involved themselves in the operating details of the business in order to know thoroughly the markets, products, and customers that were critical to the success of the business. But they did not meddle in the operating decisions. Management was assisted and advised, supplemented but not supplanted.

Recruiting Key Management

Judging from Kavanagh's experience, the right venture-capital partner during the startup and early stages of a venture can affect the survival and success of a company. Recruiting the key management team members was probably the most indispensable nonmonetary contribution of NBI's venture capital partners. (In fact, without it, there might have been no monetary contribution: Institutional Venture Associates' final decision to invest was contingent on NBI's securing a key marketing person.) Although NBI's ambitions and plans were impressive compared to those of most small fledgling firms, it had trouble enticing high-performing executives from top-notch companies to its ranks. The lead investor eventually took on that task. McMurtry, then a general partner of Institutional Venture Associates and now of Technology Venture Investors in Menlo Park, California, recruited two of NBI's three top people: Mark Stevenson, vice president of marketing, and David Klein, vice president of new business development. Their presence on the NBI team was critical to its subsequent growth and its attractiveness to other investors.

McMurtry was always available to help search for candidates and to evaluate the backgrounds and track records of any possible additions to the team. Like many other venture-capital investors, he had an elaborate network of contacts, leads, and reliable sources of intelligence and verification. Kavanagh thought he was masterful at convincing excellent people to give up all they had built up at a large prosperous company and join a new and risky enterprise. For example, when McMurtry found Stevenson, then a national sales manager for Xerox, through his contacts, Stevenson was not ready to move. In the face of this roadblock, McMurtry's reaction was to roll up his sleeves and attack the problem rather than toss it back to Kavanagh.

Kavanagh and McMurtry talked through the reasons Stevenson had given for his rejection. McMurtry was convinced that Stevenson had not really thought it through completely, particularly the financial consequences, and thus had declined for the wrong reasons. The next day, the two flew from San Francisco to Dallas to meet with Stevenson. The meeting extended well beyond dinner. The following day, Stevenson quit his job at Xerox and joined NBI as vice president of marketing. What had happened?

According to Stevenson, "There is no question that without Burt [McMurtry], I would not have moved. His professional, straightforward way convinced me. He said that he and Tom wanted to sit down with me and my wife and my two children to talk over the reasons why we should reconsider. He had the sensitivity to know that if my wife also understood these reasons, it would make all the difference. The offer really was not any different in terms of salary and stock. What he was able to do was enable me to see the offer in a different light: what it could mean to be in control of my own destiny, while achieving other personal aims." Several months later, Klein, a close former colleague of Stevenson's, also decided to join NBI, even though he had been the one who talked Stevenson out of NBI initially. He found Kavanagh and McMurtry a persuasive team: "I would not have joined if it were not for Burt. His understanding of what had to happen to make it a good deal for both of us was key. He was able to convey in a professional and credible way that he could not get rich unless we did."

Beyond recruiting top managers, McMurtry also played a key role at NBI closing deals with numerous prospective suppliers, distributors, and customers.

Unique Industry Savvy

Knowledge of the industry is essential to developing a credible business plan. For the aspiring entrepreneur, it is critical to have a thorough understanding of the markets to be served. Yet, in the case of a first startup in an industry that is only beginning to emerge, market data and boundaries are vague, and the customer elusive. It is just this environment in which venture capitalists, with extensive hands-on experience and depth of knowledge in several industries, can be instrumental in testing the reality of a business plan, its goals, and assumptions. In an emerging industry, reliable assumptions and key daily or monthly operating benchmarks, such as aging of receivables, certain costs, and margins and other ratios—especially for new customers and new products—may need to be based upon educated guesswork. But more often than not, an experienced venture capitalist will contribute to the validity of those assumptions. As Kavanagh put it, "The know-how an experienced venture capitalist can provide is not available anyplace else."

In-depth industry knowledge requires frequent contact with other CEOs, customers, and suppliers in the same business. For early-stage entrepreneurs in an emerging industry, one of the most difficult links to establish is with other CEOs. Because of their contacts and integrity, professional venture capitalists can share business perspectives otherwise inaccessible to most entrepreneurs.

A Sounding Board

According to Kavanagh, playing the devil's advocate is a third contribution of the venture capitalist. In a startup, discussing and critiquing plans and ideas prior to implementing them can help avoid costly mistakes. An entrepreneurial management team can work together so closely at times that its members begin to think alike; Kavanagh said that at NBI new product ideas, strategies, and directions began to look as if they came out of one mind. This is both a strength and a weakness. People who work together closely tend to develop a conformity of thinking; dissenters surrender to the influence of the larger body of opinion. Such convergence of opinion can be mistaken as evidence of correctness. But, although the risks of losing objectivity are large, they can be avoided by considering the outside investors' point of view.

One problem in a small company, according to Klein, is difficulty in getting "tests of reasonableness." Large companies, he found, force people with new ideas to seek reality tests, primarily because a lot of astute people are involved in the numerous layers of the approval process. This is not the case in small enterprises. At NBI, as in most small ventures, each member of the top management team had his area of accountability and acted with a great deal of independence. McMurtry deliberately made it a point to talk with each member of the NBI team, often several times a week. It was extremely valuable, according to NBI's management, to have someone who asked probing questions and played the devil's advocate. One of McMurtry's favorite questions was, "What decisions did you make last week that you were most uncomfortable with?"

Another example of the kind of benefits NBI experienced centered on the need for long-range planning and strategic thinking, even when the immediate pressures of the startup or expansion seemed overwhelming. Kavanagh stressed that it was McMurtry who "got us to do it first. He got the process on track and going a good two years earlier than we would have without his prodding. This planning can never be done soon enough."

Entrepreneurial Incentives

One of the most difficult challenges in any new venture is to create the right incentives and an entrepreneurial culture that is sustainable. This can be particularly troublesome when many of the key people are recruited from established companies. Kavanagh credits McMurtry's extensive experience with similar startup and early-stage ventures in helping to create an entrepreneurial climate and a commitment to devising an incentive system that encouraged teamwork instead of rewarding individual success. As one NBI vice president put it, "Getting promoted simply did not matter since we did not pay ourselves much anyway. All the payoffs were based on what was good for NBI." The key executives were convinced that they could achieve their financial goals if they could drive NBI to accomplish its business objectives.

The Long Haul

Being involved for the long haul is a fifth way in which venture capitalists make a contribution. For a company whose potential success is compelling enough to attract venture capital investors, it is understood that more calls for money will be made as that success becomes apparent. Unlike most other financiers, classic venture capitalists possess both the patience and bravery to go the distance. In the case of startup firms, value-added investors do more than just arrange for additional rounds of financing. They also bring in other investors who contribute more than money and a short-term interest in the enterprise. Such investors will look to fulfill and balance the material interests of the company, its customers, its suppliers, and other stakeholders rather than pursue what is most advantageous for themselves.

For NBI, McMurtry was the vital link in attracting two other highly regarded venture capitalists to participate in later rounds: William Hambrecht of Hambrecht & Quist and David Dullum of Frontenac Venture Capital. According to Kavanagh, Dullum served the company very effectively as a director and member of the audit committee. As an investor and member of NBI's board, Hambrecht played a critical role in determining the most suitable structure and timing of subsequent public offerings. Their contributions complemented McMurtry's and were considered invaluable by the management team, one of whom said, "They were smart enough and professional enough to get involved when and where they could make the greatest contribution."

Involvement

Does venture capitalists' involvement result in recognizable value? Or are they meddlesome backseat drivers? The NBI management team felt the relationship with its venture capitalists was positive. This is not always the case, and the perceived quality of the relationship often depends on whom you are talking to.

Recruiting Customers

Another value-added role that can make a major difference is that of securing key customers and suppliers. In the fragile startup and early stages, every customer is crucial. Venture capitalists can often communicate the company's purpose more objectively than can the founders. And they often know the right people to contact. Purchasing executives in larger firms are well aware of the risks of engaging a new company to supply parts, components, information, or vital services. They do not want to be the "guinea pig" first customer. A lead venture investor with other successful investments and experience in the industry can add enormously to a new company's credibility. A careful, reasoned explanation by the investor about reasons for providing a million dollars or more of startup capital can add the professional objectivity that often shifts doubt to confidence. According to the NBI team, McMurtry spent untold hours on the telephone doing just this.

When the Cannons Go Off

Roaring cannons are inevitable for most fledgling firms that grow as rapidly as NBI. By this we mean the crises, periods of doubt, even desperation that afflict entrepreneurial enterprises. The fragile process of launching and building a new business requires more of an investor than just perseverance and ingenuity. Two other virtues are also called for: patience and fortitude. When plans go awry—missed deadlines, key accounts lost, unexpected resignations, and the inevitable cash and confidence crises—nothing is more disturbing than a backer with a weak heart and a weaker pocketbook. NBI had its share of setbacks, but its managers and financial backers held together. No matter how bad things got, there was a calmness in McMurtry. "Never once," according to Stevenson, "did he step on your hands when you were lying flat on your back." There were no recriminations, or threats to withhold future financial backing, or panicky scrambles to change management, strategies, or product. In the case of NBI, the message was one of concern accompanied by a continuing, full level of confidence in the team.

VALUE-ADDED: RULE OR EXCEPTION?

McMurtry and NBI are not an isolated case of how venture capitalists add value. Another venture capitalist who adds value is Brion Applegate of Burr, Egan & Deleage. Applegate played an active role from its inception in a company called Boston Communications Group (BCG). In 1987, he worked with founder Paul Tobin and his team to identify opportunities in the still-embryonic cellular car-phone industry. He helped negotiate the acquisition of a license in southern Maine and New Hampshire that BCG built in that market as Cellular One. He also worked closely with the founders in their dealings with vendors and banks to provide the financial credibility vital to convincing creditors that BCG was a legitimate startup company with solid backing.

Along the way, at board meetings and in contact with management, Applegate was a valued confidant, cheerleader, and partner, while exercising his fiduciary role as a demanding investor. The Portsmouth Cellular One system was built and successfully harvested in 1989 at a price of $148 per capita, compared to the $9 per capita purchase price (the standard valuation method in the industry at the time). Since then, Applegate has continued to work actively for BCG in identifying and negotiating acquisitions in cellular, paging, and other telecommunications areas. He has brought in other investors to furnish know-how and contacts that he does not have. He has continued to contribute to BCG's strategic thinking and to help BCG develop banking relationships in the cruelest credit markets in a decade.

And then there are Peter Wendell and Jeff Drazen of Sierra Ventures. After 100 other venture capitalists declined to invest in Centex-Telemanagement, Inc., they helped the new company get started. Eventually, it became a highly successful firm in the telecommunications industry. In 1987, a public stock offering of 2.1 million shares raised nearly $19 million for the company. It is an especially revealing example of what is involved in adding value and the risks that must be assumed.

Drazen, with Wendell's support, became closely involved in a wide variety of decisions and tasks that were critical at the time, had to be right, and could not have been accomplished by management alone. These investors redefined the business concept and rewrote the business plan, including the development of a spreadsheet model for the income statements, balance sheets, and accounting and financial system. They recruited four Stanford MBA students to help develop a marketing brochure. They worked with management to contact customers and regulatory agencies to solve regulatory problems and learn more about the business. They devised a creative incentive structure and hired a new law firm to sort out a sticky legal problem with the existing stock classification. Furthermore, Drazen was a very active member of the board of directors. Both he and Wendell played a central role in raising both additional equity capital and debt financing from banks.

Through their formal role as outside directors but also informally through frequent contacts with management, venture capitalists may be closely involved in strategic decisions that shape the destiny of companies. Take, for instance, Advent International (AI), the world's largest venture-capital organization, with over $1 billion under management through a network of fourteen independent venture capital firms operating in sixteen countries. Advent was founded in 1981 by Peter Brooke, a leading American venture capitalist, a pioneer in the internationalization of the industry, and a long-time advocate of value-added services. Advent describes several services that illustrate how it helps companies in which it invests: financial and strategic planning; access to international markets and assistance in structuring international joint ventures; provision of both equity and debt capital, including the ability to structure off–balance sheet financing; the creation of pilot offshore manufacturing and/or purchasing capabilities; access to local government grants, subsidies, and other sources of low-cost capital; assistance in identifying opportunities for alliances with major corporations and structuring these alliances; and support in the sale, merger, or acquisition of businesses.

It is noteworthy that each of these services, particularly those involved with global markets and large companies, involves know-how that typically is not present in small companies. Such capabilities can make an investor like Advent an invaluable ally.

Our research indicated that the extraordinary contributions of venture capitalists like McMurtry, Applegate, Drazen, Wendell, and Brooke in nurturing new companies are not unique. In our research, we found numerous other examples of venture capitalists who brought industry savvy, mentoring, strategic insights, and camaraderie to entrepreneurial firms. And the entrepreneurs insisted that these contributions played an important part in making their companies successful. For their part, the venture capitalists often saw the capital as the least important part of their activities. Take this comment, for example:

Money? Sure, it's important to building a business but it's only one spoke of the wheel. You can't build a business with just money. Entrepreneurs who are looking just for money, or primarily money, if they can get it from a bank they probably should. It makes no sense to pay the price of venture capital if you don't believe you can get something extra.[2]

FOLLOW-ON RESEARCH

To examine the question of value-added in greater depth we began the most extensive research project to date on the topic. We teamed up with Harry A. Sapienza of the University of South Carolina, then a doctoral student at the University of Maryland's Dingman Center for Entrepreneurship, and gained the cooperation of Venture Economics. Our investigation extended across the country to see how the findings of our National Science Foundation study and our own knowledge of the industry matched the experiences of other entrepreneurs and venture capitalists. We conducted research on more than 120 entrepreneurs and their venture capital backers to determine their views of the importance and effectiveness of the lead investor's involvement in business development. For each portfolio company, we interviewed both the CEO-entrepreneur and the lead venture-capital investor. Their perceptions were startlingly similar.

The surveys and in-depth interviews yielded the following generalizations:

1. The most intense involvement of venture capitalists occurs in the very early stages of the business.
2. Openness of communication and personal chemistry are crucial.
3. Venture capitalists add value in a variety of ways, especially through strategic and supportive roles.
4. Most of the venture capitalist's key roles become increasingly important as the venture develops.

Although each venture's problems, challenges, and strengths differed from those at NBI, many common themes did emerge—and a few differences as well, especially when we compared startup and later-stage ventures.

In Figures 9-1 and 9-2, we highlight some of our findings to illustrate the nature of venture capitalists' involvement in a much larger sample of companies and venture firms. It is apparent from these data that venture capitalists are involved in activities deemed

FIGURE 9-1 **Ratings for Late-Stage Ventures**

	Importance		Effectiveness	
Venture capitalist's roles	*Entre-preneur*	*Venture capitalist*	*Entre-preneur*	*Venture capitalist*
	(5-point scale)		*(10-point scale)*	
Strategic				
Sounding board	4.29	4.67	8.15	8.13
Business consultant	3.96	4.42	6.90	7.58
Financier	3.46	2.96	7.22	6.73
Social/Supportive				
Coach/mentor	3.54	4.08	6.95	7.29
Friend/confidant	3.25	3.52	6.80	6.50
Networking				
Management recruiter	2.42	2.33	3.38	3.06
Professional contact	2.42	2.46	4.94	5.32
Industry contact	2.04	1.87	2.61	2.55
Overall effectiveness ratings			7.70	7.22

important by the entrepreneurs and they are effective. Revealingly, the sample did not consist only of some of the highly successful companies that led us to this further investigation but of a broad cross-section of companies—some successful and others not.

Investor Importance and Effectiveness

Each pair of lead venture-capital investors and CEO-entrepreneurs rated the importance (on a five-point scale) and effectiveness (on a ten-point scale) of the lead investor's involvement in three major roles: strategic, social/supportive, and networking. These three scales were broken down into eight separate activities, as shown in Figures 9-1 for late-stage and 9-2 for early-stage ventures. Overall, there is remarkable agreement between the entrepreneurs and venture capitalists.

The responses indicate that both entrepreneurs and venture capitalists believe that lead investors make important and effective contributions that extend beyond the mere provision of capital. What may be surprising to those obsessed with the "vulture capitalist" stereotype is that entrepreneurs actually gave the venture capitalists slightly higher effectiveness ratings than the investors gave to themselves. The responses also show the sense of the closer

FIGURE 9-2 **Ratings for Early-Stage Ventures**

Venture capitalist's roles	Importance		Effectiveness	
	Entre-preneur	Venture capitalist	Entre-preneur	Venture capitalist
	(5-point scale)		(10-point scale)	
Strategic				
Sounding board	4.25	4.37	8.05	7.67
Business consultant	4.17	4.46	8.14	7.83
Financier	4.17	4.42	8.05	8.41
Social/Supportive				
Coach/mentor	3.63	3.75	6.86	6.79
Friend/confidant	3.46	3.33	6.71	6.39
Networking				
Management recruiter	3.17	3.75	5.36	6.17
Professional contact	3.18	3.33	6.90	6.83
Industry contact	2.58	3.46	5.52	5.33
Overall effectiveness ratings			8.04	7.39

involvement and greater importance of the social/supportive and networking roles in early-stage versus later-stage companies. The research indicates that after the initial launching of the business, networking and management recruiting are not as important as the strategic and supportive roles.

Extent of Involvement

The numerical results summarized in Figures 9-1 and 9-2 are also supported by data from our interviews. Entrepreneurs often express concern over the extent to which a venture capitalist is involved in the company. The main consideration, of course, is the bottom-line effect of such involvement—whether the additional effort and support, in fact, achieve recognized value.

We found a wide fluctuation in terms of the intensity and extent of involvement on the part of venture capitalists. For the most part, however, the quality of the relationship is key. Said one entrepreneur, "Think of it as you would marriage. You don't want to go into it lightly. Think about what it would be like to work with these people day in and day out." Echoing this sentiment, a general partner in a top Boston venture capital firm said, "You've got to ask yourself: 'Can I live with this person when things get really tough?' " Another venture capitalist observed: "One of the evaluations we make is: 'Can you work with this person?' not, 'Is this person good?' "

When things work well, entrepreneurs find themselves seeking a much higher level of involvement than they ever imagined wanting. The CEO of a fast-growing high-tech firm said this about his relationship with the lead investor: "It's much more than a professional relationship. We're personal friends. . . . I wouldn't change anything—I just wish we had the opportunity to interact more." It is a well-accepted notion that the job of CEO-entrepreneur is one of the loneliest in the world. If you are the CEO, in whom can you truly confide? Our empirical data, as well as our interviews, indicate that the lead investor often fills this role.

Some relationships, of course, never develop the special chemistry needed to catapult the venture to bigger and better things, and the fault sometimes lies with the venture capitalist. As in most unsuccessful relationships, a common complaint is about the failure to communicate effectively. One entrepreneur commented, "What I can't stand is his unwillingness to listen."

The popular press has advanced the image of venture capitalists as hard-nosed, cutthroat negotiators who take advantage of aspiring entrepreneurs, but our interviews and survey data reveal a much different picture. Every profession has its share of the self-serving and the unscrupulous. An effective venture capitalist, however, must have a high level of integrity and interpersonal skill. We found that a surprisingly high percentage of venture capitalists have these qualities.

When They Are Good . . .

We wanted to go beyond the raw data and simple averages in Figures 9-1 and 9-2 to get a sense of what these numerical ratings actually mean to the entrepreneurs and venture capitalists in our study. To do so we have included typical comments from entrepreneurs and venture capitalists from the interviews. They reveal the pattern in our own and in Sapienza's research that confirmed the "add-value axiom." Time and again we found evidence of significant contributions by venture capitalists and entrepreneurs who swear that these contributions are real.

One venture capitalist most respected for his ability to pick winners and add value along the way is Don Valentine of Sequoia Capital, the California fund he founded in 1974. Even a partial list of the companies he has backed gives strong signals about his investing savvy: Apple Computer, Vitalink, Tandem Computer, Altos, LSI Logic, Oracle Software, and others. Summing up his role he says:

> Most of our talent at Sequoia lies in knowing how to start companies—knowing how to nurture them and encourage them when they are small. If the company reached $500 million a year, it probably needs somebody—a lot of somebodies with different talents, different experiences.[3]

What do good venture capitalists do differently, and what do entrepreneurs seek in the ideal venture-capital investor? To start to answer this question, we quote Sapienza's dissertation.

> It takes a rare combination of abilities and attributes to make a good venture capitalist. They have to have the ability to manage people, to analyze a wide set of information from ventures, and the time and willingness to do the analysis . . . some have it, many don't.[4]

An entrepreneur commented:

> The perfect venture capitalist is one who really understands your business and industry. . . . I think 60% to 70% of seats on the board are wasted on venture capitalists who understand almost nothing about the industry and have no operating experience. Too often they'll take someone with an MBA from MIT who knows how to do present value curves or other finance theory and put them on the board to gain experience, so you spend your board meetings educating the board about your product. Who needs that?[5]

Our own experience confirms the accuracy of this observation. An investor new to the venture capital business was about ready to co-invest in a medical venture with three large, well-respected, and established funds. One of the authors asked him, "Who is going to be on the board besides yourself, and what do they bring besides their money?" This was one issue he had not considered. Two years later, he volunteered that it had been a painful and expensive learning experience. The large lead investor had assigned a recent MBA to the board seat. This person had a health care career prior to earning an MBA and seemed like a natural fit. Yet this was the first small company or board involvement he had ever had, and he was in over his head. Our colleague simply said: "[He] learned how to be a director. We paid the tuition."

We sought to identify the specific activities of venture capitalists who were considered most effective by the entrepreneurs. These entrepreneurs' comments indicate some important dimensions of the venture capitalists' involvement. The following quotes echo and reinforce the numerical ratings in Figures 9-1 and 9-2 and the findings in our earlier NSF study:

> What I like best about [the venture capitalist's] involvement with our business is his enthusiasm for the investment. He really cares and he's really interested in what we're doing. He is always very positive and helpful and supportive. That's something that, perhaps more than any of the other things, we really need. We're faced with confusion and difficulty constantly. The moral support is invaluable.[6]

> [My lead investor] tends to be more aware of the downside problems than I am but lets me go at my own pace, rather than trying to force things, which might cause me to be less open and less willing to share information.[7]

Another entrepreneur had actually failed in a prior venture but was in a new one with the same lead investor. Nearly all new ventures experience crisis points and unexpected, adverse events. When these appear, the relationship between the entrepreneur and the investor is often tested to the limit. It is much easier for both to spread praise liberally when everything is going according to plan.

> [He] was very helpful during a crisis with a previous business— helpful in terms of just thinking out loud about it. [He] possesses a very keen insight into the state of a business and a keen insight into the viability of an industry without really knowing all the technical details of the business and the technology. I really respect that. Also he's not a shark and there are a lot of sharks in this business.[8]

One entrepreneur commented:

> When he talked to me, he told me that he thought I would really be successful, and that I could run my own business. But that if I did it with him, I'd get there faster. I'd have better PR . . . all that stuff. And he was right. I really think that he helped us in all those ways. Also, from a strategic standpoint—seeing what to do, when to do it, and how to do it.[9]

This kind of active involvement is what General Doriot envisioned as the constructive role venture capitalists ought to play in young companies. The evidence suggests that if it happens, it makes an important difference in the likelihood and extent of a new company's success. But it doesn't always work out that way. Our research also shows that not all venture capitalists add value; some make no difference at all, and some are even harmful to a venture.

When They Are Bad . . .

The evil incarnation of venture capitalism in the 1980s was the "vulture capitalist." This stereotype is exaggerated but real. Our research uncovered evidence that not all venture capitalists add value: some make no difference at all, and some are downright harmful.

The pressure cooker environment where most venture-capital-backed companies work makes the relationship between entrepreneur and investor difficult and delicate. Each has enormous expectations, and, unavoidably, some of their goals will conflict: pursuing more product development versus seeking orders and profitability; spending more heavily on marketing and distribution versus achieving earlier positive cash flow; raising as much additional capital as possible even when it is not needed versus providing capital just in time; and so on.

Prior to the 1980s, there was a tacit notion in the venture capital business that replacing the founder/entrepreneur in less than a year or so was a clear admission of failure by the investor. After all, one of the fundamental canons of classic venture-capital investing is to invest in a high-quality entrepreneur and management team. Yet, by the mid-1980s, founding entrepreneurs were being replaced regularly. One East Coast venture-capital firm reportedly fired 19 of 21 presidents in the first year of its investment. A West Coast firm reportedly replaced 9 of 10 presidents in the first year. Such wholesale sackings were totally unprecedented. As word of them got around the entrepreneurial community, it tended to reinforce the image of the venture capitalist as a cutthroat sharpie.

It is our contention that such actions flow from the structural changes noted in Chapter 2 and the changes in practice as classic venture capital evolved into merchant capital. Investors not truly apprenticed in classic venture-capital investing were unskilled in judging the quality of management teams and impatient and precipitous in replacing them. More often than not, the replacements fared no better. And simply replacing management was no substitute for the requisite value-adding know-how, willingness to pitch in, and rich industry knowledge that characterize the best classic venture-capital investors.

Our research uncovered the darker side of the venture capital story. The following comments by entrepreneurs reveal some of its dimensions.

> The big difference between the effective and the ineffective VC on my board is that the bad one has a tendency to press the panic button while [the other] doesn't do that. He supports us and refuses to panic.

> He has preconceived ideas about a particular topic, particularly from his own experience and background. He just doesn't want to hear the details. I begin to feel it's not really worth it to go into all the details to try to convince him. If we're going to have the discussion, and I have to give the details, then I feel [he] should listen.[10]

Another theme running through the criticisms of venture capitalists who don't seem to add value is captured in this comment:

> Beyond providing money, *some* of the venture capitalists should not do anything; that is, they should just provide money and financial options. People who know what due diligence is and what these various financial terms mean, which I don't know and will never pretend to know, ought to stick to it.

> They don't really understand anything else. They don't know how to run a business, and everyone would be better off if they didn't try to give their opinions on that.[11]

Two studies that focused on the role of venture capitalists on boards of directors add to our understanding of the value-added issue. One study surveyed CEOs of 162 high-tech companies in northern California, the Boston area, and north and central Texas that received venture capital financing during the period 1978 to 1988, and subsequently interviewed 98 of those CEOs.[12] The study found that those CEOs whose lead investor/director was from one of the top 20 venture-capital firms, on average, rated the value of the advice from their venture-capital board members significantly higher than that from other outside board members. However, when all directors from all venture-capital firms were taken into account, CEOs did not rate the advice of the venture capitalists any higher than that of other outside board members.

The study found that CEOs were more outspoken when their evaluations of venture capitalists were negative. Many of them expressed disappointment because their high (perhaps too high?) expectations were not fulfilled. Consider this comment: "Venture capitalists don't bring value. The typical VC has zero operating experience. Only 40% of their time is spent working with their portfolio companies once or twice a month. That is not enough time to understand the workings and intricacies of a startup business."[13]

Another CEO who headed three venture-capital-backed high-technology companies said: "When negotiating with a venture capital firm I disregard what they say about added value. My strategy is to minimize their value subtracted!"

The CEOs interviewed also gave the distinct impression that board members with significant operating experience were more valued than purely financial types with no operating experience. The areas where CEOs rated outside board members most helpful were identical to those noted in our studies cited above. These results were similar to the findings in yet another study of venture capital firms by MacMillan and colleagues.[14]

LESSONS FOR THE 1990s

These findings have practical implications for both suppliers and users of capital. What is clear from our investigations is that the successful development of a business can be critically affected by the relationship between the venture capitalist and the management team. The talents and savvy of the investors and entrepreneurs count for much more than money. And when they are in synch, the results are often stunning.

For the venture capital firm, we contend that a strategy that entails high value-added involvement with portfolio companies is a road to higher returns on invested capital. The most spectacular gains, as we have seen from numerous examples elsewhere in this book, come from investing early on: DEC, Federal Express, Apple, Genentech, and the like. One of the most difficult strategic challenges for venture capitalists in today's crowded marketplace is how to differentiate their firm from others. All our research indicates that if the investor brings only money to the table, achieving high rates of return is very unlikely. It is not an accident, in our view, that the demise of high industry rates of return during the 1980s coincided with a brand of so-called venture capital investing that was long on financial engineering and deal making and short on the value-added attributes for which classic venture capital was noted.

Not every founder-investor partnership enjoys positive chemistry. And many entrepreneurs who either overlook or fail to appreciate the substantial value-added contributions that some venture capitalists can make will opt instead for a strictly financial arrangement based on the best valuation available. But as our research has shown, this behavior is myopic.

Entrepreneurs who seek more than money must be thoughtful and selective in their quest for financial partners. If all they seek is money, then that is exactly what they will get. They must continually ask: What can the venture capitalist provide besides money? Among the danger signals for the entrepreneur, especially during startup or the early stage, are the following:

1. The investor who is spread too thin. It is very difficult for a venture capitalist to play a lead investor role and add value if he or she serves as a director to more than a half-dozen companies. Yet we have heard of investors working with a dozen or more companies at one time.
2. The venture capitalist with limited operating experience or with an overly financial orientation. These investors have limited ability to add real value.
3. A venture fund with a record of continual management replacements in its portfolio companies and more than the usual share of troubled investments.
4. A fund in the midst of raising yet another fund. The senior partners are most likely to add value to a portfolio company, but since they are also most likely to raise a new fund, their time for company involvement will be limited.
5. The investor who believes he or she can do a better job operating the portfolio company than its founders and management. Such people are suffering from delusions and will be particularly error prone.

In the 1990s, entrepreneurs will become more knowledgeable, sophisticated, and selective in seeking out financial partners. Venture capital firms will face heightened competition for the best entrepreneurial talent. Strategically, it is no longer sufficient for a venture capital firm to argue that it has a sharper focus or better-established industry niche, that it has more money to invest, that it can make more deals faster, or that it can provide access to unique corporate or international alliances. A fund may do many of these yet fail to win the hearts and minds of the cream of the entrepreneurial crop, thereby failing to deliver high rates of return. In the final analysis, if the venture capital firm cannot add more than money to the company-building process then it cannot excel.

CHAPTER 10

Venture Capital and Regional Economic Development

THE MASSACHUSETTS MIRACLE was Michael Dukakis's trump card in his 1988 bid for the presidency. Who could wonder why? In the 1980s, with Dukakis as governor, the Massachusetts economy, especially in the high-tech belt semicircling Boston, prospered as never before. The other governors marveled at the miracle. They all wished they could replicate the Massachusetts formula for economic growth in their own states. They voted Dukakis "Governor of the Year." But before he left the governor's office two years later, the state had one of the highest unemployment rates in the nation, its budget was submerged by a sea of red ink, and the state's bond rating was the second lowest in the nation—only Louisiana's was worse. The sudden plunge from boom to bust has some wondering about the potency of that most touted of regional economic cure-alls: the government-industry-academia high-tech partnership. Was the miracle really a mirage? And it extended beyond Massachusetts. For example, venture capitalists gathering for the 1990 Venture Forum conference in San Francisco were greeted by the headline "Next Governor to Face Huge State Deficit." But that time, the state was California.

What happened? Neither America's Technology Highway (Massachusetts Route 128) nor—to a lesser degree—California's Silicon Valley were able to stay clear of the economic downturn that struck the nation in 1990. We don't believe there is much wrong with their formula for high-tech prosperity. We believe the

227

end of the miracle was caused by the combined effects of a nation-wide recession, escalating state budgets, rising taxes, high interest rates, the banking crisis, and, in the Massachusetts case, a mini-computer hardware industry that suddenly flattened out—perhaps even began to decline. Before it's over, the present Massachusetts recession may match the severity of the one in 1970 to 1974, when 12,000 Route 128 engineers and scientists were unemployed. But we are confident that when the recovery comes, it will be led by high-tech companies, many of them financed with venture capital.

This chapter takes a close look at what is known about the effects of the venture capital process and high technology on regional economic growth and development. We first examine the nature of technology investing. Then we look at some specific regional models, Silicon Valley and Route 128, which give evidence of its potential and the underlying factors necessary for success. We also examine the unique characteristics of each area and compare them with more recent attempts to promote economic growth through high-tech entrepreneurship.

VENTURE CAPITAL'S ROLE IN FINANCING INNOVATION

The contribution of small, high-technology companies to technological innovation and economic development became a hot topic in the 1980s for both public- and private-sector policymakers. According to researchers, that class of small business is the source of a majority of radical technological innovations and a large share of employment growth. As Michael Dukakis and Rosabeth Kanter proclaimed in their book:

> Technological innovation provides an economic advantage and entrepreneurship helps translate this into jobs. Throughout the United States, new jobs tend to come from innovation-related growth spurts in existing enterprises and from the development of new enterprises.[1]

Their assertion was based on a study by David Birch, MIT's noted business demographer.[2] He concluded that all areas of the United States lose jobs at approximately similar rates. Regions of economic prosperity, however, differed from nongrowth or low-growth regions in their ability to create new jobs, which was in turn a function of high rates of innovation. Birch's data covered 5.6 million firms, representing 82% of all private-sector employment. In those firms, he found that more jobs tended to be created by small and new firms. Between 1969 and 1976, two-thirds of all new jobs were created by firms with 20 or fewer employees and 80% by firms with 100 or fewer employees. In addition, 80% of those new jobs were created by firms that were four years old or younger.

A 1982 Government Accounting Office study also found that there was a disproportionately large contribution to local, regional, and national economic development by venture-capital-backed firms in terms of jobs created, corporate and individual tax revenues, employee income, and export sales. The trend continued unabated throughout the 1980s. As large companies, such as those found in the *Forbes* Sales 500, lost 2.7 million jobs, firms with fewer than 100 employees more than made up for it by adding approximately 6.5 million jobs (Figure 10-1).[3]

FIGURE 10-1 **Job Loss/Creation in the 1980s**

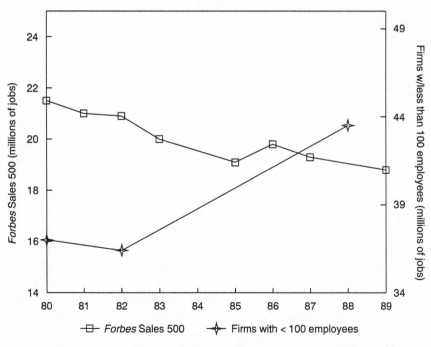

Source: "What I Learned in the Eighties," *Forbes,* January 8, 1990, p. 100.

JOB LOSS/CREATION IN THE 1980s

As presented earlier, a more detailed study, undertaken by Coopers & Lybrand and Venture Economics on behalf of the NVCA, confirms those findings.[4] Of the 235 venture-backed companies surveyed, the average firm was only 1.9 years old, employed 153 people, exported $3.34 million in goods and services, invested $3.1 million annually in research and development, and paid $723,404 in corporate income taxes. In addition, those firms had a larger equity base as a percentage of total assets (59%) than did the *Fortune* 500 companies (29%) on average. They also used their equity more efficiently to create jobs, of which 53% were highly skilled (professional) as compared to 13% for the general U.S. labor force. In terms of export revenue generation, venture-backed companies generated more than three times the export sales per dollar of equity than did the *Fortune* 500, implying that venture-backed companies help reduce the trade deficit more efficiently. In sowing the seeds for economic growth, venture capital enabled those companies to sustain growth rates of 54% in jobs, 31% in assets, 49% in R&D, 1,345% in export sales, and 209% in tax revenues. Those are impressive results, considering that the *Fortune* 500 firms lost 3.5 million jobs in the 1980s.[5] No wonder state and local governments, private institutions, and industry associations are so eager to attract high-tech companies to their own regions.

Unique Aspects of Technology Investing

Although less visible than the high-tech companies themselves, venture capital was vital to the establishment and growth of many of those budding firms. It was a crucial factor in the technological and economic development of the regions in which those high-tech companies are located. Studies of the interrelationships of innovation, technology transfer, and entrepreneurship concluded that invention alone is not sufficient to fuel the process of economic growth. Innovation and a combination of technology transfer and entrepreneurship make up the critical next step. Specialized venture-capital investing knowledge plays an essential role in that process.

One of the fundamental findings of our NSF study was that a small segment of the venture capital industry is responsible for the creation, financing, and development of a surprisingly large share of all venture-capital-backed high-technology companies.[6] Although a large proportion of venture capital firms participate in such financings through syndications of follow-on rounds of investment, a smaller subset actively generates those investment opportunities and plays a critical role in their development. That subset of venture capitalists and the entrepreneurs they invest in are responsible for the establishment of small, high-tech companies. Many of the successful new technology-based ventures involve management teams rather than a single entrepreneur. In many cases, the venture capitalist, as we have seen in Chapter 9, plays a key role in the formation of those teams. Furthermore, entrepreneurs who have successfully developed one venture move on to create still others (often financed by the same venture capitalists), thus recycling their entrepreneurial skills.

Another key finding of the NSF study is that investing in highly innovative technology ventures requires less capital than investing in the noninnovative low-technology ventures. (For simplicity, we will call them high-tech and low-tech ventures). First-round investments in high-tech ventures during the time frame studied were only 74% of the average investment in low-tech ventures. It was also true by stage: seed-stage high-tech ventures received on the average just over one-half the amount of money that went to low-tech ventures. The pattern for later-stage investments was similar. Also, larger, capital-intensive venture-capital firms are no more involved in investing in high-tech ventures than are smaller firms. The amount of capital under management was not significantly different between those venture capital firms emphasizing either high-tech or low-tech ventures.

A core group of highly skilled and experienced venture-capital firms accounts for a disproportionate share of high-tech venture investing. The 21 venture capital firms that were most active in high-tech investing—accounting for 25% of the total—represented less than 5% of the 464 firms studied. Their specialized know-how included a broad web of contacts and networks within the high-tech community, a greater degree of syndication, and a greater intensity of involvement in those fledgling firms. Heavy involvement with the portfolio companies usually occurs through the originators or lead investors, who often serve as members of the boards of directors.

Venture capitalists' investments in highly innovative technological ventures are made at a significantly earlier stage than are investments in the least innovative firms. Nearly two-thirds of the first-round investments in high-tech ventures occurred at the seed and startup stages. The number of startup investments in high-tech ventures was two and one-half times greater than was the number of startup investments in low-tech ventures, accounting for 71% of those combined startups. Seed-stage investing in high-tech ventures was three times greater than in low-tech ventures and accounted for 76% of all seed-stage investments in high-tech and low-tech ventures combined.

We saw in Chapter 9 that venture capital firms active in high-tech ventures create substantial value-added contributions to their portfolio companies as a result of their intense early involvement. Founders of high-tech ventures report that they actively seek out those venture capitalists with noteworthy reputations for their non-monetary, high value-added contributions to fledgling firms. Founders of high-tech ventures uniformly reported that it was more important whom they obtained funding from than how much and at what price. Venture capitalists who emphasize high-tech investing perform a catalytic role in finding and blending the necessary combination of people, technology, and opportunities to bring unproven ideas to commercial reality.

There is a "bird dog" characteristic to those venture capital firms that focus on highly innovative technological ventures. Contrary to the stereotype that venture capital investors sit and wait for business plans and ideas to come to them, many firms actively seek out exceptional innovators with the relevant technical expertise and the commitment to commercialize promising technologies. They bring together the talents of the business, academic, and scientific cultures that spawn highly innovative technologies.

Finally, an acceleration effect results from venture capitalists' intense involvement in the creation of highly innovative technological ventures. Innovators, entrepreneurs, and investors together compress the time span of bringing new technologies to commercial reality. Sometimes they do it so quickly that it takes your breath away. Remember, for instance, the story of Genentech (Chapter 4). It compressed ten years down to seven months in developing its first product, the genetically engineered brain hormone, somatosin.

WHERE DOES TECHNOLOGY INVESTING OCCUR?

There are definite geographical oases where founders, technologists, and venture capitalists cluster. Those locations account for the bulk of highly innovative technology-venture investing. In the NSF study, venture capital firms headquartered in California, New York, and Massachusetts accounted for more than three-fourths of all high-tech investing. By contrast, less than one-half of the investment in low-tech ventures was accounted for by firms in those three states. Independent, private, venture-capital firms accounted for 86% of all high-tech investing and are even more concentrated, by main office, in those three states. In Chapter 8, we discussed the networks created by their syndications.

Among the key building blocks for economic growth in both the Massachusetts Route 128 and Silicon Valley regions are the research and educational institutions located there. But excellent as those research facilities are, they are not sufficient to ensure the commercialization of innovative products. Figure 10-2 illustrates key precipitating and sustaining conditions that fuel the engines of economic development, whether in New England, Northern Ireland, or Eastern Europe. Societal values, government policies, research and educational institutions, and locational factors revolve around the people, capital, product/service markets, and support organizations from which new ventures are ultimately created and

FIGURE 10-2 **Precipitating and Sustaining Conditions for Economic Renewal**

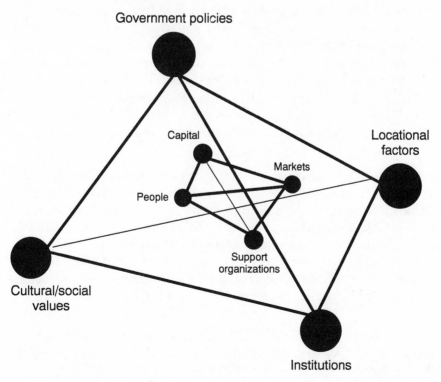

developed. It is the interaction of those elements that determines both the environment and the tangible outcomes discussed later in this chapter. For example, societal values must exist that support risk taking and also tolerate failure. The presence of successful role models not only inspires those who seek to emulate them but also sets a positive tone in the local business culture for entrepreneurial activities. As suppliers, customers, and support organizations such as banks and accounting and legal firms gain familiarity with new enterprise development and growth, they are able to perceive less risk in doing business with such ventures. Familiarity also teaches them how to deal with new enterprises, which is often quite different from how they handle well-established customers.

Massachusetts Route 128

Politicians in the Bay State were not reticent about claiming credit for the Massachusetts Miracle, but they were Johnny-come-latelies. The record shows that the real source of the state's explosive economic growth during the 1970s and 1980s was not the statehouse but across the Charles River at MIT. As Dukakis and Kanter noted:

> Some of the raw materials for the boom in [the] Massachusetts [economy] were assembled long before Michael Dukakis became governor. Route 128, the perimeter road around Boston, had long been regarded as "America's Technology Highway." The seeds for the shift to high technology had been sown by advanced research during World War II, and the Massachusetts Institute of Technology research laboratories alone spawned as many as 150 companies, some funded by the venture capital firms clustered in the area.[7]

A more detailed picture of MIT's role in the economic development of Massachusetts is provided by a 1989 study conducted by the Bank of Boston.[8] It reveals that as of 1988, 636 businesses had been established in Massachusetts by MIT alumni, creating 300,000 jobs and $10 billion in annual income for Massachusetts residents.* Annual worldwide sales for those companies totaled $39.7 billion in 1988. Many of the jobs created by those companies have been in computer hardware or computer-related fields.

---

* The difference between Dukakis and Kanter's and the Bank of Boston's numbers is because the former referred to direct spinoffs from MIT laboratories, whereas the bank studied businesses established in Massachusetts by all MIT alumni.

Figure 10-3 illustrates the declining employment growth rates for several of the state's major computer firms established in the 1950s and 1960s. Those firms are now maturing, and, consequently, their growth rates in terms of both revenue generation and new job creation are decreasing as well. The impact of the 1991 recession on both the revenues and employment levels of those firms was particularly acute. Economic revitalization will come from new technology companies established in the new industries of the 1980s, which will be growing up in the 1990s. Among the new industries cited in the Bank of Boston study are computer software, biotechnology, and advanced material technology (Figure 10-4).

Twenty of the Massachusetts biotech companies formed between 1980 and 1989 can be traced directly to MIT alumni. Also, one-third of the patents filed by the MIT Technology Licensing

FIGURE 10-3 **Employment Growth for Established Technology Companies (average compounded annual growth rate)**

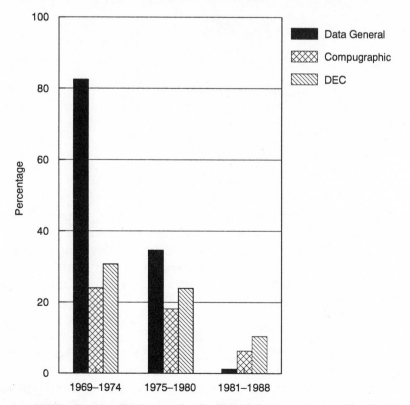

Source: "MIT: Growing Businesses for the Future," report prepared by the Economics Department, Bank of Boston, June 1, 1989.

FIGURE 10-4 **Employment Growth for Recent MIT Startups (average compounded annual growth since founding through 1988)**

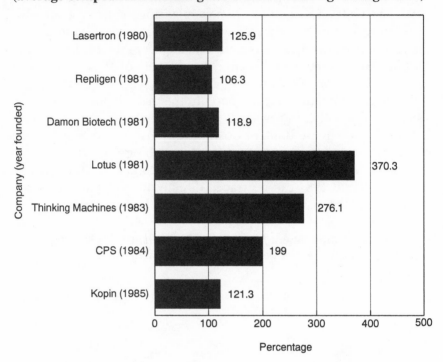

Source: "MIT: Growing Businesses for the Future," report prepared by the Economics Department, Bank of Boston, June 1, 1989.

Office in 1988 were for life sciences (biotechnology). The role of neighboring Harvard University in biotechnology is also of paramount importance in terms of basic research and innovations emanating from the Harvard-affiliated teaching hospitals and research centers such as the Dana-Farber Cancer Research Institute.

When it comes to Route 128 high tech, Harvard alumni have been much more active as investors than as founders. True, An Wang devised a magnetic core memory at Harvard and went on to found the company that bears his name, and Edwin Land left Harvard to found Polaroid. But, compared to MIT, Harvard has produced few lead entrepreneurs who founded Route 128 high-tech startups. However, when it comes to financing those types of companies, Harvard graduates have been prolific. The father of classic venture capital, General Doriot, was a professor at the

Harvard Business School when he founded ARD. Harvard MBAs, many inspired by Doriot, became venture capitalists. Advent, Arthur Rock & Company, Kleiner Perkins Caufield & Byers, TA Associates, Morgan Holland Ventures Corporation, Greylock Management Corporation, Burr, Egan, & Deleage Co., and Sequoia Capital have achieved spectacular successes with high-growth companies (Figure 10-5).

Silicon Valley

Since the mid-1950s, more than 3,000 technology-based firms have located in Silicon Valley—an environment unusually supportive for high-technology entrepreneurs.[9] Similar in many ways to the development of Route 128, early growth in the valley can be traced to a strong association with research and innovation coming out of Stanford University. The development of Silicon Valley's economy was tightly linked to the electronics industry, beginning with Lee de Forest's first successful demonstration of the triode vacuum tube in 1912[10] and evolving into the transistor technology that Shockley brought to the West Coast from Bell Labs in the mid-1950s. Semiconductor development occurred in the late 1950s, integrated circuits in the mid- to late 1960s, and microprocessors in the early 1970s. The economic growth from those innovations in electronics technology resulted in a dramatic shift in employment and industry in the region. In the mid-1950s, total employment was approximately 100,000, primarily in agriculture. With the establishment of Shockley's company in 1955 in Palo Alto, and other companies like it, employment grew steadily to 275,000 by mid-1960. By 1975, there were 470,000 jobs in the county; by 1984, 750,000. As of 1985, Silicon Valley was adding jobs at the rate of 40,000 per year.[11]

Several forces propelled Silicon Valley's development. Early growth depended on the government, which supported basic research and procured electronics, primarily for defense. From about the mid-1960s, commercial markets for advanced electronics began to be more important. As we saw in Chapter 4, venture capital was key to the formation and financing of many of those companies.

In a concentrated effort to blend cutting-edge research with applied electronics technologies, the Center for Integrated Systems at Stanford University was established in 1982 to integrate solid-state circuit research and fabrication with computer systems applications, building on departmental research programs, continuing government support, and broad-based industry sponsorship and participation. Stanford's Departments of Electrical Engineering and

FIGURE 10-5 **Harvard Alumni Venture Capitalists**

Peter Brooke	TA Associates, Advent International	Boston, MA
Richard Burnes	Charles River Partnerships	Boston, MA
Craig Burr	Burr, Egan, Deleage & Co.	Boston, MA
Frank Caulfield	Kleiner Perkins Caufield & Byers	San Francisco, CA
Frank Chambers	Continental Capital Corporation	San Francisco, CA
William Congleton	Palmer Partners	Boston, MA
Charles Coulter	American Research & Development	Boston, MA
Daniel Gregory	Greylock Management Corporation	Boston, MA
John Hesse	Plant Resources Venture Funds	Boston, MA
Franklin Johnson	Asset Management Company	Palo Alto, CA
James Morgan	Morgan Holland Ventures Corporation	Boston, MA
Thomas P. Murphy	Partnership Dankist	Stamford, CT
Thomas Perkins	Kleiner Perkins Caufield & Byers	San Francisco, CA
Jack Peterson	Venture Founders	Boston, MA
Charles Prothro	Southwest Enterprise Associates	Dallas, TX
Arthur Rock	Arthur Rock & Company	San Francisco, CA
Thomas Stephenson	Sequoia Capital	Menlo Park, CA
Charles Waite	Greylock Management Corporation	Boston, MA
Peter Wendell	Sierra Ventures	Menlo Park, CA

Computer Science annually produce 80 Ph.D.s and 280 masters students, many of whom have been closely involved with the center.[12] Those engineers emerge with specialized, multidisciplinary skills appropriate for the development of emerging electronic technologies. Stanford's pivotal role in regional development was its recruitment of the brightest science and engineering students and its stimulating research assistantships. Stanford strongly encouraged its students to think commercial and to join existing and newly formed high-tech companies in the area.

But we are getting ahead of the story. In 1912, when De Forest, a researcher at Federal Telegraph Company in Palo Alto, first amplified an electrical signal with a vacuum tube, Stanford University was only 20 years old. It was still "a minor league, country club school" in 1920, when Fred Terman graduated with a degree in electrical engineering.[13] Terman, son of Stanford psychology professor Louis Terman, went to MIT for a doctorate. There, the legendary Vannevar Bush became his role model. Bush, who later became dean of engineering, vice president of MIT, and a leading science adviser to the government in World War II, was one of the founders of Raytheon. He understood the value of MIT professors working closely with high-tech companies. When Terman graduated with his Ph.D. in 1924, he accepted an appointment at MIT but never took it up. He went home for a vacation, fell ill, and decided to stay in Palo Alto because its sunny climate was better for his health. He became a professor of Stanford's radio engineering department, as electronics was then called.

According to Rogers and Larsen, "without Fred Terman, Silicon Valley might never have happened." Terman took back to Stanford the MIT model for an academic-industrial partnership. He inspired and encouraged two of his former students, William Hewlett and David Packard, to start their electronics company to exploit a variable frequency oscillator that was the basis of Hewlett's thesis in Terman's 1938 graduate seminar. Terman loaned them $538 to start producing the oscillator and helped them arrange a $1,000 loan from a Palo Alto bank.[14] Was he, we wonder, Silicon Valley's first angel?

From that beginning, a synergistic university-industry relationship developed at Stanford over the years. In 1951, then–Vice President Terman and President Wallace Streling created the Stanford Industrial Park on university land. It was the first of its kind. Years later, it became the prototype for other university technology parks around the world. Varian Associates, a Stanford University spinoff, became the first tenant. Hewlett-Packard moved there in 1954. By the early 1980s, all the available space was leased to about 90 tenants employing 25,000 workers.[15]

Stanford's high-tech park formed the nucleus of what we now call Silicon Valley. It has the most sophisticated infrastructure for high-tech entrepreneurship of any region in the world. A necessary ingredient of that environment is venture capital for highly innovative technology companies. As we pointed out in Chapter 8, the most concentrated cluster of high-tech venture-capital firms in the world is on the edge of Stanford's campus. Silicon Valley is the global capital of classic venture capital.

VENTURE CAPITAL COMPLEXES AND THE REGIONAL FLOW OF CAPITAL

Silicon Valley and Route 128 are two of seven U.S. venture capital complexes identified by Richard Florida and Martin Kenney in 1988.[16] The complexes were: California (San Francisco/Silicon Valley), Massachusetts (Boston), New York, Illinois (Chicago), Texas, Connecticut, and Minnesota (Minneapolis), each characterized as technology oriented, finance oriented, or hybrid. In understanding venture capital's role in regional economic development, it is useful to take a closer look at those regions and to examine where and how the capital formation and investing occurs.

California (San Francisco/Silicon Valley)

The California venture-capital complex consisting of the San Francisco/Silicon Valley area is—as we have already noted—dominated by technology-oriented investing. It has both a high degree of locally invested venture capital and, as noted, a large concentration of high-tech businesses. More than three-quarters of the money raised by venture capital firms located in the region is invested in state. The rest goes primarily to New England and Texas. The California complex also attracts capital from other regions. Approximately 50% of the funds invested by firms in the Mid-Atlantic and Rocky Mountain regions also went to California companies. Venture capital firms in New York, New England, and the Pacific Northwest, on average, invest approximately 40% of their funds in California. In total, outside capital invested in the California complex outnumbers internally raised capital by a factor of three times.

> Venture capital in the Silicon Valley area evolved gradually alongside the high technology enterprises that sprung up there. Venture capital thus became an integral part of what we term a social structure of innovation (Florida and Kenney 1988): an interactive system comprised of technology intensive enterprises, highly

skilled human capital, high caliber universities, substantial public/ private research and development expenditures, specialized networks of suppliers, support services such as law firms and consultants, strong entrepreneurial networks, and informal mechanisms for information exchange and technology transfer.

The synergies among the various elements of this social structure created a unique window of opportunity for the emergence of technology-oriented investing apart from traditional financial institutions. The growth of technology venturing then proceeded along a learning curve characterized by the gradual accumulation of investment and management skills on the part of venture capitalists and entrepreneurs alike. This in turn facilitated the development of extended entrepreneurial networks that became conduits for sharing information, making deals, and mobilizing resources. As a central component of such networks, venture capital thus played an important role in incubating entrepreneurial activity, attracting entrepreneurs, and accelerating rates of new business formation.[17]

New York and Illinois (Chicago)

New York and Chicago, Illinois, are finance-oriented centers and net exporters of capital to other regions. Venture capital firms in those regions are typically tied to major financial corporations or other institutional sources of wealth. In New York, more than 40 funds are linked to financial institutions. Most of their investments go to other regions: 38% to California, 17% to New England, 9% to Texas, with only 20% going to in-state companies. Total inflows from other regions equal less than half the capital raised in New York state. Many New York firms have branch offices on Route 128 and in Silicon Valley to facilitate long-distance investing.

Chicago follows a pattern similar to New York's. Twenty-three firms control half of all the venture capital raised in the Midwest. The flow of funds is 80% to other regions, primarily California, and is frequently co-invested with firms from other regions. The ability to co-invest is an important strategy for venture capital firms that do not have branch offices located in the technology-oriented complexes. As mentioned, lead investing is extremely time and effort intensive and thus not practical from a remote location. However, firms located in the finance-oriented complexes still play a critical role in providing part of the much larger follow-on capital that is required to support ventures beyond the initial investment stages.

Massachusetts (Boston) and Minnesota (Minneapolis)

The Boston and Minneapolis venture capital complexes are technology-oriented hybrids. Both contain a high number of local sources and users of venture capital. Local technology companies also attract capital from other regions, and venture firms invest frequently in outside regions as well, most notably California. Boston was the first region in the United States to possess any degree of organized venture capital. As early as 1911, the Boston Chamber of Commerce was active in providing finance and technical assistance to new enterprises. And, as detailed in Chapter 1, ARD was founded in 1946 as the first institutional venture fund. ARD became an incubator for other venture-capital firms, including Boston Capital Corporation, Palmer Partners, Greylock, Charles River Partnerships, and Morgan Holland. Funds flow in the region is roughly breakeven; a sizable portion of capital is exported to other regions but inflows from other regions balance them out.

Boston's economy is also much more diverse than that of Silicon Valley. In addition to high technology, many old-line manufacturing companies provide substantial employment in the state. In addition, Boston is home to many large firms in the financial services industry, the defense industry, real estate, and education (426,000 students attend 124 public and private colleges and universities[18]). And many knowledge-based consulting and information businesses are headquartered in the Greater Boston area (Bain & Company, Temple, Barker & Sloane, Boston Consulting Group, Monitor, Arthur D. Little, DRI/McGraw-Hill, and Venture Economics, to name a few).

In the words of Florida and Kenney, Minneapolis is the "best example of a nascent entrepreneurial center which has the potential to develop into a full-fledged technology complex."[19] This center consists of a small number of tightly networked venture-capital firms such as Pathfinder Venture Fund, North Star Ventures, and Northwest Venture Capital, which invest heavily in the Minneapolis area. As we noted in Chapter 4, venture capital investing and high-technology development in Minneapolis–St. Paul can trace their origins to 1946, when Engineering Research Associates opened for business in a St. Paul glider plant. CDC, Medtronic—manufacturer of heart pacemakers—and Cray Research came along later. Minneapolis was also the site of First Midwest Small Business Investment Corporation, the first SBIC licensed under the Small Business Investment Act of 1958. It was followed by Northwest Growth

Fund a year later in 1960. There is regular co-investment in the Minneapolis area with funds from other regions, particularly from the Chicago complex. Forty percent of investments by venture capital firms in the area are in companies located in the region.

Connecticut and Texas

Connecticut venture capitalists consist of three groups. The earliest venture-capital activity was by wealthy individuals. Sherman Fairchild, whose wealth came from family investments in IBM, provided the backing for Fairchild Semiconductor in 1957. Much later, in 1972, retired IBM chairman, Thomas Watson, Sr., founded Partnership Dankist. Anderson Investment Company was founded in 1969 by Harlan Anderson, co-founder of DEC. Thomas Murphy of Partnership Dankist later went on to form the Fairfield Venture Capital Group, an informal assemblage of 30 to 40 venture capitalists and private investors.

Connecticut has also been home to the three largest, industrial corporate-subsidiary venture-capital organizations. GEVENCO, General Electric's now-defunct venture group, was founded there in 1968; Xerox Venture Capital was founded in 1974; and SOHIO's Vista Ventures organization was founded in 1980. In addition, many private venture-capital partnerships are located in Connecticut. The hybrid nature of the investing means that approximately one-third of the investments remain in the New England area, with a slightly smaller percentage going to California (28%).

Texas has four centers of venture capital activity: Dallas, Houston, San Antonio, and Austin. Dallas is the largest with approximately $285 million under management and is home to Sevin Rosen Management, a highly successful firm. Branch offices for several major Boston, New York, and California funds are also located in Dallas. San Antonio has $86 million under management; Houston, $66 million; and Austin, $62 million. At the time of the Florida and Kenney study, more than 75% of Texas investing was energy-related, but interest in biotechnology investing has been on the upsurge since the establishment of the Texas Research Park in the San Antonio area. Although slightly less than half (45%) of funds invested by Texas firms remain in state, capital inflows from other regions more than balance the outflows.

EMULATORS, IMITATORS, AND INCUBATORS

There is no doubt that a vigorous local venture-capital community was a necessary element in the building of Route 128 and Silicon Valley. But as we have seen, it took much more than venture capital to build those two regions. Their high-tech entrepreneurial genetic code evolved, Lamarckian fashion, over many decades. What are the elements of that code? How do they interact with one another? And can the code be replicated? Policymakers in many regions are betting that they have the answers to those questions. First we will take a look at some of the things they are doing. Then we will examine the genetic code of high-tech economic development.

Venture Incubators

Incubators are perhaps the most visible public policy initiative aimed at building pockets of high-tech entrepreneurship. Rather like baby chicks, newly hatched companies are nurtured and sheltered until they are ready to fly off into the real world. That is what's supposed to happen. The difficulty with trying to hatch out startup companies in an incubator is that there's no way of knowing which eggs will produce chicks that die after one day or which will never get to the fledgling stage and be able to fend for themselves.

Entrepreneurial incubators are grounded in the notion that if the right ingredients are brought together—capital, facilities, support staff, organizations, and so forth—the resulting mixture will be an ideal breeding ground for new ventures. Formal venture incubators are essentially "factories for manufacturing new ventures."[20] These factories foster creativity and innovation by encouraging interaction among independent entrepreneurs housed under one roof. Entrepreneurs often share common administrative services and receive financial support, either outright in exchange for equity or indirectly through reduced rent and utilities. Funding may be provided by government agencies, local communities, established corporations, wealthy individuals, venture capitalists, private entrepreneurs, or some combination thereof.

The incubator's function is to integrate the elements of the entrepreneurial environment, to streamline the startup organizational tasks, and to help create an infrastructure for doing business. In theory, this improves the cost effectiveness of investors' capital and increases the chances of survival by making information available to both entrepreneurs and service providers.

Among the first incubators were the Business and Technology Centers (BTCs) organized by Control Data Corporation.[21] They were the vision of William Norris, the famous computer pioneer who founded CDC. Based on his experience as an entrepreneur, he hoped to make incubators a commercial success. Sad to say, CDC's incubators never became viable. When the company hit hard times, its incubators were one of the first things it jettisoned.

Today, incubators come in many types and sizes, from tiny rural low-tech ones to big—relatively speaking—urban high-tech ones. As of January 1990, *The Wall Street Journal* reported, U.S. venture incubators numbered 346 in 41 states. That is up from only 84 in 1985.[22] The Commonwealth of Pennsylvania has been a notable leader in this economic development program, having 40 incubators, the largest number of any state. Since 1983, it has invested $17 million of state funds in some 300 companies that employ 2,000 people. The incubator at Crozer Mills alone has 31 tenant companies employing 110 people; it was financed in 1983 with $1.7 million. Secretary of State Ray Christman referred to that program as "the vehicle for the new transformation" of an area. In addition, $35 million from the State Employees Retirement System has been used to fund startup companies.[23]

Other Government Initiatives

Other examples of government initiatives abound. Iowa State University, for instance, recently consolidated ten research centers into a single consortium, receiving $150 million from the state for advanced silicon research.[24] The U.S. Department of Energy supplied another $30 million, and Iowa will continue to provide $30 million annually. The state-run Iowa Product Development Corporation (IPDC) has financed 42 startups in two years, and Edge Technology, privately financed by six large Iowa corporations, has provided more than $2 million to startups. Figure 10-6 lists some university-government-industry initiatives around the United States.

State government venture-capital sources such as the IPDC and the Ben Franklin Partnership in Pennsylvania are modeled after pioneering initiatives undertaken in Massachusetts in the late 1970s—Massachusetts Capital Resource Company (MCRC), founded in 1978, and Massachusetts Technology Development Corporation (MTDC), founded in 1979. These two firms provide high-risk capital for companies that are sometimes unable to obtain financing from conventional sources, whose development may promise local job creation. While MCRC focuses on manufacturing

FIGURE 10-6 **U.S. Programs for Encouraging High-Technology Development**

Massachusetts
> Centers of Excellence, MTDC, MCRC, MIT: AI Lab, Microsystems Industrial Group

Pennsylvania
> Ben Franklin Partnership—advanced technology centers at
> - University Park (Penn State)
> - University of Pittsburgh and Carnegie-Mellon
> - Lehigh
> - University City Science Center (University of Penn, Drexel, Temple)

Research Triangle
> Duke, NC State, UNC–Chapel Hill—Microelectronics Center of North Carolina

Stanford University
> Center for Information Systems, Stanford Research Park, Center for Integrated Systems

Arizona State University
> Center for Solid State Electronics Research
> Arizona State University Research Park

University of Utah
> Utah Innovation Center, Utah Innovation Foundation, Utah Technology Finance Foundation

Florida State University
> Central Florida Research Park

Rensselaer Polytechnic Institute
> Rensselaer Technology Park

Princeton University
> Forrestal Park

Texas A&M University Research Park

Chicago Technology Park
> University of Illinois and Rush Presbyterian–St. Luke's Medical Center

Iowa
> Iowa Product Development Corp. (public), Edge Technology (private)

firms with growth potential, MTDC concentrates on technology-based startup companies for which "capital gaps" exist, in order to attract larger private venture-capital investment. For example, as of the end of fiscal 1989, every dollar invested by MTDC in Massachusetts-based technology companies had attracted an additional $4.63 in initial private co-investment funds. Those investments subsequently leveraged an additional $152.2 million. MTDC portfolio companies have, in turn, created more than 3,700 jobs in the state, with a total annual payroll of $133 million, generating $6 million in state income tax revenues and $37 million in federal income tax revenues.[25] Similarly, MCRC, which is typically a later-stage investor through a broader range of financing instruments (subordinated and senior debt, as well as equity) has invested cumulatively $233.7 million in more than 150 businesses employing more than 10,000 people.[26]

At the federal level, the National Science Foundation has been a key provider of funding for basic research and technology development centers. Figure 10-7 lists some of those centers and their locations.

Similar programs exist outside the United States. Technology transfer and new-venture promotion schemes, some founded prior to the 1980s, are on the rise in many countries, all extolling the virtues of industry-government-university partnerships. The outcomes of these programs range from miserable failures such as government-inspired venture capital in Australia to shining successes such as the St. John's Innovation Centre in Cambridge, England. Figure 10-8 lists many of these efforts.

A Caveat about Government Involvement

Other states eager to emulate Silicon Valley and Route 128 scramble for funds to finance promising technologies. A striking example recently occurred in Utah. In 1989, the University of Utah stunned the world with its announcement that two of its chemists, Pons and Fleischmann, had found fusion in a test tube. The next best thing to perpetual motion, the discovery held the promise of cheap, clean energy. But physicists, including Nobel laureates, were skeptical—the discovery broke basic laws of physics well known to every MIT senior. But before other scientists could repeat Pons and Fleischmann's findings, the Utah state legislature, no doubt propelled by all the hype, hastily funded a cold fusion research center with millions of taxpayer dollars. In the months that followed, some universities claimed to have confirmed the Utah discovery; others

Figure 10-7 **NSF-Funded Research Centers**

Columbia University	Engineering Research Center for Telecommunications
MIT	Center for Biotechnology Process Engineering (some NIH support also) Polymers (processing)
Purdue University	Center for Intelligent Manufacturing Systems
University of California, Santa Barbara	Center for Robotics Systems in Microelectronics
University of Delaware	Center for Composites Manufacturing and Engineering (affiliated with Center for Composite Materials, Rutgers University, New Brunswick, New Jersey)
University of Maryland, College Park	Center on Systems Research (affiliated with Harvard University, Cambridge)
Carnegie-Mellon University	Steel making
Case Western Reserve	Polymers (applied)
Colorado School of Mines	Steel processing
Dartmouth College	Ice research
Florida State University	High magnetic field research
Georgia Institute of Technology	Materials handling
Iowa State University	Nondestructive testing
Lehigh University	Innovation and research management Process modeling
New Jersey Institute of Technology	Toxic/hazardous waste management
North Carolina State University	Telecommunications
Northeastern University	Tribology Electromagnetics
Ohio State University	Welding
Oklahoma State University	Flexible material handling
Pennsylvania State University	Dielectrics

FIGURE 10-7 **Continued**

Purdue University/North Carolina State University	Plant molecular biology
Rensselaer Polytechnic Institute	Computer graphics
Rutgers University	Ceramics
Texas A&M University	Hydrogen technology
University of Arizona	Optical circuitry Microcontamination control
University of California, Santa Barbara	High-speed image processing
University of Massachusetts, Amherst	Polymers (properties) Process design
University of Minnesota	Biological process technology
University of North Carolina	Monoclonal lymphocyte technology
University of Rhode Island	Robotics
University of Tennessee	Management of control engineering
University of Texas, San Antonio	Biomolecular research
University of Washington	Process analytical chemistry
Washington University, St. Louis	Computerized chemical engineering
West Virginia University	Fluidized bed research
Worcester Polytechnic Institute	Automation technology

found it to be false. The science community was divided. It appeared that the more elite the laboratory, the less likely it was to find cold fusion. (One wag observed that you could only find it if your university had a great football team.) As it soon turned out, the elite scientists were correct. Cold fusion was a mirage.[27]

There is an important lesson in the cold fusion fiasco: only excellent science counts on the frontiers of knowledge. And excellent science is not forthcoming at the government's command, as Washington politicians, keen as ever to spread the pork around, seem to believe. Consider the furor caused by the NSF's recent decision to award funding to Florida State University for the development of the new National High Magnetic Field Laboratory.

FIGURE 10-8 **International Technology Centers**

Australia
   Victorian Economic Development Corp (VEDC)
   Centre for Innovative Development (Royal Melbourne Institute of
   Technology)
   Australian Innovation Corp, Nascent Technology Ventures
   (NaTeVs) Program

Canada
   Sheridan Park, Toronto, Ontario
   Innovation Place, Saskatoon, Saskatchewan
   Edmonton Research & Development Park, Edmonton, Alberta
   Calgary Research Park, Calgary, British Columbia
   Discovery Parks, Vancouver, British Columbia
   Research Technology Park, Waterloo, Ontario

England
   The Cambridge Science Park, Cambridge
   St. John's Innovation Centre, Cambridge
   Aston Science Park, Aston University, Birmingham
   South Bank Technopark, London

Germany
   New Technology-Based Firms (NTBF) Scheme
   Research Center for Innovation and New Enterprise (BIG),
   Berlin

The Netherlands
   Dutch Inventors Center, Rotterdam

Northern Ireland
   The Shannon Innovation Center, Limerick City

While National Science Foundation review panels said MIT had
better physicists, the state of Florida pledged a package of financial and political support that gave the Tallahassee campus the
edge.[28]

Frank Press, president of the National Academy of Sciences,
commented that

From the national point of view, the government gets the best
return by investing in the best institution; on the other hand, with
funding help, regions have come from behind and become world-
class centers of scientific research. Texas is a good example of
that.[29]

Critics argue that the politicization of the science-funding
process and regional rivalries within the United States threaten the

status of the nation's top research universities by allocating funding for reasons of political expediency rather than scientific excellence. The danger is real. If initiatives do not support world-class innovations that lead to commercial products, both the local economic and national competitiveness goals will be compromised. Research into technology commercialization tells us that superb research—more often than not government funded—is the key to breakthrough discoveries. Then, after the basic discovery has been made, market-oriented product development in private industry takes over, pushing the leading edge of technology in market-driven directions. Let's hope the Florida State scientists make world-class discoveries and that, if they do, there will be enough would-be engineer-entrepreneurs locally to turn those discoveries into world-beating commercial products.

The lessons learned from the classic venture-capital complexes described in this chapter have not been lost on the Europeans and Asians. It's no accident that one of the most successful complexes outside the United States is in Cambridge, England, adjacent to Britain's premier science and engineering university. The age of the high-tech entrepreneur is just dawning in Japan. Capitalism is on the rise throughout the world. The stakes in the global high-tech race are much too high to place politically inspired bets on long-odds outsiders instead of odds-on favorites. Frankly, when it comes to magnetic research, we would place our bets on MIT's magnificent winning track record in that area. If Florida State doesn't come through, the United States will have frittered away precious R&D dollars.

THE GENETIC CODE OF HIGH-TECH ECONOMIC DEVELOPMENT

The genetic code for economic development is far from simple. If our research shows one thing, it is that economists and policymakers—apart from a few enlightened ones—have not understood that reality. Entrepreneurs and the enterprises they form are at the center of economic development. It would be convenient if they could be created and stimulated simply through tax law changes, lower interest rates, and federal grants to universities. Unfortunately, the process of economic development is far more complicated.

Figure 10-2 illustrated the basics of the economic development process, grouping the various factors into two sets: external and internal. Societal values, government policies, institutions, and location are the external factors that determine the environment. People, capital, and support organizations are the internal factors. We like to think of the external factors as molecules and the internal factors as the nucleus of the entrepreneurship process. The interaction of those molecules with one another and with the nucleus ultimately determines whether a region has the right stuff for high-tech entrepreneurship. Let's look at the molecules.

Government Policies

Policies set by federal and local governments influence the economic renewal process on several fronts (Figure 10-9). An obvious element is support for basic research at colleges and universities. Along with direct support for those programs, as well as government-run research institutes, Small Business Innovation Research grants fund leading-edge technological development. On a more basic level, effective primary and secondary education, along with jobs-skills training and retraining, influence the economic development

FIGURE 10-9 **The Government Policies Molecule**

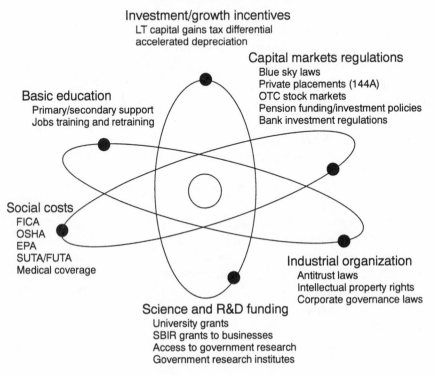

Investment/growth incentives
LT capital gains tax differential
accelerated depreciation

Capital markets regulations
Blue sky laws
Private placements (144A)
OTC stock markets
Pension funding/investment policies
Bank investment regulations

Basic education
Primary/secondary support
Jobs training and retraining

Social costs
FICA
OSHA
EPA
SUTA/FUTA
Medical coverage

Industrial organization
Antitrust laws
Intellectual property rights
Corporate governance laws

Science and R&D funding
University grants
SBIR grants to businesses
Access to government research
Government research institutes

process. And, of course, tax rates are perhaps the most important macroeconomic policy that stimulates economic activity. The capital gains tax, for instance, affects the amount of money that is available for investment in businesses.

Government regulation encompasses a whole host of rules governing capital formation and the function of organized capital markets. SEC regulations control the methods by which capital is raised and the disclosure and reporting requirements, as applicable. Pension funding levels and asset allocation restrictions also fall within the realm of government policy. Antitrust laws have a powerful but subtle impact on the ability of growing companies to compete globally. Many of those well-intended laws and regulations are impediments to market forces. Laws governing intellectual property protection and antitrust law affect the incentive both to innovate and to share new technology in the marketplace.

There are also social costs to consider, especially when they compare unfavorably to those of competitors in a region. Some social costs are state and federal unemployment programs, mandatory health plans, workers' compensation insurance, and safety and environmental quality regulations.

Societal Values

Societal values establish the extent to which entrepreneurship is accepted or encouraged (Figure 10-10). Most important, a society must have a culture that prizes its entrepreneurs. Its successful entrepreneurs must be visible so that they can be role models. While success must be lauded, failure must not be condemned—indeed, it must be socially acceptable. Positive societal values lessen the blow of failure and make it possible for an entrepreneur to rejoin the work force at an experience-based level or, as is often the case, to try again. An entrepreneurial society has investors, bankers, lawyers, workers, suppliers, and customers that know the importance of entrepreneurs. Most of all, a region needs to catch the entrepreneurial fever that, according to one well-regarded diagnosis, was the most important single factor in the rise of Silicon Valley.[30]

Institutions

Institutions play a large role in the renewal process as the locus for research and innovation. Included in that group are universities, research institutes both public and private, and large companies (Figure 10-11). All of them act as spawning grounds for innovation.

FIGURE 10-10 **The Cultural/Societal Values Molecule**

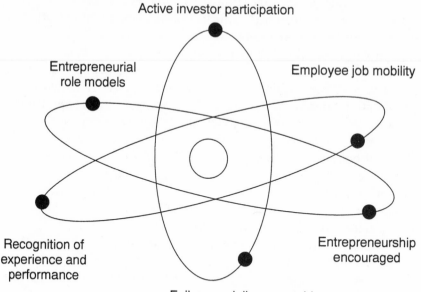

A key virtue of the institutional elements is the cross-fertilization and cooperation of clusters of industry, academic, and government efforts, particularly in the computer science, biotechnology, medical/health, materials science, electronics, and engineering fields.

Within universities, societal influences again come into play. Supportive value systems that encourage faculty participation in new ventures, outside consulting opportunities, and royalty arrangements, along with a willingness to share resources with industry all play a part in accelerating the innovation process. European academics are astonished when they learn that MIT's electrical engineering faculty has a dozen or so millionaires whose wealth stems from companies they've founded.

Some universities—Harvard, for example—go so far as to invest part of their endowment in venture capital funds or in the direct funding of new ventures. Others invite industry participation through symposia and business development workshops such as the MIT Enterprise Forum, where entrepreneurs present their business plans to a panel of experts in front of an audience. To facilitate the financing of small businesses by wealthy individuals, the University of New Hampshire started the Venture Capital Network, which is essentially a dating service for entrepreneurs and potential

FIGURE 10-11 **The Institutions Molecule**

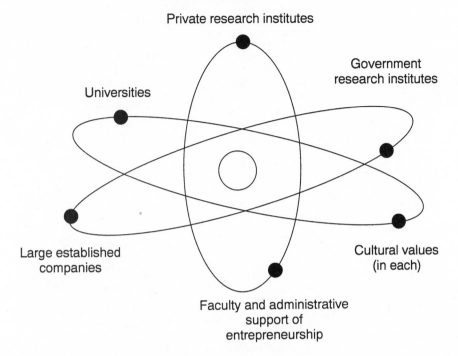

Private research institutes

Government
research institutes

Universities

Large established
companies

Cultural values
(in each)

Faculty and administrative
support of
entrepreneurship

investors; the network recently moved to MIT. Universities across the country help numerous small businesses each year through their Small Business Institutes and Small Business Development Centers.

Locational Factors

Some of the locational factors that help set the environment for renewal are the local business climate, proximity to resources, and quality of life issues (Figure 10-12). The local business climate includes elements previously mentioned: taxes, regulations, and blue sky laws governing securities transactions.

If a region's competitive advantage lay solely in its ability to provide low-cost facilities, housing, commercial real estate, and labor, then Silicon Valley and Route 128, where real estate costs are among the highest in the nation, would definitely not qualify. Fortunately for those two regions and similar ones that are emerging, other factors are more important to high-tech entrepreneurs. High among them is proximity to resources such as suppliers, well-educated workers, customers, and institutions.

Consider, for instance, how a typical Route 128 company gets

FIGURE 10-12 **The Locational Factors Molecule**

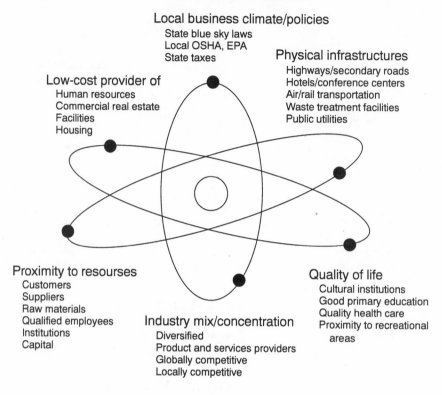

Local business climate/policies
State blue sky laws
Local OSHA, EPA
State taxes

Physical infrastructures
Highways/secondary roads
Hotels/conference centers
Air/rail transportation
Waste treatment facilities
Public utilities

Low-cost provider of
Human resources
Commercial real estate
Facilities
Housing

Proximity to resourses
Customers
Suppliers
Raw materials
Qualified employees
Institutions
Capital

Industry mix/concentration
Diversified
Product and services providers
Globally competitive
Locally competitive

Quality of life
Cultural institutions
Good primary education
Quality health care
Proximity to recreational
areas

started. A would-be entrepreneur leaves his existing employer to start a company. Almost always, the new company is located in the area where the entrepreneur previously worked. It's where the entrepreneur lives, and it's where the entrepreneur has the most of his contacts. More likely than not, the entrepreneur's wife also works in the same area. Starting a new business is difficult enough without the added burden of relocating. Their present quality of life is important to the entrepreneur and his family. They are accustomed to excellent schools, world-class hospitals, and cultural institutions, restaurants, shopping, and outdoor recreation nearby.

No matter how hard they try, most other areas in Massachusetts and adjacent states find it extremely difficult, if not impossible, to lure Route 128 high-tech entrepreneurs to their regions. Even with enticements such as low-cost space, municipally guaranteed bonds, favorable tax treatment, and job training programs, local governments can seldom offer enough to pull a would-be entrepreneur away from Route 128. True, some companies migrate to nearby regions. (Southern New Hampshire with its allure of no personal income tax and no sales tax is a favorite.) But Route 128 firms generally do not migrate, until they have established themselves locally. The same is true on the West Coast, where established companies are locating plants in places such as Boulder, Portland, and Seattle.

The Nucleus: People, Capital, and Support Organizations

At the nucleus of the economic development model are people, capital, and direct-support organizations (Figure 10-13). When the environmental conditions are just right, entrepreneurship takes over. New companies start up. They create employment. A few of their employees leave and start their own companies. Investors finance startups, harvest their successful investments, and finance yet more startups. Direct-support organizations such as teachers,

FIGURE 10-13 **The People, Capital, Support Nucleus**

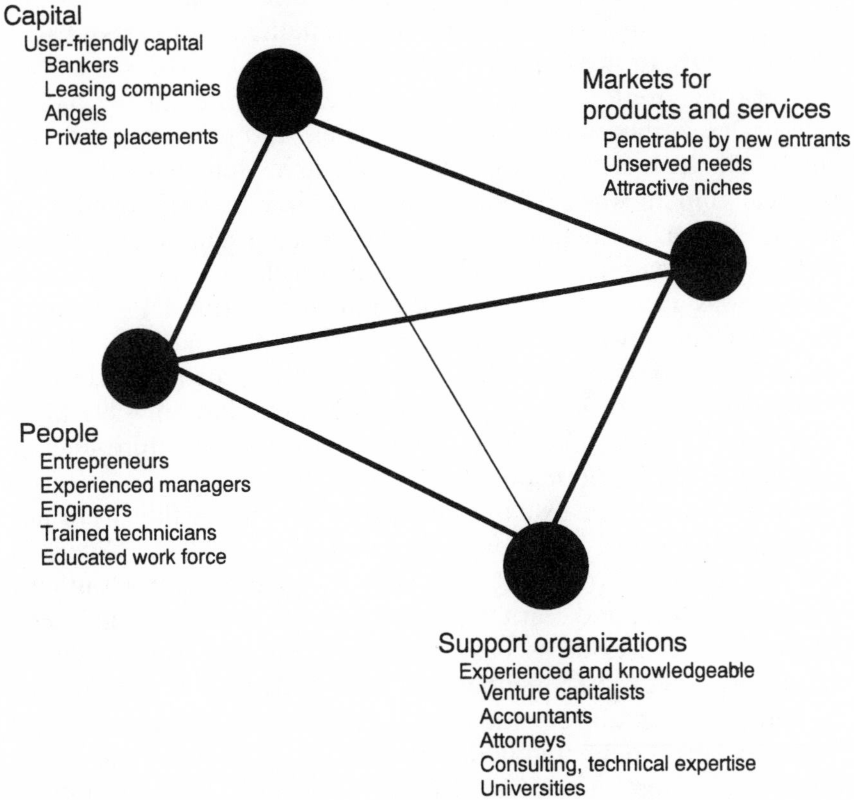

Capital
  User-friendly capital
  Bankers
  Leasing companies
  Angels
  Private placements

Markets for
products and services
  Penetrable by new entrants
  Unserved needs
  Attractive niches

People
  Entrepreneurs
  Experienced managers
  Engineers
  Trained technicians
  Educated work force

Support organizations
  Experienced and knowledgeable
    Venture capitalists
    Accountants
    Attorneys
    Consulting, technical expertise
    Universities

suppliers, accountants, lawyers, and consultants become skilled at meeting the needs of entrepreneurial companies. A region becomes a self-sustaining, high-tech entrepreneurial metropolis.

CAN A HIGH-TECH ENTREPRENEURIAL REGION BE PLANNED?

The most successful high-tech entrepreneurial metropolises were not deliberately planned by governments. Indeed, some say that the first one, Route 128, managed to develop despite handicaps imposed by local and state government. One of the authors vividly remembers a visitor to his venture-capital-backed startup when it was only a few weeks old in December 1969. It was a Massachusetts state employee, not visiting—as one might have hoped—to ask what the state could do to help. Instead, it was an inspector demanding evidence that we had filed all the necessary tax forms with the state. We had filed them, but he hadn't bothered to check the state's records. The next visit from a state employee was several years later. He wanted to know how the state had helped our company with its exports. It hadn't. Nonetheless, he asked if it would be OK to say that it had.

Massachusetts has one of the highest tax rates in the nation when sales, ordinary income, capital gains, and property taxes are combined. In the late 1970s, many executives felt that the state's political climate was so unfavorable that they banded together in self-defense to form the Massachusetts High-Technology Council to lobby and campaign on behalf of high-tech businesses. Its first success was Proposition 2½, styled after California's Proposition 13, which limited property taxes to 2½% of the market value of an asset. There is no doubt that the council has made Massachusetts more supportive of high-tech business. Nonetheless, in 1991 Massachusetts has the fifth-highest income tax and the third-highest inheritance tax in the nation.

There are other examples of high-tech regions that were not deliberately planned, among them, Austin, Dallas, Colorado Springs, Portland (Oregon), Phoenix, Orange County, southern New Hampshire, and San Diego. Our genetic code for a high-tech entrepreneurial region is based primarily on how Silicon Valley and Route 128 evolved, neither of which resulted from government planning. So can this genetic code be consciously replicated? That is, can planners deliberately design and develop a high-tech entrepreneurial region? A number of regions are betting that the answer is yes. But they need to be patient; there is no royal road to high-tech entrepreneurship. The Research Triangle in North Carolina is a good example. It is a 6,000-acre high-tech research park that was opened in 1960 in the Raleigh–Durham–Chapel Hill metropolitan area, home of Duke University, North Carolina State University, and the University of North Carolina. It resulted from a deliberate government decision to capitalize on the intellectual talent at those three universities and build a solid core of entrepreneurial, high-tech companies in the region. After a slow start, a turning point came in 1965, when IBM stepped in with an important R&D center.[31] For the next two decades, it attracted many R&D laboratories from well-known companies, but there were few entrepreneurial spinoffs. That situation slowly improved as the right mix of physical and institutional structures (capital, research universities, and so forth) gradually developed enough to support a self-sustaining high-tech metropolis. Indeed, Raleigh–Durham, Charlotte, and Wilmington–Jacksonville, North Carolina, placed ninth, eleventh, and thirteenth, respectively, on *Inc. Magazine*'s 1990 list of Most Entrepreneurial Cities in America.[32] North Carolina has come a long way since 1960, when its per capita income and industrial wage rate were near the bottom of the U.S. rankings.

Another example of a deliberately planned high-tech complex is the attempt to revive a declining industrial base in Troy, New York. That city is the home of Rensselaer Polytechnic Institute (RPI) and forms a metropolitan area with Albany and Schenectady, where the State University of New York at Albany and General Electric's renowned R&D center are located. RPI has one of the best high-tech incubators in the world adjacent to its campus and nearby on its land in North Greenbush is its 1,200-acre Rensselaer Technology Park. That park, opened in 1981, is doing very well at the end of its first decade.

The University of Utah Research Park in Salt Lake City is another example of planned development. Opened in 1970, it is home to a number of high-tech companies.

There are signs that the Philadelphia area is currently undergoing an entrepreneurial transformation. Pennsylvania's Ben Franklin Partnership, now with eight years of experience, is beginning to succeed in spawning many new technology-based enterprises. Its success is the more remarkable for occurring in an entrepreneurial culture that traditionally has underachieved despite the presence of excellent educational and research institutions and capital sources.

Thus, we think the evidence is encouraging. Parts of the genetic code of high-tech entrepreneurial development are being replicated by a few regions. We will know that the complete code has been cloned when this can be said of those regions:

> A lot of things are in place here. The banks understand it more than anywhere else. You've got universities that are feeding out ideas more than anywhere else. You've got realtors who understand how it all works and are willing to speculate and gamble on small companies where they won't elsewhere. And then, most important, you've got entrepreneurs here. The point is, there's almost nobody in Silicon Valley who doesn't know someone else that's made a million dollars. At least! Whereas there is almost no one in Chicago who knows anybody that has ever come close to making a million dollars. And that's all the difference. Out here, they know it can be done. In Chicago, it doesn't even occur to them.[33]

That is what Tom Perkins, the consummate venture capitalist, said about Silicon Valley's entrepreneurial culture. The same observation holds true for Route 128. Add "You've got venture capitalists who understand it better than anywhere else," and you've got the full-blown high-tech entrepreneurial metropolis prescribed by our model.

CHAPTER 11

Factors Influencing the Flows of Venture Capital

THE LIFEBLOOD of the venture capital process consists of three essential components: entrepreneurial deals, money to invest in those deals, and a return on the money invested in them. When returns are running high, new money flows into funds, and, provided that the deal flow keeps pace, the industry is euphoric. Such was the situation in the late 1960s and the early 1980s. But when the flows are out of balance, as happened in the mid-1970s when the flow of new money was reduced to a mere trickle or the late 1980s when returns fell well below expectations, the industry becomes despondent. Any discussion of the factors that turn the flow of venture capital on and off must focus on what affects the three decision makers responsible for the money, the deal flow, and the returns—that is, the investors who put up the money, the entrepreneurs who form companies to invest it in, and the venture capitalists who raise the money, seek out entrepreneurs, and put deals together. Prominent among the factors influencing those three constituents are the capital markets, government policies, technologies, and industries (see Figure 11-1). Other factors also cited as important determinants of the flows of venture capital are the ERISA rules governing pension fund managers and SEC regulations. Capital markets, especially the IPO market and interest rates, affect the flows. The discovery and development of new technologies stimulate the venture capital industry because more than half the deals are in technology-driven companies. And the state of an industry influences the flows—for

FIGURE 11-1 **Factors Influencing the Flows of Venture Capital**

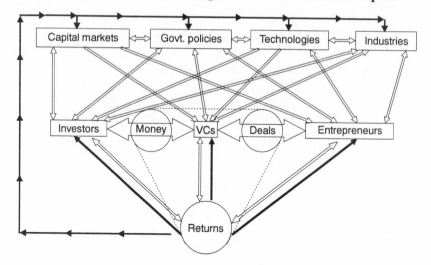

Source: W. Bygrave, in D. L. Sexton and J. D. Kasarda, eds., *The State of the Art of Entrepreneurship* (Boston: PWS-Kent, 1992), p. 457.

example, the emergence of new industries such as the personal computer can spur investments.

In the next sections we discuss the major, measurable factors influencing the flows of venture capital. Econometric analyses of these influences follow. Then we look at the relationships between the flows of venture capital and public policy, capital markets, new technologies, and changes in industries.

MEASURABLE FACTORS INFLUENCING VENTURE CAPITAL FLOW

Capital Gains Tax

Within the venture capital industry, it is almost universally believed that the federal capital gains tax rate is the most important influence on the flows of venture capital. Representative Daniel E. Lungren, for instance, wrote this in his foreword to a 1984 U.S. Congress report, *Venture Capital and Innovation:*

> Since the larger availability of [post–1978 venture capital] funds resulted essentially from reduced taxation of capital gains, the consequences of increasing the capital gains tax rate *or* removing the differential in taxation of capital gains and ordinary income

holds serious ramifications for our country's ability to maintain its technological leadership.[1]

As recently as 1990, when asked, "Was it truly the capital gains tax change in '78 that sprung all the venture capital loose after 1978, or was it there anyway, waiting to happen?" Ben Rosen replied:

> It was a combination of things. Yes, the old rate was oppressive, almost confiscatory. The reduction—eventually to 20%—was a big factor in helping to shake loose the supply of capital, but also the supply of entrepreneurs. . . . Lowering the capital gains tax made entrepreneurs more willing to start companies. Also, it made it easier to recruit people to come over to those start-ups. [What else in the combination of things?] Simply that technology moves forward in cycles, and at the same time as the tax adjustment, two immense technologies happened to be coming to the fore—the microprocessor and biotechnology, each poised to spawn hundreds of new companies. But the point is, if we'd had a 70%* capital gains tax rate, I can assure you there would be no new industries as we knew then today in the entrepreneurial sector.[2]

Perhaps the capital gains tax does not deserve all the credit; nonetheless, Rosen's comment is representative of venture capitalists' collective wisdom. The 1969 tax bill, which increased the capital gains tax rate, was widely criticized by venture capitalists for impeding the flows of new venture capital in the early 1970s. Similarly, decreases in the capital gains tax rates have been cited as improving those flows. For example, as a result of the 1978 Steiger Amendment and the 1981 tax bill, the maximum capital gains tax rate for individuals declined from 49% to 20%. During that period of declining capital gains tax rates, venture capital flows exhibited unprecedented increases.

The 1986 Tax Reform Act eliminated the preferential capital

---

*The 70% capital gains tax rate applied to personal holding companies. It was rarely paid, because, as one tax partner in a Big 6 accounting firm commented, any individual who paid at the 70% rate needed a new tax adviser. According to a 1984 congressional study, "through various stages and with the Revenue Act of 1976, the 25% alternative tax on capital gains was severely limited, and the maximum effective capital gains tax rate was almost doubled to 49.125%." At that time the maximum tax rate on ordinary income was 70%.

gains tax rate. This should have a strong negative impact on individual investors, a slightly negative impact on corporate taxpayers, and no impact on tax-exempt investors (for obvious reasons). Prior to the Tax Reform Act of 1986, individuals were allowed to exclude 60% of long-term capital gains from taxes. If the taxpayer was in the highest tax bracket (50%), then the maximum overall rate charged on long-term capital gains was 20%. Following the 1986 act, taxpayers no longer had a long-term capital gains tax exclusion and had to pay at their marginal tax rate—as high as 33% for some high-income taxpayers (the marginal rate rose from 28% to 33% because of the phase-out of exemptions). In other words, capital gains taxes increased by as much as 65% for individual investors. Corporate taxpayers also suffered. They did not have the opportunity to take a 60% long-term capital gains exclusion prior to the 1986 Tax Reform Act; nevertheless, they had been allowed an alternative 28% tax rate on excess long-term capital gains over short-term capital gains. This rate was used whenever the marginal tax rate exceeded 28%. The 1986 Tax Reform Act reduced the top statutory tax rate from 46% to 34%, but it also eliminated the alternative tax rate. Consequently, the top rate charged on corporate long-term capital gains rose from 28% to 34%—a 21% increase.

The following statement reflects what the venture capital industry expected to happen to the flows of venture capital as a result of the Tax Reform Act of 1986:

> Now that the initial shock of the Treasury Department's proposed tax reform program has abated, it is time to analyze its effect on the business development process. That is easy. In a word: disaster![3]

Economists are divided on this issue. Some agree with the position of venture capitalists;[4] others argue that changes in the capital gains tax have little direct effect on the flows of venture capital.[5] Econometric studies have suggested that the capital gains tax is only a minor influence.[6] Yet those studies have been challenged by other observers of the venture capital industry as the work of number crunchers:

> Since *Venture Capital*'s first editorial on the Treasury's capital gains tax proposal, there have been a number of rationalizations that this tax change will not adversely affect the venture capital industry and new business development. Most of this thinking has

been based on simplistic statistical analyses which display a lack of understanding of the critical role played by the entrepreneur.[7]

Stock Market Indices

The stock market indices and the amount of money raised by IPOs may influence the flows of venture capital in a direct manner. A hot new issues market has the most favorable effect on venture capital returns.[8] That in turn would be expected to lead to increases in the flows of funds to venture capitalists because of improved prospects of attractive initial public offerings for their portfolio companies. Low stock prices or a declining IPO market might be considered a harbinger of an oncoming recession and thus discourage investors from participating in venture capital funds. Although a public offering of a typical venture-capital investment may not be realized for five years or thereabouts, it is assumed that the public perception may be negatively biased by existing market conditions.

Interest Rates

Short-term Treasury bills and long-term Treasury bonds are risk-free alternatives to investments in venture capital funds. Furthermore, since short- and long-term government rates are indicative of the cost of borrowing bank debt, rising interest rates may cause competing sources of external financing, such as venture capital, to look more attractive to growing firms. Consequently, during periods of high interest rates, investment of venture capital in portfolio companies would be expected to rise.

THE INTERACTION OF FACTORS AND FLOWS

Now we will look at how changes in the factors discussed above actually correlated with the flows of venture capital over the last twenty years or so. Figures 11-2 through 11-4 illustrate the range and variation of the factors included in the analysis. Figure 11-2 shows the flows of new venture capital into venture capital firms as well as the flows of venture capital into new investments. Data were collected from *Venture Capital Journal* and include aggregate amounts from more than 500 venture capital firms and annual investments in portfolio companies, which numbered approximately 1,500 in 1987. Data prior to 1969 were not available.

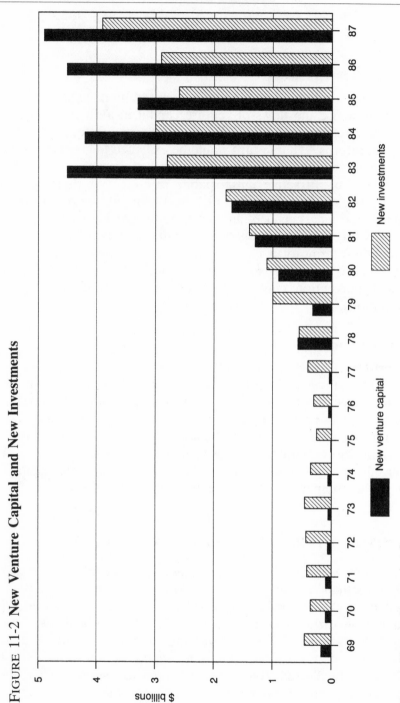

FIGURE 11-2 New Venture Capital and New Investments

Source: Venture Economics, Inc.

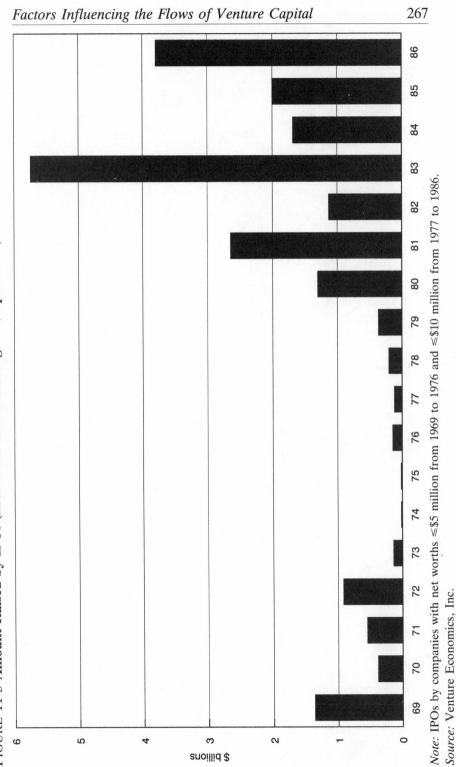

FIGURE 11-3 **Amount Raised by IPOs (firm commitment offerings ≥ $1 per share)**

Note: IPOs by companies with net worths ≤$5 million from 1969 to 1976 and ≤$10 million from 1977 to 1986.
Source: Venture Economics, Inc.

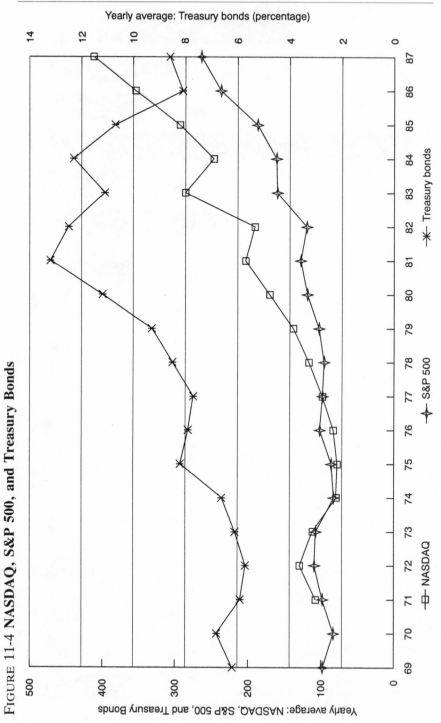

FIGURE 11-4 NASDAQ, S&P 500, and Treasury Bonds

New venture capital flows (funds committed* to venture capital firms) were as low as $10 million in 1975 and as high as $4.9 billion in 1987. New investment flows (funds flowing out of venture capital firms into portfolio companies) were as low as $250 million in 1975 and as high as $3.9 billion in 1987. Both new venture capital and new investments seem to have followed similar patterns of ebb and flow during the 1969 to 1989 period. However, since 1983, more funds flowed into venture capital firms than flowed out. It resulted in a venture capital surplus, which declined from $1.7 billion in 1983 to approximately $1 billion in 1987. Perhaps part of the surplus reflected a desire of venture capitalists to increase reserve holdings the better to accommodate second- and third-round funding requests. Alternatively, it could be argued that venture capitalists were becoming more conservative (selective?) in their investments and were awaiting more promising projects. Of course, part of the gap is explained by the fact that not all the new money invested in venture capital funds flows into them in the year in which it is committed. Hence, when new commitments rise from one year to the next, inflows of new money will lag behind in any one year.

Figure 11-3 shows the amount raised by IPOs during the 1969 to 1986 period. The IPO index for 1969 to 1976 was derived from the public offerings of companies with net worths of $5 million or less. To allow for inflation—albeit crudely—the net worth limit was raised to $10 million from 1977 to 1986. To be included in these statistics, the offering price had to be at least $1 per share, the offerings had to be firm commitment underwritings and not best efforts, and the stocks had to be for nonfinancial companies.

The data in Figure 11-3 indicate that the amount raised with IPOs parallels the amount of new venture-capital funds raised shown in Figure 11-2. This is especially apparent at the peaks and valleys. For instance, in 1975—the low point for new venture capital and investments—the amount raised with IPOs was a mere $16 million. Similarly, in 1983 a record 611 IPOs raised a whopping $5.7 billion. Although such perfect correlations did not occur in other years, the general pattern seemed to hold. Figure 11-4 illustrates the NASDAQ index, the Standard & Poor 500 index, and the yield on Treasury bonds. Long-term interest rates as measured

---

*Money committed to a venture capital fund actually flows to the fund in installments over the following few years. Venture Economics tracks only commitments year by year. Hence, the data used in analyses are annual commitments, not actual flows.

by the yield on Treasury bonds during this period ranged from a low of 6% in the early 1970s to a high of more than 13% in the early 1980s.

Econometric Analysis

Relationships between the inflows and outflows of venture capital and external factors have been studied with regression analyses—a statistical technique widely used in finance and economics. The principal findings of one of those studies are as follows:[9]

1. The inflow of new venture capital was correlated to the NASDAQ index and the amount raised through IPOs.
2. There was no statistically significant relationship between the changes in the capital gains tax rate and the inflows of venture capital. That was a real surprise and will be discussed later in this chapter.
3. The outflow of venture capital as investments in portfolio companies was correlated to the NASDAQ index and the amount of money flowing into venture capital firms.
4. There was no statistically significant relationship between changes in the capital gains tax and the outflows of venture capital. Again, that will be discussed later.

Those findings are represented graphically in Figure 11-5, which shows the annual inflows of venture capital, the NASDAQ index, and the major changes in the differential between the maximum tax rate on ordinary income and the maximum tax rate on capital gains tax.* It shows that the inflows were strongly correlated with the NASDAQ index. It also shows no consistent correlation between the four major changes in the tax-rate differential and the inflows of venture capital.[10] (The 1969 and 1978 changes are positively correlated; the 1981 and 1986 changes are negatively correlated.)

Changes in Capital Gains Tax Rate

The most startling finding of econometric models is that the correlation between the inflow of venture capital and the changes in the federal capital gains tax rate in 1978 and in 1986 is not statistically significant. This finding was not expected because a similar study of the flows of venture capital through 1982 found that the

---

*It is assumed that the difference between the tax rate on ordinary income and capital gains determines where an individual invests, rather than the absolute rate of either tax, all other things being equal.

FIGURE 11-5 **New Venture Capital, NASDAQ, Tax Rate**

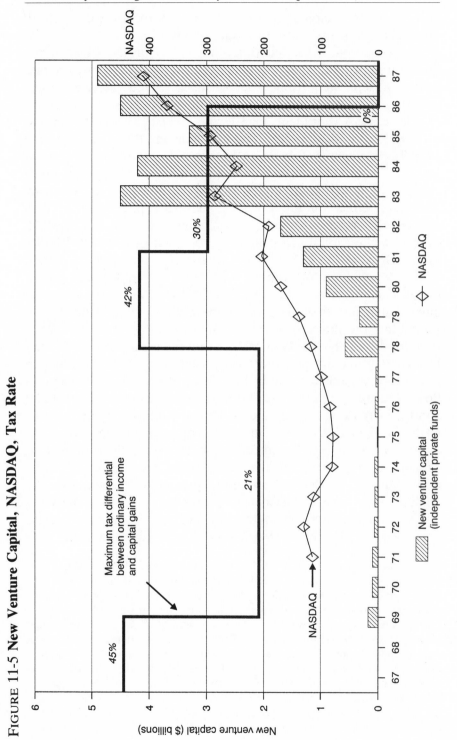

flows of venture capital were correlated with the 1978 decrease in the capital gains tax rate—the exact opposite.[11]

What accounts for this difference? First, in the study of the flows through 1982, the 1978 changes in the capital gains tax rate were not separated from other changes in federal regulations, primarily the Department of Labor's less stringent interpretation of the ERISA "prudent man" rule, which occurred simultaneously.* Second, data are now available for the years after the 1986 Tax Reform Act made an unfavorable change in the capital gains tax rate. This change was not accompanied by any other changes in government policy that were believed to have any noticeable effect on the flows of venture capital. Hence, it is possible to separate—at least by inference—the effect of the 1978 change in the capital gains tax rate from that of the 1978 ERISA ruling. Because the 1978 changes in federal policy were correlated to the flows of venture capital while the 1986 change was not, it seems reasonable to infer that the ERISA ruling was probably more important than the reduction in the capital gains tax in stimulating the flows of venture capital in 1978. That inference is supported by the post–1978 relationship between the flow of venture capital and changes in the capital gains tax rate. A reduction in the capital gains tax rate in 1981 was followed by an increase in flow of venture capital in 1983 but by decreases in 1984 and 1985; and the increase in the tax rate in 1986 was followed by an increase in the flows in 1987. Thus, since 1982, apart from one year, 1983, there has been a negative correlation between the flows of venture capital and the changes in the capital gains tax rate, which is the exact opposite of what industry gurus predicted. Furthermore, the analysis offers a very plausible reason for the increase in the flows in 1983 that does not involve the 1982 decrease in the capital gains tax rate. In 1983, the NASDAQ index was robust, and the IPO

*The change in the ERISA regulation to eliminate some of the ambiguities of the 1974 prudence rule was proposed in 1978 and became effective in 1979. (The ERISA prudence rule deals with the due diligence that a pension fund manager must perform before investing in a portfolio company.) It should be noted that other federal policy changes may also have increased the flows of venture capital. Among them were improvements in SEC regulations, beginning in 1978, that were intended to lower the cost of access to private and public capital for small businesses, and the Economic Recovery Tax Act of 1981 (ERTA), which contained a number of tax changes to spur investment. Venture capitalists, however, rate those changes much lower than the changes in the capital gains tax rate and the ERISA prudence rule as causes of the post–1978 surge in venture capital availability.[12]

market was the hottest ever; both factors could have contributed to the increase in the flows of venture capital.

It should also be noted that there was no apparent correlation between the venture capital invested in portfolio companies and the changes in the capital gains tax rate.

Why did the changes in tax rates not have as positive a correlation with the flows of venture capital as many believed they would? Individual taxpayers pay considerably more taxes on capital gains under the new Tax Reform Act of 1986 than was previously the case; yet the amount of new venture capital increased from $3.3 billion in 1985 to $4.5 billion in 1986 to a record high of $4.9 billion in 1987.

Figure 11-6 may illustrate a reasonable explanation of this paradox. It depicts how the profile of investors in private venture capital funds has changed dramatically. Whereas in 1979 (the first year that detailed data were available), only 56% of all investments in new venture capital came from nontaxable investors (i.e., pensions, endowments, and foreign investors), in 1986, approximately 66% of all investments came from nontaxable investors. Furthermore, although corporations and insurance companies are subject to capital gains tax, the impact of changes in the capital gains tax rate on those two groups of venture capital investors has been less dramatic than it has been for individual investors and wealthy families. The last group is the most affected by such changes, but it contributed only 12% of the new venture capital in 1986 versus 23% in 1979. So it is no surprise that there was no significant relationship between the overall flows of venture capital and changes in the capital gains tax. The bulk of new venture capital was from entities that either paid no capital gains taxes or were only slightly affected by the changes in that tax.

Given the proliferation of individual retirement plans during this period, an absolute increase in pension fund investments should not be surprising. Portfolio managers acting under the "prudent man" rule may simply be diversifying their growing portfolio holdings in all reasonable investment opportunities. Since venture capital funds have historically appreciated at a rate greater than other investment options (e.g., government certificates, S&P 500 stocks), some funds will naturally flow into this area.[13]

Changes in Capital Markets

The inflow of venture capital is correlated first and foremost with the NASDAQ index and secondly with the IPO market. As the

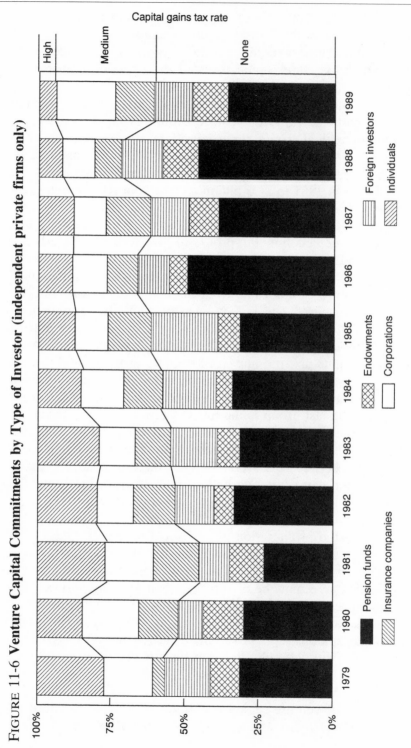

Figure 11-6 Venture Capital Commitments by Type of Investor (independent private firms only)

Capital gains tax rate

High Medium None

Pension funds
Insurance companies
Endowments
Corporations
Foreign investors
Individuals

1979 1980 1981 1982 1983 1984 1985 1986 1987 1988 1989

100% 75% 50% 25% 0%

strength of the IPO market depends to a large extent on the strength of the over-the-counter market, it is clear that the inflow of venture capital is influenced by the health of the OTC market. Thus, the investment of venture capital in portfolio companies is strongly correlated with the inflow of new capital and with the NASDAQ index.

Let us look at the returns on securities over five-year holding periods (Figure 11-7). (We have chosen the five-year holding period because it approximates the time from the initial investment of venture capital in a portfolio company and its initial public offering.) By 1968, the five-year return on small company stocks peaked above 30%—more than three times the five-year return on the S&P 500 stocks. Investors' appetites for small company stocks seemed insatiable, and venture capital was booming.

But by 1970, the five-year return on small company stocks had plummeted to 7.5%. It bottomed out in 1973 at −12.2%. From there it rose steadily, just breaking into double digits in 1977. Thus, the five-year return on small company stocks was either in single digits or negative for every year but one from 1970 through 1976. It had not stayed that low for such a prolonged period since the Great Depression. Investors lost their taste for small company stocks. The IPO market for venture-capital-backed companies collapsed. Venture capitalists were unable to reap their favorite harvest. The industry slumped badly.

Fortunately, at least as far as stock market cycles are concerned, what goes down must go up. The five-year return on small company stocks rose above 20% in 1978 and stayed there through 1984. In three years, it was above 30%, peaking just short of 40%. The rolling return on small company stocks had never before been above 20% for a string of seven years. The longest run before that was the period 1944 to 1947, which—perhaps not by chance—coincided with the birth of the venture capital industry. No wonder investors' appetite for small company stocks revived as the 1970s ended, turning into what some have called a feeding frenzy in 1983. Venture capital boomed as never before.

Alas, by 1987, the five-year return on small company stocks again fell into the single digits, and the return on venture capital fell along with it. The inflow of new venture capital, which hit an all-time peak in 1987, has now declined somewhat, but there is no sign of a disastrous plunge like the one that accompanied the fall in the return on small company stocks at the start of the 1970s. This is probably because the venture capital industry is more mature

FIGURE 11-7 **Returns on Securities Held Five Years**

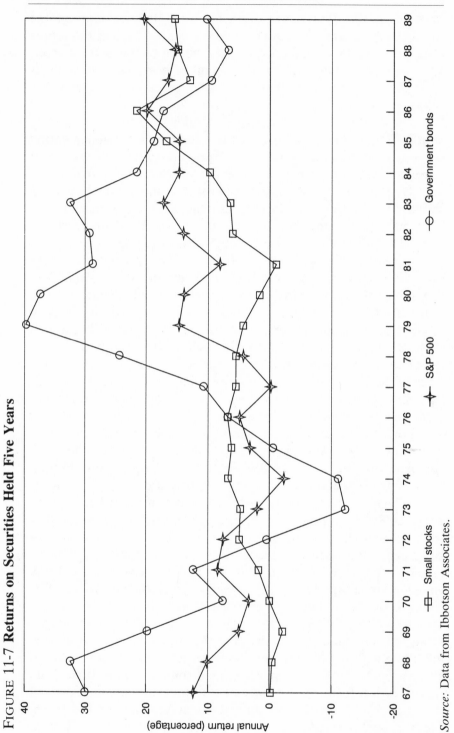

Source: Data from Ibbotson Associates.

and those who invest in it have more sophisticated information about returns and their cycles. After all, the industry is now more than 40 years old and has been through several cycles.

The difference between the rolling five-year returns on small company stocks and the Standard and Poor 500 stocks is shown in Figure 11-8. A similar graph for the rolling ten-year returns is shown in Figure 11-9. Those two figures when viewed alongside Figure 11-2 show how the decline and rise in the inflow of venture capital tracked the decline and rise in the differential in the five-year return on small company stocks and the S&P 500 stocks during the 1970s.

A MODEL FOR THE FLOWS OF VENTURE CAPITAL

The major factors believed to influence the inflows of new venture capital to independent private venture-capital funds from 1978 to 1989 are shown in Figure 11-10. The rising inflow of venture capital from 1978 to 1980 coincided with (1) an increase in the number of venture-capital-backed IPOs, (2) an increase in the differential between the maximum tax rate on ordinary income and capital gains,* and (3) the ERISA "prudent man" and "safe harbor" rules.

Small company stocks are publicly traded on the over-the-counter market. The state of that market determines the climate for initial public offerings by small companies, which, in turn, directly affects the returns on venture capital. Thus, the health of the OTC market and the IPO market for venture-capital-backed companies is by far the most important influence on the flows of venture capital.

As we have mentioned, the changes in the capital gains tax rate in 1978, 1982, and 1986 had less direct influence on the flows of venture capital than the changes of the ERISA prudence rule in 1978. This is not to say that the capital gains tax does not influence the flows of venture capital. Some believe that it affects the stock markets. If that is so, then it has a strong influence on the health of the over-the-counter market and hence indirectly

*We have shown the differential between the maximum tax rates for individuals on ordinary income and capital gains because that is what determines where a rational decision maker invests. When the differential is high, rational decision makers will put more of their portfolios in investments with the potential for capital gains, and, when it is low, they will put more of their portfolio in investments that produce ordinary income, all other things being equal.

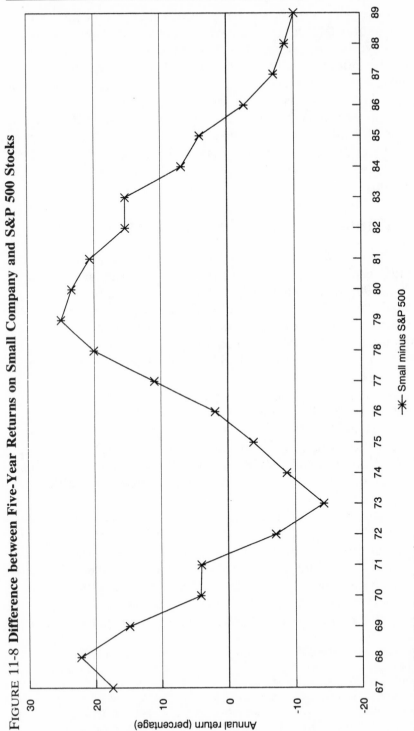

FIGURE 11-8 Difference between Five-Year Returns on Small Company and S&P 500 Stocks

Source: Data from Ibbotson Associates.

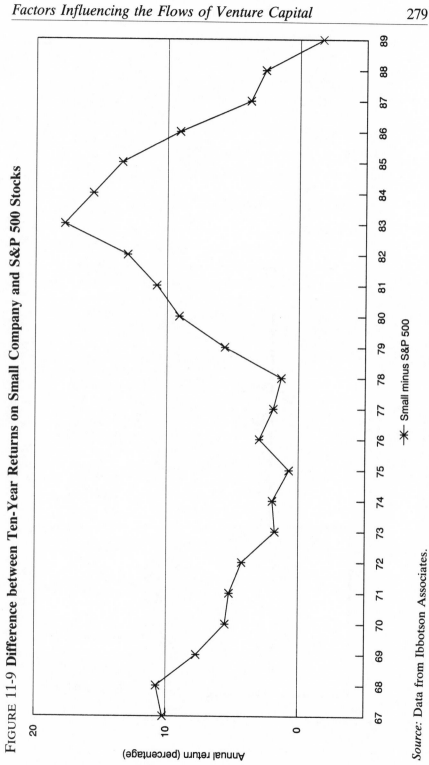

FIGURE 11-9 **Difference between Ten-Year Returns on Small Company and S&P 500 Stocks**

Source: Data from Ibbotson Associates.

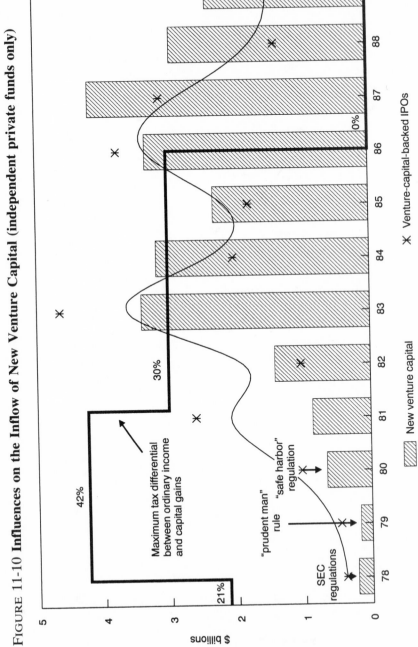

FIGURE 11-10 **Influences on the Inflow of New Venture Capital (independent private funds only)**

affects the flows of venture capital. Other changes in government regulations that facilitated the venture-capital investment process were the improved SEC regulations in 1978 and the ERISA "safe harbor" regulation in 1980.

What we have not shown in Figure 11-10 are technology and deregulation. The late 1970s and the early 1980s saw tremendous technological innovation in such industries as computers, communications, genetics, medical diagnostics, and electronics. As Rosen and many others have observed, it provided unprecedented opportunities for venture capital investments. Without doubt, Apple Computer's spectacular 1980 initial public offering, in which venture capitalists made $243 for every $1 invested just four years earlier, spurred venture capital investments in personal computer hardware and software companies. Similarly, Genentech's equally spectacular 1980 IPO, which skyrocketed from an issuing price of $35 per share to as high as $89 on the first day of trading, aroused widespread interest in biotechnology startups. It was also a period of government deregulation in such industries as telecommunications, airlines, and transportation. And what is more, it was a period when the government took a hands-off approach to acquisitions and mergers. Those technology cycles and government policies were as important—or possibly more important—than the factors shown in Figure 11-10.

The increased inflows of venture capital after the 1986 increase in the capital gains tax were a real—and very pleasant—surprise to the industry. It confounded almost everyone involved in the venture capital industry. For example, 95% of the independent private venture-capital firms responding to a 1983 U.S. congressional survey of the venture capital industry cited the capital gains tax as one of the causes of the post–1978 surge in venture capital availability, 88% listed the easing of the ERISA "prudent man" rule as a cause, and 77% pointed to the improved IPO market as yet another cause.[14] Other factors such as SEC regulations, inflation, and other provisions of the Economic Recovery Tax Act were not rated as nearly as important.

Why is it that econometric models such as those discussed here concur with intuitive opinions about the impact of the IPO market and the ERISA revision on the flows of venture capital yet differ with them concerning the impact of the capital gains tax rate? There are three possible explanations.

First, in 1983, venture capitalists did not entirely foresee the extent of the participation of tax-exempt institutions, especially pension funds, in venture capital in the 1980s. A second explanation is that venture capitalists' judgments about the importance of reductions in the capital gains tax rate are biased by their own self-interest. After all, in the venture capital process, the general partners' personal wealth is increased by reductions in the capital gains tax rate, because they pay individual income tax rates on their 20% share of the capital gains from their partnerships. And the sums involved are substantial. For example, in 1983, partners of venture capital funds expected to achieve a 30% annual compound rate of return, which would have yielded a capital gain of about $150 billion on the 1983 pool of venture capital. About $30 billion of that gain would have gone to the general partners. Thus, for each percentage point of reduction in the capital gains tax rate, the general partners would have saved $300 million in individual capital gains taxes. Is it any wonder that in the euphoric summer of 1983 when expectations were running high, venture capitalists told U.S. Congress researchers that reduction of the capital gains tax had the most potential to aid capital formation?

Third, we have focused on venture capital firms and therefore, by implication, on their sources of funds, which increasingly are institutions that are either tax-exempt or not much affected by recent changes in the capital gains tax. In light of this, let us recall the quote from *Venture Capital Journal,* which pointed out the critical role of entrepreneurs. We did not explore the effect of tax policy on the willingness of entrepreneurs to venture into the market independently with new products and processes. Nor did we deal with its effect on wealthy individuals who invest directly in small companies. There can be no doubt whatsoever that entrepreneurs and the wealthy individuals who invest in them are directly influenced by changes in the capital gains tax rates. A few of the companies started by those entrepreneurs subsequently raise money from the organized venture-capital industry. Hence, reductions in the capital gains tax increase the flow of deals, if not the flow of money, for the venture capital industry.

Overseas Venture-Capital Industries

There appears to be qualitative support for the findings of econometric models overseas. Outside the United States, the largest venture capital pools in 1984 and the highest venture-capital activity for the period 1981 to 1984 were in the United Kingdom and the Netherlands, both of which had healthy second-tier stock markets.[15] The United Securities Market (USM) was launched in London in

1980 and the Parallel Market was launched in the Netherlands in 1982. By the end of 1985, 443 companies had joined the USM, while about 40 companies were being traded on the Parallel Market. According to a 1983–1984 study by the Joint Economic Committee of Congress, the United Kingdom had the highest long-term capital gains tax rate (30%) of any of the eleven nations listed, whereas the Netherlands (along with five other countries) had the lowest (0%).[16] That evidence from the United Kingdom and the Netherlands seems to be consistent with our model, which says that a healthy second-tier market is a more important direct influence on the flows of venture capital than is the capital gains tax.

IMPLICATIONS

It would be dangerous to develop tax policy based on econometric models that simply look at the factors that directly influence the inflow of venture capital without further research on the impact of tax policy on deal flow, seed capital, and investment from all players in the industry. According to a U.S. congressional survey conducted in 1983, venture capitalists believed that of all the federal government proposals to aid U.S. capital formation and innovation, further reduction of the capital gains tax had the greatest potential.[17] When it comes to investing money, investors' beliefs and expectations are paramount. Hence, it would be foolish to change the capital gains tax without listening to the opinions of the venture capital industry. Let's not forget one of the important messages from Chapter 4: individuals play a pivotal role in the financing of fledgling companies. Silicon Valley might not have existed had it not been for the loans and investments of individuals: Hewlett and Packard began with a loan from their professor, Terman; Shockley, the co-inventor of the transistor, started Shockley Semiconductor Laboratory with financial backing from chemist-entrepreneur Beckman; when Noyce and Moore left Shockley with other members of the "Shockley Eight" to launch Fairchild Semiconductor, they obtained backing from industrialist Fairchild.

However important tax policy may be in directly encouraging venture investments, there can be little doubt that by far the most important government policies are those that foster a flourishing stock market for small company stocks and a nurturing environment for the development of new technologies. No government policy can excite entrepreneurs and investors as viscerally as a spectacular IPO. When four-year-old Apple computer went public in 1980, it made instant millionaires out of Jobs ($165 million), Markkula ($154 million), Wozniak ($88 million), and Scott ($62 million), who owned 40% of Apple. Rock's venture capital investment of $57,600 in 1978 was suddenly worth $14 million—an astronomical compound return of more than 500% per year or 17% per month. The combined acumen of all the financiers in the United States could never create one new high-tech industry without America's superb scientists and technologists who, as we showed in Chapter 4 and will discuss again in Chapter 12, depend on the federal government for support.

CHAPTER 12

The Road Ahead

IN HIS RECENT BOOK, *The Competitive Advantage of Nations,* Michael Porter makes a potent argument for the entrepreneurial process—which he describes as comprising innovation, change, entrepreneurship, and domestic rivalry: "Invention and entrepreneurship are at the heart of national advantage. . . . Our research shows that neither entrepreneurship nor invention is random."[1]

Innovative entrepreneurship is America's best chance of realizing a national competitive advantage in the twenty-first century. As this book shows, innovative entrepreneurship of the kind that built our semiconductor, computer, and biotechnology industries is where classic venture capitalists can make their greatest contribution. In this final chapter we will argue that venture capital itself is a vital element of the entrepreneurship equation and that as a nation we must do more than just tolerate venture capital. We must actively foster it.

Government policies can be a powerful—probably the most powerful—promoter or inhibitor of venture-capital-backed entrepreneurship. It is a long-term process; policy initiatives taken in the 1990s will have an effect on entrepreneurship and innovation well into the next century.

CLASSIC VENTURE CAPITAL PROS AND CONS

We have seen how venture capital acts as an important accelerator in the commercialization of new technologies. As in the cases of Intel, Apple, and Genentech, when the right opportunity comes along, classic venture capitalists are able to marshal society's resources to speed innovation and nourish new industries. They are able to mobilize otherwise dormant capital to build new companies, which in turn create hundreds of thousands of jobs and thereby generate large local, state, and federal tax revenues.

Let's look at more of David Birch's statistics. The U.S. economy created 21 millon jobs in the 1980s. Just 5% of the young and rapidly growing companies accounted for 77% of those jobs, and 15% accounted for an astonishing 94%. But while small businesses were putting Americans to work in the 1980s, giant corporations were laying them off in droves. As we mentioned in Chapter 10, *Fortune* 500 companies eliminated more than 3.5 million jobs in the 1980s. In one year alone, 1988, 3.6 million new jobs were added overall, while 400,000 jobs were eliminated by the *Fortune* 500. Today, only 5% of the U.S. work force is employed in *Fortune* 500 manufacturing plants.[2]

Birch predicts that almost 60% of all U.S. job growth in the next decade will be in six states: California, Florida, Texas, Georgia, New York, and Massachusetts. It's no accident that four of them, California, New York, Massachusetts, and Texas, account for the lion's share of classic venture capital under management in the United States. We are not suggesting that classic venture capital deserves all the credit for job growth. As a matter of fact, it only accounts for a fraction of it. But we do believe that venture-capital-backed startups are the cream of the crop—the pacesetters of advanced, knowledge-based economies that can transform whole regions. They produce the rising tide that lifts all the boats.

According to David Brophy, venture capital is an important ingredient in the transition to a knowledge-based economy. It is unlikely that a country or area can be competitive in commercial exploitation of innovative processes, products, and services without a strong local venture-capital community.[3] We saw earlier how classic venture capital was a necessary ingredient in the mix of entrepreneurs, scientists, and financiers that built high-tech industries in Silicon Valley, Route 128, and San Diego. We have also seen how the top venture-capital-backed high-tech companies account for a disproportionate share of technology, market, and product innovations. As we noted earlier, government studies indicate that roughly half the innovations in the U.S. economy come from smaller companies. And they do it with an efficiency that puts large firms to shame: smaller companies produce about twice as many innovations both per R&D dollar and per R&D scientist as do giant firms.[4]

What's more, although they are thrifty, venture-capital-backed companies certainly do not stint on R&D dollars. According to a *Business Week* article, the top ten spenders in R&D per employee were Genentech, Genetics Institute, Chips and Technologies, Weitek, Amgen, Telematics International, BMC Software, Alza, Centocor, and MIPS Computer Systems. Nor do they shave R&D spending to improve the bottom line. The top ten R&D spenders, as a percentage of sales, are Genetics Institute, Centocor, Chiron, Genentech, Alza, Telematics International, Continuum, Hogan Systems, BMC Software, and Cypress Semiconductor.[5] Those two lists read like a Who's Who of venture-capital-backed companies.

When economic times get tough, the giants are the first to pinch on R&D and investment in new plant and equipment. In 1990, U.S. corporations increased R&D by a paltry 2.2% in real dollars, making it the second-smallest real increase in 16 years. Numbers prepared by the Organization for Economic Cooperation and Development show that, on a currency-adjusted basis, R&D spending by U.S. corporations actually fell 1.6% in 1990, while other nations posted increases—France, 7.5%; Italy, 3.3%; Canada, 2.9%; and Germany, 2.8%.[6] Furthermore, the Council on Competitiveness reported that in 1990, the United States ranked dead last among the world's seven richest nations for the third year in a row in terms of its share of GNP devoted to investments in new factories and equipment.[7]

When it comes to productivity, the best venture-capital-backed companies leave the giant corporations in the dust. Look at the computer industry. Apple and Compaq rank first and second with productivity per employee of $451,600 and $317,500, respectively, compared with IBM's $184,600 (no wonder IBM's CEO, John Akers, is peevish). They even put the Japanese and Germans to shame. Their nearest Japanese competitor, NEC, is at $198,200, and their only significant German competitor, Siemens-Nixdorf, trails way behind at $106,700.[8] True, Apple and Compaq subcontract more of their manufacturing. Even so, it does not explain all the difference.

The nation cannot hope that its competitiveness will be restored by giant corporations—the sort that Congress loves to protect and subsidize. Instead, the nation must put its faith in its new and emerging companies. It's those kinds of companies that classic venture capital has historically served so well. But our research makes us concerned about the viability of classic venture capital. The incentives and competitive structure of the industry have been altered. If the trend since the mid-1980s were to persist through the 1990s, there might be little or no classic venture capital in the next century.

Classic venture capital is too important to America's long-term economic viability for the threat of its extinction to be ignored. Classic venture-capital investing is very sensitive to changes—both direct and indirect—in public policies, as we observed in Chapter 11. It cannot be taken for granted. It must not be allowed to wither because of Washington's benign neglect.

Vulture Capitalists?

As might be expected, not everyone sees it that way. One of the leaders of the semiconductor industry, Andrew Grove, the outspoken president of Intel, characterizes many entrepreneurs as little better than thieves who steal intellectual property from their employers. And the venture capitalists who fund them are, in his opinion, "the financial equivalent of ambulance chasers."[9] It seems incongruous to hear that point of view from the president of a company that itself was once a classic venture-capital-backed start-up. But what Grove and others such as Intel's chairman, Moore, and Advanced Micro Devices' chairman, Jerry Sanders, are grousing about is "vulture capitalists" who entice employees to leave their companies and start new firms based on their former employers' proprietary know-how. It was that kind of wheeling and dealing in the semiconductor industry that Charles Ferguson apparently had in mind when he accused venture-capital-backed startups of destroying America's ability to compete with the Japanese. Ferguson, an MIT academic, consultant to Intel, and ex-IBMer, has championed large corporations as America's best hope in its competitive struggle with Japan's technology giants.[10] This crusade earned him the dubious title of "vocal Cassandra of American microelectronics" from that stalwart of free enterprise, George Gilder.[11]

Ferguson has since modified his position. He now advocates that the United States should compete by adopting the practices of Japanese keiretsu. Under the arrangement he proposes, giant corporations such as IBM, Xerox, DEC, and Motorola would lead trading groups, which would channel innovations to startups and guarantee them markets and distribution.[12] Where and when, we wonder, would the microprocessor, or the personal computer, or overnight package delivery, or bioengineered insulin, have been born if U.S. industry had been organized along the lines of Ferguson's suggestion?

Industrial Policy versus Free Enterprise

The debate, of course, is not about big corporations versus startups. Rather, it concerns whether the United States should have an industrial policy. There are those who refuse to believe that more than 2,000 U.S. venture capitalists allocate society's resources efficiently and effectively under free competition. Rather than trust the judgment of the invisible hand of the venture capital marketplace, these disbelievers favor industrial planning by Washington bureaucrats. In Robert Reich's opinion, the invisible hand is spreading "chronic entrepreneurialism," which threatens to destroy the U.S. semiconductor industry.[13] It's a disease that some policymakers would like to see contained by a national industrial policy. According to Gilder, such ideas are produced by "a mind-set haunted by the ghost of Marxism";[14] for instance, a rash of industrial policy plans inundated Congress in 1982 and 1983. Many of those plans reflected an attempt on the part of the liberal establishment to chart a new economic policy for America.

We prefer to let the record speak for itself. Venture capital has served this nation well. As we hope this book demonstrates, venture capitalists play a key role in establishing new high-tech industries that no other country can match, not even Japan—the paragon for the advocates of U.S. industrial policy. Our classic venture capitalists perform spectacularly well when new technologies are at the early, innovative part of the life cycle. They help give new U.S. industries a head start over their overseas rivals. But if, as is often the case, U.S. industries lose their competitive edge as companies age, is that the fault of venture capitalists who finance their defecting entrepreneurs? Or is it the fault of managers who, as their companies grow big and lethargic, abandon the competitive spirit of the entrepreneur and adopt the asset preservation stance of the oligopolist?

Take, for example, Intel's recent attempt to ensure a continuing monopoly for its 80386 microprocessor. It went to court to try to prevent Silicon Valley rival Advanced Micro Devices from marketing a competing 386 chip. So far, the courts have ruled in AMD's favor. AMD 386 chips are now being used in PCs, and, according to technical reviews, they outperform Intel's and are just as reliable. Intel has responded by competing more aggressively both with a vigorous marketing campaign and by accelerating the introduction of its 486SX processor.[15] If the 386 competition between Intel and AMD is what Grove had in mind when he said that U.S. semiconductor firms "are in a demolition derby and some of us are going to die,"[16] then we think he is misinterpreting what's happening. That is, the sort of domestic rivalry that limbers up U.S. companies and makes them better able to compete with the Japanese.

On the other hand, the "roller derby" argument says that unfettered domestic competition means a fragmented industry with many relatively small entrepreneurial competitors, none of them big enough to compete against the Japanese. That spells ruin for the U.S. semiconductor industry. Bigness is best when competing with the Japanese, because, the argument goes, the bigger the business, the greater its economies of scale and, hence, the lower its per-unit costs of R&D, production, marketing, distribution, and capital.

The fact is that in manufacturing industries where the Japanese beat the Americans, it's the Japanese who have to contend with intense domestic competition. What's more, the Japanese domestic market is substantially smaller than the American market. Consider cameras. While Kodak dominated its U.S. competitors after World War II, infant Japanese companies had to contend with plenty of domestic competition in a nation still struggling to get back on its feet. Look at automobiles. There are three times as many different auto manufacturers in Japan as in the United States. The picture repeats itself with motorcycles, televisions, radios, electrostatic copiers, and camcorders. Competition has made the Japanese more competitive. We will take unfettered entrepreneurial competition every time over an oligopoly. Oligopolists should heed what General MacArthur is reported to have said, "There is no such thing as security in this world. There is only opportunity."[17]

OUTLOOK FOR VENTURE CAPITAL IN THE 1990s

An entirely changed venture-capital industry is emerging. Ten years ago, 80% of the world's identifiable venture capital was in the United States. Today, that figure is below 40%. Other nations are now investing in venture capital at a much faster rate than the United States is. What might that imply for the creation of new industries in the next century? The two industrial nations we fear most are paying attention to venture capital. Japan's industry is blossoming. And Germany has suddenly awakened, moving up to number three in Europe. We shudder to think what that might foretell for America's economy. If Japanese and German venture-capital firms become as successful as their U.S. counterparts at building new industries, America could lose its principal competitive advantage. It could decline to a second-rate industrial power.

There are other reminders of a very different environment in the 1990s. The bloom is off the rose for LBOs and MBOs. Valuations have dropped precipitously according to Merrill Lynch. The severe constipation of bank credit has created a buyer's market. For entrepreneurs and venture capitalists, it's the best of times and the worst of times: it's an excellent time to buy but an awful time to sell a company.

WINNING STRATEGIES: 1960s AND 1970s VERSUS 1980s

In Chapter 2, we examined the structure of the venture capital industry and how it changed. The implied strategies of venture capital firms have changed significantly as well. In its glory days of the 1960s and 1970s, classic venture capital heeded these maxims:

1. Invest in the management team and the market potential.
2. Stress value-added company building.
3. Concentrate on startup and early-stage companies.
4. Be a lead investor.
5. Invest for ten years, maybe longer, but harvest when appropriate.
6. Raise a new fund once your present fund is performing well.
7. Deal-making and transaction skills are important but not central to the value creation process.

But in the 1980s a new strain of venture capitalists suddenly sprang up, merchant capitalists who (dare we say it?) turned out to be a greedier, speedier breed. Many adopted some of the following strategies:

1. Raise new funds while the money is flowing instead of when you need the money.
2. Rely on financial engineering for quick entry and exits.
3. Exploit hot IPO markets to harvest early and often.
4. Co-invest; do not be the lead investor.
5. Look to later-stage LBO and MBO deals for larger minimums and faster returns.

6. Invest in publicly traded stocks that seem to be underpriced.
7. Worry less about the management team (you can shape it later). Worry more about the fiduciary expectations of the limited partners.
8. Trade the horse before the horse dies!

Strategies in the 1980s grew less venturesome and more impatient. The new merchant capitalists lost sight of who their primary customers were; many behaved as though limited partners were the real customers. Entrepreneurs took second place in their affections.

LOOKING AHEAD TO 2000

In Chapter 1, we examined the major changes that occurred in the industry in the 1980s. Now we will offer our prognosis for venture capital in the year 2000 if current trends continue. Remember, ten years ago, few people could have foreseen the state of the industry as it is today; our crystal ball may be murky, too. With that caveat, here are our speculations:

1. Market mechanisms cull underperformers from the industry. The U.S. shake-out ends by the mid-1990s, with about 40 or so top performers earning returns higher than 20%.
2. The U.S. industry, with $45 to $50 billion under management, ranks third behind Europe and Japan, respectively.
3. A shake-out begins in the European venture-capital industry, mirroring what happened in the United States five or so years earlier.
4. A new technology wave (parallel to the microprocessor and the biotechnology era of the 1970s) precipitates a surge of interest in startup and early-stage investing.
5. The 1980s' style of merchant capital steadily loses ground to creative financial strategies and alternative sources of capital.
6. Increasingly savvy entrepreneurs seek only the 50 to 75 venture capital firms known for value-added skills and committed to structuring deals in ways that equitably share risks and rewards with management.
7. Mergers with strategic partners—like those pioneered by biotechnology companies—become the harvest of choice because IPO markets are too unpredictable.
8. More and more, seed-stage companies are built with the intent of merging with giant corporations rather than going public.

As a result, they concentrate on building R&D assets rather than generating quick profits.

9. A unique form of venture capital emerges in the erstwhile Eastern bloc nations and the former Soviet Union with hundreds of links to Western venture capital and investment banking, especially in Germany.

10. Competition for deals, capital, and venture capital know-how becomes global.

If America is to keep its lead in the twenty-first century in the creation of dynamic new industries, it must change some national attitudes and policies. High-tech industries emerged and flourished in the United States because its economic climate was favorable for technology entrepreneurs and their venture capital supporters. America must ensure that it not only preserves but also enhances that favorable climate. It has these characteristics: a culture that prizes entrepreneurs, a population second to none in education, and a government that generously supports pure and applied science, that fosters entrepreneurship with enlightened policies, and that enables schools to produce the best-educated students in the world.

It's a tall order. But it's the only prescription for leadership in a knowledge-based world. It will require companies that are focused, fast, flexible, and flat (the so-called four Fs): focused on market niches for high-value products; fast to respond to changing technologies and markets; flexible in the way they get things done; and flat, that is, structured with as few levels of hierarchy as possible.[18] It will be the "era of the other," in which, as Regis McKenna observed, the fastest-growing companies in an industry will be in the segment labeled "others" in a market-share pie chart.[19] By and large, there will be newer entrepreneurial firms rather than large firms with household names.

Not long ago, Rosabeth Kanter said that giant firms would have to "learn how to dance" if they were to compete successfully with the 4F generation.[20] Ross Perot, the founder of EDS, was more direct. He said that making General Motors entrepreneurial was like teaching an elephant to tap-dance. But it seems to us that instead of tap-dancing on their own, giant firms prefer waltzing with entrepreneurial partners. Big firms are relying increasingly on strategic partnerships with entrepreneurial firms, many of them venture capital backed, in order to get access to desirable R&D. It is a trend that is well under way. Hoffmann–LaRoche, hurting for new blockbuster prescription drugs, purchased a majority interest in Genentech and is buying the highly regarded biotechnology called PCR (polymerase chain reaction) from Cetus for $300 million.[21] Eli Lilly purchased Hybritech. IBM has recently entered into strategic agreements with Apple, Borland, Go, Intel, Lotus, Metaphor, Novell, Stratus, Thinking Machines, and Wang for the purpose of gaining computer technologies. One observer has even gone as far as to suggest that the way of the future for U.S. industry is with giant firms concentrating on M&D—marketing and development—and relying on smaller, entrepreneurial firms for their R&D.[22]

Needed: 50 Million Entrepreneurs

Just to keep up with population growth, let alone the number of new immigrants, the U.S. economy must generate about 10,000 jobs every working day. That amounts to 2.5 million new jobs each year—at least 125 to 150 million new jobs between now and the year 2050. Where are those jobs going to come from? It's our belief that the trend of the 1980s will continue: small, entrepreneurial firms will generate most of the new jobs. Projecting present trends on the births, survivals, and job creation rates of startup firms, we estimate that the nation will need at least 50 million—perhaps as many as 100 million—new entrepreneurs over the next fifty or so years.

We are confident that entrepreneurs will rise to the challenge, provided that society enables them to do so. Unfortunately, we see very disturbing trends suggesting that society's faith in entrepreneurship is waning. Yet, when it comes to the creation of new industries, entrepreneurship goes hand in hand with creativity and technology. In our opinion, those three areas—creativity, technology, and entrepreneurship—are America's most distinctive competencies in the world of business.

Let's look at how well the United States is doing at furthering creativity, technology, and entrepreneurship from the point of view of culture, education, and government.

Culture Robert Noyce stands alongside the all-time greats of technological entrepreneurship. For good reason, he was dubbed "mayor of Silicon Valley." Yet when he died suddenly on June 3, 1990, the media for the most part ignored his passing. *The Boston Globe*, the leading newspaper for Route 128, did not carry an obituary. Nor did the three national TV networks—whose operations owe their very existence to the fruits of Noyce's inventiveness—do much better. Here was a man who did more than any other entrepreneur to build the $50 billion semiconductor industry, which in turn drives a $500 billion electronics industry. But most Americans were unaware of his death unless they read the *New York Times* or *The Wall Street Journal* or lived in California. What a contrast to Rex Harrison's death one day earlier. The major claim to fame of that British star of stage and screen was as Henry Higgins, the professor who taught Eliza Doolittle to speak the king's English in *My Fair Lady*. The TV networks eulogized him on evening news programs.

We think the news coverage of those two deaths is symbolic—relatively speaking—of how little society appreciates its entrepreneurs. It wasn't always that way. One of the authors is old enough to remember, as a child in England, the day Henry Ford died. The event made headlines in the English newspapers. What has happened? Well, one thing is certain: it has become fashionable for some thinkers to debunk the image of the self-made entrepreneur operating under the discipline of the free market as the hero of the U.S. economy. According to Reich, "the self-made man as the force behind the vast mobilization of the economy from 1870–1920 was a myth that became a cultural ideal."[23] And recall how Ferguson cast entrepreneurs in the role of villain in his scenario—for a tragedy—for the U.S. semiconductor industry.

What's more, when it comes to technology, the mass media are quick to criticize. Day after day, the media carry alarming stories about the ills brought upon society by technology: acid rain, the greenhouse effect, nuclear power, oil spills, airplane crashes, cancer, and so on. Every hiccup, no matter how trivial, at a nuclear power plant is solemnly reported. In early 1991, TV viewers were awestruck by the success of Patriot missiles blasting Scud missiles out of the skies over Israel and Saudi Arabia—in real time on live TV. It was a technological tour de force. But no sooner was the Gulf War won than the media trotted out self-styled experts to highlight the shortcomings of the Patriot missile. It would be easy to get the feeling that American technology is failing the nation. What a contrast to the optimistic attitude of society in the post–World War II era. Grateful to scientists and engineers for such wartime triumphs as radar, penicillin, and atomic bombs, the nation was in love with science and technology. That love affair was a crucial part of America's favorable economic climate through the 1960s.

No wonder our youth is turning away from industry and science. A 1981 survey of Harvard freshmen found that only 7% intended to become scientists, whereas 24% were planning careers in law.[24] It foretold a disturbing trend in the 1980s: a shortage of science graduates and a surfeit of lawyers. How can our country hope to compete with Japan when 24% of our finest young minds want to be lawyers? Do we really need 281 lawyers per 100,000 people, when Japan makes do with only 11 and even Britain gets by with only 82? Can a society litigate its way to greatness?

A few years ago, one of the authors addressed the tenth anniversary gathering of the David Syme Business School of the Chisholm Institute of Technology at the Melbourne Opera House. "What advice do you have," he was asked, "for a nation that desires economic growth?" He told the audience: "When your nieces and nephews, your daughters and sons sit on your knee and ask what they should do when they grow up, what do you tell them? A doctor, a lawyer, a dentist, a teacher, a public servant. Why not an entrepreneur, or a venture capitalist? If you want to light the fire of economic progress, these are the flames."

Education Americans must be educated to their full potential if they are to succeed in today's knowledge-based society. Yet there is universal agreement that we are graduating students who are inadequately educated. The problem is particularly acute in mathematics and science—the very basis of an advanced society. It is an appalling story of failure across the board from the poorest inner-city elementary schools to the most elite graduate schools.

Amar Bose is an archetypal MIT professor–entrepreneur. Partly out of his frustration with the hi-fi systems then on the market, he founded, in 1964, the hi-fi corporation that bears his name. Today, his company has 3,000 employees in the United States, Europe, and the Far East. Annual revenue is over $350 million. It leads an industry comprising approximately 450 sound-system manufacturers. Bose Corporation has the best-selling speaker in Japan. It competes very successfully in Germany.

Bose is an educator-engineer-entrepreneur worth listening to. He continues to teach engineering at MIT, the school he entered as a freshman in 1947 and never left. He has a passion for education. But he is concerned that U.S. standards have declined to the point where it will be extremely difficult for America to catch up with the educational systems of its archrivals in the global economy, Japan and Germany. According to Bose, students in his MIT course today are able to cover about two-thirds of the material that students covered 20 years ago.

In science and mathematics, excellence matters above all else, but not, apparently, when it comes to admission to top universities. Highly competitive schools, especially in California, have been systematically rejecting Asian-American candidates not—as might reasonably be expected—because their SATs and GPAs are too low. On the contrary, it's because their scores are too high. They are being rejected in the pursuit of racial diversity in student populations.[25] What message does that convey to high school students who are contemplating a career in science? What does it imply for America's future?

Here are some education statistics that give cause for concern: In primary school Japanese children spend 52% more time in class than do Americans and in junior high 60% more. When it comes to homework, the Japanese in primary school spend 8.3 hours per week on it versus 1.8 hours for Americans; in junior high 16.2 versus 3.2 hours; and in high school 19 hours versus 3.8 hours. Alan Blinder, a Princeton economics professor, used those statistics to estimate that 12 years of Japanese education are equivalent to 22.3 years of American education.[26] Only 46% of graduating U.S. high-school seniors have seventh-grade math skills or better; 28% of high school students do not graduate. Students are failing miserably in science, geography, history, languages—indeed everything, it seems, except sports. Which work force is better prepared to meet the challenge of the knowledge-based revolution now transforming the economies of developed nations, the American or the Japanese?

It's true that American education emphasizes creativity. And that's just as well, because it may be our only remaining competitive advantage, according to such observers as Bose. But it would appear that we may be in danger of losing that advantage because of how we educate most MBA students.

As *Fortune* 500 companies find themselves bedazzled by Japanese manufacturing brilliance, American business schools have responded by introducing more courses dealing with improving operating efficiencies. In so doing, they run the risk of inculcating MBAs with an incremental improvement mentality—the kind that produces suggestion boxes brimming with production refinements rather than ideas for creating daring new products and processes. Of course, we must fine-tune existing operations to make them as efficient and effective as possible. Perhaps we can match Japan's manufacturing wizardry—although U.S. automobile manufacturers' inability to catch up to the Japanese suggests that's doubtful, at best. But left-brain logical analysis won't put U.S. industry ahead of its foreign competition. There is much more to good thinking than that. We need more right-brain imagination. Unfortunately, MBA courses tend to emphasize analysis at the expense of intuition and creativity. As Doriot once remarked, there is no idea that an MBA cannot analyze to the point where it's not worth pursuing. Or as Fred Smith of Federal Express put it, an MBA builds a career in a large organization by saying no more often than saying yes. Dean LeBaron, head of Batterymarch Financial Services, went further when we asked him if business schools were teaching students the right skills. He replied there is nothing a new MBA can do that a microprocessor can't.

America's best hope for a competitive advantage will come by doing what it does best: creativity, technology, and entrepreneurship. No other nation comes even close to equaling the United States in those areas, but they are not taught well, if at all, in most schools of business. True, some schools have made great strides with entrepreneurship courses. But in most schools, creativity is ignored. And technology is neglected, even at business schools surrounded by technological companies. At a time when America needs its brightest MBAs in manufacturing industries, we are not doing enough to excite those students about careers in technology-driven companies.

According to a 1988 *Business Week* survey, recruiters for high-tech manufacturing companies rated Harvard as their favorite hunting ground for MBAs.[27] But their bag appears to have been rather meager. Consider these statistics from the *1988 HBS Placement Report*.[28] Thirty-three percent of the Harvard Business School's incoming class had degrees in science or engineering, but only about 10% of its graduating class entered high-tech manufacturing companies, while almost 50% entered finance or real estate companies. It appears that, in the mid-1980s, Harvard was turning scientists and engineers into financiers and realtors. And if that is what was happening at the favorite business school of high-tech recruiters, it seems reasonable to infer that most other schools were doing worse.

To paraphrase a lovely verse from the Book of Common Prayer, have we taught the things we ought not to have taught, and left untaught the things we ought to have taught? Ask any MBA student about Boesky, Icahn, Milken, Kravis, Pickens, and

Trump, and you will learn more about leveraged buyouts and real estate deals than you ever wished to know. But ask a student about Fleming, Shockley, Bardeen, Watson, Crick, Fermi, and Townes, and you will, more often than not, draw blank stares, even though the discoveries of those Nobel laureates led to products that transformed our very existence. One of us heard a professor teaching a computer course at a well-known business school—not Babson or Harvard, we hasten to add—tell his MBA students that Sony invented the transistor. Not one of the students challenged that statement. And they were in Boston, the hub of high tech!

Is there something fundamentally wrong in business schools with both what we teach and how we teach it? Our students largely ignore scientists, engineers, and entrepreneurs who move society forward by creating new products, new companies, new jobs, and new industries, but they idolize financiers whose primary "creation" for mankind is junk bonds. Does anyone believe that KKR's leveraged buyout of RJR is something to be admired? It was as monstrous a case of megagreed as there has ever been, even by the gargantuan standards set by Wall Street in the 1980s. To satisfy that greed, plants may be closed, jobs may be destroyed, capital investment may be curtailed, R&D budgets may be pared down, and so on. Of course, Henry Kravis—a man who has never run a manufacturing company—will tell you that he is doing it to restructure American industry. What's worse, our students will believe that story if we say it is so.

Are we overstimulating students' greed glands by glamorizing the exploits of financial swashbucklers while downplaying the daring deeds of high-tech entrepreneurs? We should be producing students who admire job-creating entrepreneurs rather than job-destroying financial manipulators. Whom should they admire more: Ken Olsen, the founder of DEC, who heads a company with 120,000 employees worldwide, or Henry Kravis, the junk-bond artist, who destroys jobs? There should be no contest. Yet many students prefer to emulate Kravis because he has amassed a personal fortune reported to be in excess of $300 million in about a decade of wheeling and dealing, whereas Olsen has accumulated a fortune of about the same size after a lifetime devoted to building a company brick by brick and to leading the minicomputer industry.

The future of the U.S. economy is secure if venture capitalists continue to put their trust in builders like Olsen. There is definitely no future if we put our faith in what Reich called "paper entrepreneurialism," the manipulation of assets and liabilities on paper.

That kind of financial engineering produced the spectacle of Kravis and H. Ross Johnson brawling over the right to purchase RJR for more money than classic venture capitalists have invested in all the high-tech startups since the beginning of time! If business schools continue to produce graduates better suited for financial engineering and cost cutting than for creating innovative new products and building new companies, the outlook for America in the next century will be bleak indeed.

Role of Government   While the government doesn't direct industrial policy, it does play many crucial roles in high-tech entrepreneurship. It funds research and development in university and government laboratories; it is a customer; it supports education; it passes laws that foster entrepreneurship, and sometimes—although never with deliberate intent—it passes laws that inhibit entrepreneurship. For now, let's look at the vital role of government in the development of technologies. Elsewhere, we write about rules and regulations.

The military is the arm of government that spends the most on research and development. The organized venture-capital industry itself came into existence because of all the technologies that had been developed with military money during World War II. The first investment of the first venture-capital company was $200,000 invested at the end of 1946 by ARD in High Voltage Engineering Corporation, which was founded by five men who had worked together at MIT during World War II.* HVE's initial product was a high-energy X-ray machine that had been developed to examine weapons.

The digital computer came into existence because of the need to speed up the computation of gunnery tables. Even the fastest mathematician took hours to compute one trajectory using an electromechanical calculator, and each table contained thousands of trajectories. The wartime need to speed things up led to military-funded ENIAC at the University of Pennsylvania during World War II. From the very beginning of the computer industry, the government was a major customer for computers. Indeed, it was

---

*The lead entrepreneur was John Trump, the president was Denis Robinson, and the chief scientist was Robert Van de Graaff. For trivia buffs, Trump was Donald Trump's uncle.

the Census Bureau that took delivery of the first commercial computer, UNIVAC, the direct descendant of ENIAC.

Similarly, it was the U.S. Air Force that saw the need for interactive computing. That is why it funded the SAGE defense system to protect the United States against surprise attack from the air. MIT's Whirlwind was the heart of the SAGE system. In a manner of speaking, DEC was an offshoot of the SAGE project.

From those early beginnings with ENIAC and Whirlwind in the 1940s and early 1950s, the military has pushed relentlessly to arm itself with the very best electronic warfare equipment. The Gulf War of 1991 provides ample evidence of the prowess of that equipment. The awesome power of those electronic systems had the world spellbound. Patriot missiles intercepted Scuds in flight and blasted them from the sky. Laser-guided bombs plummeted down the heating and ventilating shafts of communications centers. Tomahawk cruise missiles launched from ships in the Persian Gulf flew hundreds of miles and struck within ten yards of their intended targets in Baghdad. Artillery officers used GRiD laptops to compute shell trajectories on the battlefield.

Forty years or so after ENIAC and Whirlwind were born, their offspring fought the first computer war—on-line, in real time. Perhaps a more apt name would be the microprocessor war because it was the computer on a chip that provided so much of the brains of the systems. Whirlwind—the finest computer in 1950—required 20,000 electronic tubes, filled a huge room, and required immense amounts of power. It was hardly the kind of thing that could be taken onto a battlefield, let alone flown in the air. Semiconductors changed all that. Almost as soon as the transistor had been invented, the military recognized its immense advantages over vacuum tubes in electronic circuits. About ten years after its invention, the U.S. Department of Defense was purchasing about 40% of all U.S. semiconductor production.

Clearly, military spending was important in the growth of the semiconductor industry and played a role in the development of Silicon Valley.[29] Just as clearly, military spending was important in the development of the computer industry. In 1990, total sales of military electronics in the United States were estimated to be $55 billion, or 21% of the nation's $225 billion electronics industry. About 25% of the Pentagon's $214.5 billion budget was spent on developing, testing, buying, and maintaining weapons.[30] And the military continues to be a major force in the development of new technologies. Although Silicon Valley and Route 128 companies are not as dependent on military spending as they were in the 1950s and 1960s, the military continues to play a crucial role as it pushes technologies to their limits.

Military spending may have taken the lion's share of government spending on R&D, but the importance of nonmilitary spending in the development of science and technology should not be overlooked. There is no better example than biotechnology. The United States is preeminent in this revolutionary industry because the U.S. government has been far more generous than any other nation with its support for research in biological sciences. According to a 1984 U.S. congressional study of the international biotechnology industry, the United States was supporting basic biotechnology research to the tune of about $500 million per year compared with about $60 million each by Japan, Britain, France, and West Germany.[31] That same study claimed that America enjoyed its lead in the biotechnology industry because of the financial and tax incentives provided by the government, the amount of government support for R&D, and the degree to which government policy ensured that there were sufficient well-trained experts.[32] Undoubtedly, U.S. support for the basic life sciences provided a fertile breeding ground for scientists and their discoveries, but the revolutionary industry would not have sprouted up in the 1970s without what was then a singularly American pursuit: channeling venture capital to risky, high-technology startups founded by scientists with the entrepreneurial bug.

THE TWENTY-FIRST CENTURY

The next century poses enormous opportunity—and risk—for the United States. As we see it, entrepreneurship will have to produce the majority of the jobs that must be generated just to maintain stable employment. Washington, however, seems to be betting more on osmosis and serendipity than on deliberate initiatives to create those jobs. We agree with Porter that there is a "legitimate role for government in shaping the context and institutional structure surrounding companies and in creating an environment that stimulates companies to gain competitive advantage."[33] We would be the last to argue for heavy-handed regulations and policies. To borrow management scholar James March's metaphor of organizational design, we see the purpose of government initiatives to encourage entrepreneurship as placing snow fences to deflect the drifting snow rather than building snowmen.[34] It's time to adjust those snow fences. As Robert Fildes, CEO of Cetus, wrote, "We must get [Washington] to see that when we decide to cut back on research funding, fail to provide incentives for long-term investments and protect investors from Wall Street's excesses, or fail to fund technical education, we are affecting our industrial sector—and our future quality of life—in a very detrimental way."[35]

Support for Basic Sciences and Research and Development

The miraculous wave of technology products during the 1970s gave birth to some of the fastest-growing new industries and companies the world has ever seen. The federal government, more than any other single source, was responsible for that wave through investment in basic science in universities and national laboratories, support of R&D in industry, and purchase of products. The beginning of the 1990s, compared with the 1970s, has been relatively quiescent when it comes to technology waves. But the next major wave is sure to come as long as Washington continues to support basic science and R&D.

We cannot predict what the next wave will be. Indeed, ever since the first industrial revolution began in Britain in the 1760s, when a wave of new technologies suddenly swept across the nation, it's been impossible to predict revolutionary technology. Experts can even be wrong about their own fields:[36]

> [The nickel-iron battery will put] the gasoline buggies . . . out of existence in no time. (Thomas Edison, 1910)
> Man will not fly for fifty years. (Wilbur Wright to his brother Orville, 1901)
> I think there is a world market for about five computers. (Attributed to Thomas Watson, chairman of the board of IBM, 1943)
> There is not the slightest indication that [nuclear] energy will ever be obtainable. It would mean that the atom would have to be shattered at will. (Albert Einstein, 1932)

Governments have a special knack for getting it wrong:

> [Edison's ideas] are good enough for our transatlantic friends . . . but unworthy of practical or scientific men. (Report of a committee set up by the British Parliament to look into Edison's work on the incandescent lamp, circa 1878)
> When the last [U.S.] census was taken, to wit 1880, the census man did not consider the electric lighting investment of sufficient

importance to warrant him collecting the data. Today the investment is $107,000,000. And how long has it taken for this vast sum to be attracted to the electric light field? Only six years!"[37] *Scientific American,* March 1888.

Throughout the 1970s, when companies such as Altair, Ohio Scientific, Commodore, Atari, and Radio Shack were pioneering in the fledgling microcomputer industry, Ken Olsen did not believe there was a market for personal computers. In his view, they were toys for playing electronic games. He didn't believe that anyone seriously needed one at home.[38] Nor did he believe that there was any future for personal computers in the office. He is reported to have said, "The personal computer will fall flat on its face in business."[39] If Olsen, an entrepreneur-engineer without peer in the computer industry, could be so wrong in his prediction, it would be foolhardy for us even to try. Nor do we have much confidence that government experts can do any better. But Washington can target general areas of science and technology that appear to have the most promise. And in these times of huge budget deficits, it is of paramount importance that it continue to support, as generously as possible, basic science and research and development. Here is one example of an area that needs more attention.

Materials science is a huge industry, estimated to be about $150 billion worldwide, including, among other things, ceramics, metals, semiconductors, superconductors, insulators, plastics, and solar cells. The field is bursting with excitement and new discoveries. High-temperature superconductivity, discovered by now–Nobel laureates Bednorz and Muller at IBM's Swiss research laboratory not much more than five years ago, is one such discovery;[40] it is already the most cited technology in the science literature.[41] And no wonder; one day, it might permit electricity to be transmitted with virtually no losses. If that promise can be realized, it will trigger a revolution as important as any in the history of electricity.

Research into materials requires extensive facilities. Of course, there is a remote possibility that a lone investor will produce a radical breakthrough in this field. For instance, 80-year-old Alvin Marks in Athol, Massachusetts, thinks he has a way to generate electricity inexpensively at a projected production cost of one cent per kilowatt hour compared with fossil fuel at about five cents per kilowatt hour. Marks's patented process uses polarizing film, Lumeloid, to produce electricity from sunlight. The electricity industry thinks Marks's process is sufficiently promising for the Electric Power Research Institute (EPRI) to fund his research with $100,000. Skeptics, however, doubt that it will ever be commercially viable.[42] If he pulls it off, Marks will have beaten very long odds indeed, because materials research requires so much equipment that it is virtually impossible to conduct it on a shoestring, as Marks did before he was backed by EPRI.

Marks and his like excepted, materials research requires huge investments that only well-financed companies and governments can afford. It is research that Washington, somewhat belatedly, has recognized that it must support more generously, in light of America's declining competitive position relative to Japan and Germany. Federal nondefense spending on materials R&D has fallen by 17% in real dollars since 1980. The Bush administration is planning to boost its funding of materials research by hundreds of millions of dollars. But will that be enough? The Materials Research Society claims that government and industry in America must increase R&D funding by $1.25 billion per year just to stay competitive.[43]

The difficulty for Washington is the abundance of projects clamoring for funding—cancer cures, neurobiology, AIDS research, the human genome project, the supercollider, the manned mission to Mars, fusion, environmental concerns, artificial intelligence, the national aerospace plane, the strategic defense initiative, and so forth. One of the biggest challenges facing Washington is deciding which projects to support. Nevertheless, today more than ever, we cannot afford to let up on funding for basic science and R&D.

Haphazard as the U.S. government's funding may appear to be in comparison with the Japanese strategy of targeting specific technologies, it has served the nation well in creating a technological lead in many new industries. The real challenge is in maintaining and consolidating that lead. To do that requires sustained investment in growing companies, a supportive regulatory environment, respect for intellectual property, and well-educated workers. We will now look at how those factors affect entrepreneurial businesses and make proposals for policy initiatives that we believe could improve the climate for entrepreneurship.

Investment

The key to stimulating investment is the cost of capital and its availability. In the summer of 1991, there was some good news amid the gloom about the crises in the banking and insurance industries: the stock market hit record highs, interest rates were trending downward, and inflation remained low. Consequently— and perhaps this is the best news of all—the cost of funds for big businesses was at its lowest point in many years. According to Shearson Lehman Brothers, the weighted average cost of debt and equity, adjusted for inflation, tax, and accounting differences in the United States (5.9%) was slightly lower than in Japan (6.1%), although it remained higher than in Germany (4.8%). That was an astonishing reversal from the mid-1980s. For instance, in 1985, the comparable costs of capital were 9.7% in the United States, 5.9% in Japan, and 3.9% in Germany.[44] Small wonder that investment by U.S. big business in the 1980s was anemic.

With low cost of capital, labor costs among the lowest of the advanced industrial nations, and improving manufacturing productivity, some observers believe that the stage is set for the rest of the world to worry again about America's business prowess.[45] Presumably, they mean big business, because capital for seed and startup companies—if it is available at all—is still too expensive. The banking industry crisis has hit smaller businesses particularly hard, not just in the United States but also in other countries such as Britain and Australia. Entrepreneurs are blaming banks for the demise of their businesses. Sometimes feelings run very high, as in the case of an embittered small-businessperson who was recently on Australian television touting the slogan "Shoot a banker, save a business."

Bear in mind that startup businesses in general cannot borrow money from banks or, if they can, only when they have collateral. Those fortunate enough to get a loan pay interest much higher than the bank's prime rate. Also, startup companies have no earnings to invest in themselves nor have publicly traded stock. Instead, they must rely on family, friends, wealthy individuals, and venture capital firms for funds. Thus the most obvious way to increase the availability of capital and to lower its cost is to cut the capital gains tax for investments in startup businesses.

Capital Gains Taxes By eliminating the favorable treatment of capital gains, the 1986 Tax Reform Act deterred investments in high-risk, long-term, illiquid investments, diverting money from classic venture-capital investments to less risky short-term, liquid investments. Simply put, it reduced the amount of money invested in new companies. That flaw in the 1986 act can be rectified by enacting a capital gains tax differential that encourages investments in small startup and early-stage ventures.

No tax issue is more polarizing than whether capital gains should be treated more favorably than ordinary income. Both sides make extravagant claims. According to one article advocating a cut in the capital gains tax, "There would be no recession today if the financing of small young companies had not collapsed after 1986, when tax reform raised the top capital gains rate to 33%."[46] Others claim that there is scant evidence that a cut in the capital gains tax will increase investment and that, if it does, the increase will be too small to make a noticeable difference in the overall economy. Furthermore, they claim, it benefits mainly the rich at the expense of the poor.

In the 1988 presidential election, George Bush and his economics adviser Michael Boskin championed a cut in the capital gains tax—a measure opposed by Michael Dukakis and his adviser Larry Summers. To date, President Bush has been unable to persuade Congress to pass his proposals for a lower capital gains tax. Proponents and opponents generally divide along party lines, with Republicans in favor and Democrats—except for a few Sun Belt renegades—opposed. In October 1990, with his popularity running high, President Bush was fervently insisting on a cut in the capital gains tax while at the same time approving a hike in other taxes. Democrats successfully framed it as a rich-versus-poor issue. The proposal for a capital gains tax cut was shelved. Kevin Phillips claims that the issue is the Republicans' Achilles' heel, citing a December *Wall Street Journal* poll that found the majority of Americans favored increasing the capital gains tax, not decreasing it.[47] Phillips may be right, to judge from President Bush's dampened ardor for the capital gains cut. True, he mentioned it—almost perfunctorily—in his January 1991 State of the Union address and occasionally since then, but his efforts are desultory compared with the fervor of his 1990 crusade.

Those favoring a cut in the capital gains tax need to take a new tack if they are to get the support of American voters and Congress. We believe that job creation is the issue that will get voter support. Who could begrudge Olsen a break on his capital gains tax when he founded a company that employs more than 120,000 people worldwide? We believe any proposal to reduce the capital gains tax must concentrate on investments in entrepreneurial small businesses. After all, small businesses generate most of the new jobs, and they—in contrast to big businesses—badly need more plentiful supplies of capital and at lower cost.

Any capital gains tax reduction most definitely must not encourage—as did previous cuts in capital gains rates in the late 1970s and early 1980s—financial engineering and real estate wheeling and dealing. It was excesses in those areas that were responsible for the savings and loan disaster. Who stood to benefit most from the capital gains in the deals that S&Ls partially financed? Milken, Keating, and their ilk. And who is now burdened with extra taxes to pay for their excesses? Every taxpayer in the nation, including small savers who put their faith in S&Ls, some people whose jobs were eliminated to help pay the crushing debt heaped on some LBOs, and some retirees whose pensions were slashed when LBOs ran into trouble. Can you blame most voters for not believing that cuts in the capital gains tax bring them benefits?

We hasten to stress that some LBOs and some MBOs are very beneficial. Consider, for example, Lau Technologies of Acton, Massachusetts. It was formed in March 1990 as a leveraged buyout by Joanna Lau, three co-founders, and 21 employees of Bowmar-ALI. Lau and her team increased the company's annual revenue from $7 million to $22 million in just 18 months.[48] That is the type of leveraged buyout that we would encourage.

Our proposal for a tax break for investment in small entrepreneurial businesses will, above all else, produce social benefits by creating badly needed jobs. As a reward for generating those jobs and renewing the economy with new goods and services, there would be direct financial benefits for three stakeholder groups: first, entrepreneurs themselves; second, individual investors; and third, professional venture capitalists and their limited partners. The focus of our proposal is on startup and early-stage investments in operating companies, i.e., companies producing products and not shuffling assets on paper. The changes it suggests would reward patient investors who seek to create long-term value. We believe that the capital gains tax should be cut to half the maximum rate on ordinary income, or even eliminated entirely, for investments meeting all three of the following criteria (real estate wheeler-dealers and holding companies would be excluded):

- The investments are in small companies with less than $25 million of net tangible assets at the time of the investment.

- They are in companies with sales in the prior twelve-month period of less than $20 million.
- They are held for at least five years.

Losses on those types of investments would be deductible from gross income. In addition, there would be a lifetime exemption for small business owners on the first $1 million of capital gains realized from the business in which they work full time.

On August 17, 1991, President Bush, refusing to take action that would have extended benefits for the unemployed, observed that the way to fix unemployment would be a capital gains tax cut, which would quickly create jobs. Then why not tie capital gains tax benefits directly to job creation? It would make a cut much more acceptable to workers—after all, it is one of the main justifications for favorable tax treatment of capital gains. But it might not be acceptable to investors. The last politician who proposed to do that was Dukakis in 1989 as governor of Massachusetts. His proposal was met with howls of protest from Massachusetts investors, so he dropped it. Nonetheless, we believe it is feasible. The fact is, every business already has to report periodically the number of its employees to various state and federal agencies. And we know of at least one venture-capital firm, Massachusetts Capital Resource Company, that reports to the Commonwealth of Massachusetts the number of jobs it creates or preserves by investing in its portfolio companies.

Our proposed cut will benefit all sizes of startups from the smallest mom-and-pop business to the more high-tech venture. It's the latter that this book is all about, so let's examine how our proposed cut would boost investing in the early-stage companies that classic venture capital has long favored. Would-be entrepreneurs would be more likely to leave well-paying jobs if they knew that the reward for building a business would be taxed at a very favorable rate compared to ordinary income. Consider a person like Bill Foster, who founded Stratus Computer in 1980. He left a top management position at Data General. By that time, the "golden handcuffs" of the corporate world were on him: excellent salary and fringe benefits and a lot of stock options. With the cost of rearing and educating a growing family, it's difficult to walk away from the corporate life and risk all the family savings, as Foster did. A big differential in favor of capital gains versus ordinary income would make starting a company more enticing for would-be entrepreneurs like Foster. What's more, if they were successful, they would be better rewarded when they realized their capital gains.

Most entrepreneurs get the seed money to start their businesses from their own savings, family and friends, and "angels." Angels are an extremely important source of startup capital. Bill Wetzel, the University of New Hampshire authority on this topic, estimates that angels invest as much as $30 billion annually, which is an order of magnitude more than professional venture-capital firms invest. Those angels are not extraordinarily wealthy. They are upper middle class with median incomes around $100,000 per year.[49] More often than not, they are entrepreneurs themselves. An important source of their wealth is the capital gains tied up in their own businesses and other startups in which they are invested. Hence, a cut in the capital gains tax would be an incentive for them to harvest some of their investments. That would increase the amount of angel money available for investment in new startups. What's more, a capital gains tax cut, plus the ability to deduct all losses from gross income, would improve their overall rate of return from startups compared with other less-risky investments.

Few entrepreneurs ever get capital from the professional venture-capital industry, but those that do are often the pacesetters for an industry. Classic venture-capital investing in seed and early-stage companies would increase if our proposal were implemented because (1) more high-potential entrepreneurs would take the plunge, (2) more money would be available from entrepreneurs themselves, their family and friends, and angels—Apple, Federal Express, Genentech, and Intel started out with money from these sources, (3) wealthy individuals who invest in venture-capital limited partnerships would benefit, so they would be more inclined to invest in venture capital funds, and (4) the after-tax returns to venture-capital general partners would increase, so they would have a greater incentive to seek out and invest in early-stage deals.

The only certainty about the current capital gains tax situation is that it will be changed. Only the how and when are in question. Since the capital gains tax was introduced in 1918, it has been changed in a major way at least eight times. Some nations thought of as far more taxing than the United States actually have lower capital gains tax rates (Figure 12-1). Consider the following: Switzerland, Italy, South Korea, Taiwan, and West Germany have zero tax on long-term capital gains, while Canada, the Netherlands, and France have lower rates. Of course, as we pointed out in Chapter 11, we are not

FIGURE 12-1 **International Comparison of Capital Gains Tax Rates**

Country	Maximum tax rates on capital gain		Long-term holding period
	Short term	Long term	
United States current law	33%	33%	More than one year
President's proposal	Ordinary rates	15%	7/1/89–12/31/92—more than 12 months 1/1/93–12/31/94—more than 24 months After 12/31/94—more than 36 months
United Kingdom	40%	40%	Not applicable (gains are adjusted for inflation over period of ownership)
Switzerland	0	0	Not applicable
Canada 1989 post-1989	19.91% 22.40%	19.91% 22.40%	Not applicable (individuals are eligible for a lifetime exemption of $100,000)
Japan	20% of the net gain or 1% of the gross sales price	same	Not applicable
The Netherlands	20% Generally there is no tax on capital gains. However, there is a 20% tax on the gains from a substantial interest in a company.	20%	
West Germany	56%	0	Six months
Australia	50.25% (49% + 1.25% medicare levy)	50.25%	Not applicable (basis indexed for inflation if asset is held longer than 12 months)
France	16% Gains are taxable only if they exceed FF288,400 (approximately $45,000) per family in a tax year.	16%	Not applicable

claiming that capital gains taxes are the sole influence on a nation's venture capital industry. The United Kingdom, for instance, has one of the highest capital gains taxes (40% maximum rate) yet the European Venture Capital Association, in its 1991 yearbook, states that "the UK probably has the most favorable legal and fiscal environments for venture capital in Europe."[50] In 1990, there was more venture capital in the United Kingdom than in all the other European countries combined. Even so, the chancellor of the exchequer in his 1991 budget acknowledged the need to provide some capital gains tax relief for entrepreneurs and managers and adopted a tapering mechanism based on a proposal by the British Venture Capital Association.[51] Perhaps the U.S. Congress will follow suit. In August 1991, New York Governor Mario Cuomo, standard-bearer of liberal Democrats, proposed that the federal capital gains tax be cut to 10% for assets held five to six years. To pay for it, he suggested that the top rate on ordinary income be increased from 33% to 38% and that possibly the tax rate for short-term capital gains be increased as well. By February 1992, President Bush was once again pushing for a capital gains tax cut to revive the economy and, at the same time, stimulate his bid for a second term in the White House.

Regulatory Policy

The United States and the United Kingdom have the largest pools of venture capital in the world because they have the most favorable regulatory environments for facilitating venture capital of any of the advanced nations. Nonetheless, there is room for improvement.

Consider, for example, biotechnology products, which for the most part are finding applications in areas that are highly regulated. The Food and Drug Administration (FDA) has been unable to cope with the increased flow of new products. Washington regulators find it all too convenient to take the politically expedient route of caving in to small, vociferous groups who seek to ban or at least delay the introduction of biotech products because of their superstition that those products pose a very dangerous threat to the human race. For a multinational pharmaceutical corporation that is a serious impediment, but for a small biotech company, it can spell financial ruin. As the late Soichiro Honda, a consummate global entrepreneur, said about government officials, they "tend to become an obstacle when you try something new."

Even worse is what happens after the FDA approves something. Once on the market, biotech products—drugs in particular—

face product liability suits with the potential of damage awards so huge that they cannot be covered fully by insurance. Some awards are so high that they can wipe out a small business. But Congress—where lawyers are overrepresented but small-business owners and scientists are scarcely represented at all—has stubbornly rebuffed all attempts to impose limits on product liability claims. Plaintiffs deserve to receive adequate recompense for actual damages. But when juries award damages lavish enough to impair even a company as rich as Croesus, it's time for Congress to act.

Intellectual Property

In an advanced knowledge-based society, respect for intellectual property is essential. A biotech startup, for example, spends the early years of its life developing products. It burns a great deal of cash to build that intellectual property. It may be five years or more before it has a commercial product. At that point, it is very vulnerable to a predator stealing its intellectual property.

The patent office needs to speed up its processing of patent applications without lowering its standards. Currently, in an attempt to speed things up, it is issuing some doubtful patents. Competing companies then sue each other to settle the matter. Litigation has emerged as the fastest way to make money in biotechnology.[52]

Even patent protection may not prevent a well-heeled competitor from riding roughshod over a small company's rights. The costs of a patent suit and the three to five years that it is likely to be tied up in the legal system simply preempt a credible defense by many small firms. There are numerous examples of this. One of the most notorious involved the CAT scanner, which was invented and patented by Godfrey Hounsfield of EMI in Britain. It did more to revolutionize medical diagnosis than anything since the invention of X-ray apparatus at the turn of the century. It earned Hounsfield the Nobel Prize—surely, there could be no better validation of a patent. Yet within a few years of its commercial introduction, EMI had competitors both great and small in the United States, Germany, Israel, Japan, and the Netherlands. Among them were giants such as General Electric, Siemens, Philips, Johnson & Johnson, and Pfizer. EMI sued. But by the time the U.S. courts decided in its favor, EMI had been forced out of the CAT scanner market and acquired by Thorn. If that happened to EMI, a large British firm, imagine what could happen to a small company.

Well-Educated Workers

The mass-production age was dominated by production lines on which workers were treated as automatons. It was the era of the machine. Today is the age of knowledge-based industries and of the thinking worker. Now industries run on gray matter not muscle. A superb educational system is a must for this era.

The news about education is discouraging. Achievement levels decline even as we direct greater financial resources to our schools. It seems to us that the more we spend, the worse the overall education level of our graduates. On a per-pupil basis, we are spending more in real dollars to educate our children than ever before in U.S. history, but by any objective measure, the quality of our graduates is declining. If dollars held the key to a good education, New Hampshire SAT scores would be among the lowest in the nation, not, as is the case, among the highest. In education, as in most of its public spending, New Hampshire is thrifty. To be candid, it's downright stingy compared with, say, Boston. But we'll leave that debate to others. Here is a proposal that we think will help industry find the educated workers it needs.

Investing in human capital   In the era of mass production, public policy favored investment in plant and equipment. In the knowledge-based era, policy must favor the formation of human capital. Just as we gave tax incentives such as accelerated depreciation and investment tax credits to companies that invested in plant and equipment, we should today give similar credits for investments in human capital. We propose that companies in certain industries should be allowed to assume payment of all the student loans that a worker has accumulated before being hired. Companies would be allowed to capitalize the loans as assets on their balance sheets. They would be given a 10% tax credit against such loans and would be able to write them off on a five-year accelerated depreciation schedule.

Let's see how this would work. An engineering student graduates with debt that has financed his or her education. A high-tech company hiring that graduate can, if it so chooses, assume responsibility for paying off that debt. If the graduate leaves the firm before the debt is paid off, he or she is responsible for paying off the remainder of the debt. The next company to hire that student can also take over the remainder of the debt.

This benefit would not apply to all graduates in all industries.

It definitely should not benefit, for example, lawyers. With 50% of the world's lawyers generating 18 million lawsuits every year, the U.S. legal profession needs no encouragement. Our proposed incentive would target mathematicians, scientists, engineers, technicians, production workers, and others who work in product companies.

Teaching entrepreneurship　Some academics say entrepreneurship cannot be taught. Of course, we cannot guarantee to produce a great entrepreneur from our entrepreneurship courses any more than a music professor can promise to produce a Mozart or a physics professor an Einstein. But give us a student with entrepreneurial traits—determination, dedication, and inspiration—and we are confident we will produce a better entrepreneur. A business school with no entrepreneurship courses is as incomplete as a medical school with no obstetrics courses. Without entrepreneurs, there would be no businesses, and hence no business schools. Yet only 500 to 600 four-year colleges and universities worldwide offer at least one entrepreneurship course.

We suspect that the number of courses dealing with Marxism dwarfs those dealing with entrepreneurship. Even though former Soviet students have toppled the statues of the Marxist's pantheon, Karl Marx remains, ironically, one of the few European males in good standing with the politically correct movement on American campuses, and *Das Kapital* is still required reading in many courses. We would hope that the work of Schumpeter, whose book explained why entrepreneurship is the force that moves a free enterprise economy forward, will be more widely read as communism gives way worldwide to free enterprise.

Some universities are making great strides in celebrating entrepreneurs and their accomplishments. Babson College, for instance, created the first Global Academy of Distinguished Entrepreneurs in 1977. To date, 48 of the world's most famous entrepreneurs have been inducted into this Hall of Fame. Among them are Ken Olsen (DEC), Berry Gordy (Motown Industries), Sandra Kurtzig (ASK Computer), Ray Kroc (McDonald's), Soichiro Honda (Honda Motor Car Company), Heinz Nixdorf (Nixdorf Computer), Mary Wells Lawrence (Wells, Rich, Greene), William McGowan (MCI), Amar Bose (Bose Corporation), Byung-Chull Lee (Samsung), Kazuo Inamori (Kyocera Corporation), Diane Von Fürstenburg (DVF, Inc.), An Wang (Wang Laboratories), John Johnson (Johnson Publishing), Trammell Crow (Trammell Crow

Company), Nolan Bushnell (Atari), Fred Smith (Federal Express), Peter Sprague (National Semiconductor), Don Burr (People Express), Paul Fireman (Reebok), and Fred Hamilton (Hamilton Brothers Petroleum).

The Kenan Institute of the University of North Carolina houses the Hall of Fame for Ernst & Young's Entrepreneur of the Year winners. Its co-sponsors are Merrill Lynch and *Inc. Magazine.*

There are numerous business plan contests sponsored by universities throughout the country. The Association of Collegiate Entrepreneurs (ACE) has chapters on many campuses nationwide. The fastest-growing number of endowed chairs in U.S. universities and colleges are for professors who teach entrepreneurship. Those chairs mostly have been donated by successful entrepreneurs, who are among the most generous of all benefactors. They understand how important it is to get students excited about free enterprise and entrepreneurship.

VENTURE CAPITAL IN PRACTICE: STRATEGIES FOR THE 1990s

A Flawed Marriage: Pension Funds and Classic Venture Capital

Recently, we visited with an organizer of a new venture-capital fund aimed at classic venture-capital investing in environmental businesses. He reported a conversation with a pension fund money manager who had some potential interest in the new fund—until the money manager learned that the fund was targeted at around $30 million with each investment in the $1 to $1.5 million range. "The fund is too small; you can't invest enough money for us, the payback is too long, and our money will be too illiquid and too risky," concluded the money manager. In other words, it wouldn't enable him to meet the objectives by which his performance was measured. His response summarizes a fundamental pattern of the 1980s that led to increasing fund size, larger investments per company, and pressure for earlier cash distributions to limited partners. We also suspect that the 2.5% to 3% management fees were another reason for larger fund sizes.

Contrast the preceding scene with the policy of two other funds that are concentrating on classic venture-capital deals in the 1990s. The policy of both is to have: no institutional backers; instead, all the limited partners are individual investors. The strategy of these funds is to avoid pension funds and institutional investors at all cost. Why? We detect from our on-going analysis of the industry the existence of a new theory of merchant capital, which is incongruous with classic venture capital. In essence, the pension industry in the early to mid-1980s was sold by fund organizers (and it bought) the "classic venture capital" promise but ended up owning merchant capital that produced savings bank rates of return, or, in some instances, even worse. In a few instances, returns exceeded expectations, but such cases were all too rare. The venture capital mitosis in the 1980s turned out to be a mutant cell, as we have argued, consisting of the two distinct types.

Incongruous Compensation and Rewards for Money Managers

One result of all this is a major incongruity between the nature and requirements of classic venture-capital investing and the prevailing measures of performance and methods of rewarding institutional money managers. The pension fund industry needs to examine this mismatch carefully and to devise new motivational standards and incentive systems. The way it currently stands, applying existing performance measures to money managers responsible for investments in classic venture-capital funds is like tying Michael Jordan's bonuses to the number of yards gained rushing and bases stolen! If money managers are awarded annual bonuses based on their quarterly investment performance and realized cash-on-cash distributions and year-end returns, we see little hope that pension funds and institutional money managers will do anything but favor merchant capital funds and others over classic venture-capital funds. The current compensation practices in the pension industry are diametrically at odds with the longer holding periods, illiquidity, higher risk, more difficult and complex valuation requirements, deal flow sources and deal sizes, potential rates of return, and value-added investing strategies of classic venture capital. Such a mismatch can only lead to disappointment and failure. Wouldn't it make sense for the industry to recognize these two distinctly different capital markets and devise dual-reward mechanisms to match the unique requirements of each? Why not motivate fund managers with a capital-gain-driven bonus and thereby encourage and reward long-term, classic venture-capital investing?

Already there is a case to be made that many in the pension fund industry may be making an inadvertent, longer-term strategic blunder by opting out of participation in venture capital funds for

the wrong reasons. First, the prevailing mismatch between performance and reward measures and the requirements of classic venture
capital is encouraging counterproductive practices. Since they cannot win in their short-term incentive system, pension fund managers
are passing up precisely those longer-term opportunities in classic
venture capital that offer the highest ultimate return and make the
most difference to the economy and the nation. Second, savvy
classic venture capitalists who have recognized these paradoxes are
in increasing numbers simply eliminating pension funds from their
short list of desired limited partners. Their reasoning is clear: we
cannot deliver the short-term performance results by which pension
fund managers are measured that would justify their investment in
our fund. In other words, they make lousy financial partners.

New Incentive Structures for Venture Capital Pools

One of our colleagues has characterized the formation of a new
venture-capital fund as "the immediate transfer of wealth from the
limited partners to the general partners!" This insightful observation may not amuse the suppliers or users of venture capital, but
it strikes at the heart of another incongruity: the prevailing incentive
structure for fund organizers and their dismal performance in the
1980s. It is not surprising that at this writing pension funds are
abandoning investing in venture capital to a degree very reminiscent
of the early 1970s. To reverse this trend, there needs to be a better
match between institutional sources and venture capital funds. One
way to achieve this to encourage bolder and more aggressive incentives structures, such as:

1. *A graduated carried interest structure* with a threshold rate
of return to the limited partners of 10% to 12% (roughly five
percentage points over prime) before any carry is realized; a 10%
carry if the cash-on-cash return is up to 15%; a 20% carry up to a
20% return; a 30% carry up to a 30% return; a 35% carry up to
a 35% return; and a 40% carry for a fund that achieves a return
of 40% or higher. Only general partners who believe they can
achieve superior performance would be willing to make such a bet,
and the downside for limited partners would be very small.

2. *Proportionate gains and losses* for both limited and general
partners. This would create an incentive structure quite different
from current practice. Presently, general partners bear only 1% of
the losses but typically enjoy 20% of the gains. If general partners
also bore 20% of the losses, we contend that the pattern of too
much money chasing too few good deals in the 1980s would have

been severely curtailed, since overinvesting and excessive risk taking would also penalize in a meaningful way the general partners.

3. *A fixed management fee* that reflects the true economics of managing a partnership, rather than a percentage of capital under management. When combined with a graduated carry this would put the performance incentive in line with the actual risks. It would eliminate the prevailing incentive to raise larger and larger funds, since the evidence indicates that this effectively undermines classic venture capital. (It may also turn out that it may not help the ultimate returns of merchant capital either.) A fixed fee would eliminate windfall earnings by general partners simply because they could raise a larger fund and enjoy certain economies of scale while achieving a performance that is weak to miserable. It would also discourage new entrants hoping to benefit from the inherent windfalls of the traditional approach.

4. *Limited partners on the fund advisory board* whose primary concern is with portfolio valuation. This practice has already been adopted by some funds. A classic venture-capital fund ought to meet no more frequently than semi-annually, possibly even annually, rather than quarterly. Once a majority of its investment portfolio reaches the harvest stage, the partners and advisers might opt to meet more frequently to confer on the tricky decisions surrounding exit strategies and timing.

5. *New valuation standards* that recognize the differences between classic venture capital and merchant capital. Anyone knowledgeable about the industry today can recognize that we are dealing with an apple and an orange. Determining the value early on of a portfolio of startup companies is extraordinarily difficult and subjective. One portfolio consisting of very young companies with a cost basis of $10.5 million was estimated to be worth as little as $9.5 million to as much as $21 million by different experts.

Gatekeepers

The so-called gatekeepers who advise pension fund managers and other institutional money managers on where to invest monies targeted for venture capital funds are playing an increasingly influential role in the industry, yet it may be that they add a layer of cost but no real value to the venture capital process. Further, they may make an already quite imperfect market even more imperfect by guaranteeing that the vast majority of capital ends up in the follow-on funds of a chosen few. They may play a useful role in matching pension funds with merchant capital funds, but, unfortunately, this appears to be at the expense of classic venture-capital funds.

Structural Impediments to Classic Venture Capital

Historically, high rates of return on venture capital have coincided with peaks in the NASDAQ index. In the United States in 1969, 1983, and 1986, hot IPO markets created an abundance of harvest opportunities and, in the 1980s, sustained high valuations long enough to enable investors to achieve liquidity after the expiration of Rule 144 and any underwriter lock-up requirements. In the United Kingdom and France, the USM and second market bolstered venture capital returns. However, the OTC and unlisted securities markets are simply too fickle and uncontrollable to make harvest strategies that depend upon IPOs anything but a perpetual nightmare. Strategic partnerships with major corporations, which are growing in popularity as an alternative to IPOs, offer some relief, but they are only a partial solution.

Some significant new proposals merit our encouragement and support. Two critical areas were noted by Alan Patricof in a piece in *Pensions and Investments:* (1) the underwriting system, and (2) the accessibility of appropriate trading markets.[53] Both the American Stock Exchange and the National Association of Securities Dealers are considering proposals that address these two areas. The AMEX, according to Patricof, has suggested developing "an incubator market" with lower listing standards where the securities of fledgling companies could be traded. NASD is considering markets for the thousands of companies that have long been traded sporadically on the pink sheets.

We agree with Patricof that the SEC's introduction of Rule 144A in April 1990 was important in bringing institutions into the marketplace earlier, forestalling the need for IPOs and giving corporations a new tool for spinning off subsidiaries. This freed up a potential $100 billion in private placement money for securities of young companies that previously were difficult to sell under SEC rules. Following Rule 144A, the NASD set up the PORTAL market, and the AMEX is considering a similar move. Potentially, this could enable 4,000 institutions with $100 million or more to trade in what had been illiquid investments. While 144A has been slow to take hold, it certainly represents a step in the right direction. Initiatives such as these, once established in the United States, could be transferable to other nations, creating further sorely needed liquidity for venture investments.

THE ROAD AHEAD

Disillusions and disenchantment usually follow periods when the
true meaning of a task is ignored and forgotten. Venture capital
seems to have shifted from a constructive, difficult task to a new
method of speculation. Capital gains have become a primary goal
instead of considered as a reward for a constructive task well
done. Manufacturing capital gains seems to be of far more importance than manufacturing products. As a matter of fact, in many
cases the latter seems to be of little importance.[54]

That's how Doriot expressed his concern about changes for
the worse in the venture capital industry when he wrote to stockholders on February 4, 1972, in anticipation of ARD's merger with
Textron. The words could easily have been written at the end of
the 1980s. Let's hope they are not a prophecy for the 1990s. The
greatest challenge facing venture capital firms today is to achieve
superior rates of return—rates that are adequate for the risk involved. We have always argued that venture capital is the art and
craft of the exceptional. In order to achieve exceptional returns in
the 1990s, venture capital funds face a major strategic challenge:
how to differentiate themselves in the marketplace for risk capital.
They can do it if they focus on value-adding as their most important
competence.

Earlier in this book, we presented the Porter-Sahlman-
Stevenson analysis of the venture capital industry (see Figure 2-
15). What is the picture in 1991? We see the following changes in
Porter's five forces already taking place (Figure 12-2): (1) Within
the industry, competition may be lessening, because some firms,
unable to raise new funds, are actually leaving the business. (2)
The threat of new entrants has diminished. In 1990, new funds
raised just $139 million, compared with $1.75 billion raised by
follow-on funds.[55] (3) Limited partners—the major suppliers of
capital to venture capital firms—have adjusted their expectations
for returns to more realistic levels. Returns of 15% are now acceptable as opposed to the expectations of 25% or higher that were
common in the late 1980s. However, limited partners are less
inclined to invest in venture capital funds, so the amount of money
raised in 1990 was well below peak levels. They are also demanding
better terms. Some now have gatekeepers to advise them on which
funds to invest in and on what terms. In 1990, gatekeepers were
involved with 19% of all new capital commitments versus only 10%
in both 1988 and 1989. Their influence on pension funds is especially

FIGURE 12-2 **Determinants of Venture Capital Industry Profitability, 1992**

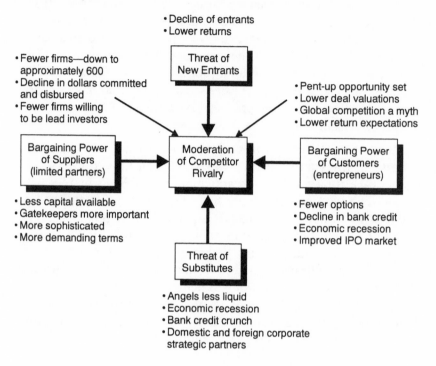

• Decline of entrants
• Lower returns

Threat of New Entrants

• Fewer firms—down to approximately 600
• Decline in dollars committed and disbursed
• Fewer firms willing to be lead investors

• Pent-up opportunity set
• Lower deal valuations
• Global competition a myth
• Lower return expectations

Bargaining Power of Suppliers (limited partners)

Moderation of Competitor Rivalry

Bargaining Power of Customers (entrepreneurs)

• Less capital available
• Gatekeepers more important
• More sophisticated
• More demanding terms

• Fewer options
• Decline in bank credit
• Economic recession
• Improved IPO market

Threat of Substitutes

• Angels less liquid
• Economic recession
• Bank credit crunch
• Domestic and foreign corporate strategic partners

pronounced. In 1990, they directed 35% of pension dollars committed to venture capital funds, up from 25% in 1989.[56] (4) Small entrepreneurial firms—the customers for venture capital—are hurting for capital because of the credit crunch brought on by the recession and the banking crisis. This has enabled venture capital firms to drive harder bargains with their portfolio companies and should translate into higher rates of return. We are not sure yet if the number of startup firms that deserve to receive venture capital is increasing. (5) Bank debt as an alternative to venture capital for financing late-stage deals has decreased, but corporate financing as a substitute for deals at all stages has increased as big companies seek strategic partnerships with innovative small firms.

We ask the reader to refer to Figures 1-8 and 6-2 and to reflect on Figure 12-2. Looking ahead, what predictions can be made from these data and patterns concerning (1) the flows—i.e., supply—of venture capital, and (2) the rates of return during the coming decade? When the current shrinkage of supply and shake-out are over, most likely by or during 1993, we would expect both the supply and rates of return to improve. In fact, with the lowered valuations and decreased competition among venture capital firms in 1990–1991, combined with a strong IPO market in 1991, this is already happening. We speculate that investors who came in to funds from 1989 to 1991 are quite likely to achieve a substantially better rate of return in the 1990s. Even entering 1992, this evidence suggests it is still a good time for limited partners to invest in venture capital funds with proven records. On balance, the industry in the early 1990s looks very similar to what it was in the early to mid-1970s: it is the best time in over a decade for both limited and general partners. An overreaction and withdrawal from venture capital investing by money managers now will result in missed opportunities for superior returns in the 1990s.

Our research shows that successful startup and early-stage investing—the heart and soul of classic venture capital—is actually more *management-intensive* than *capital-intensive*. This carries important implications for the operating strategies of venture capital firms. Firms that focus on the basic strategy of classic venture investing are most likely to achieve superior returns. But those firms will have to:

1. Concentrate on the quality of the management and the market potential of their portfolio companies.
2. Seek the more active role of the lead investor.
3. Focus on where they as general partners can bring the most know-how, wisdom, and contacts.
4. Devise creative harvesting alternatives to IPOs. Strategic partnering, which has proven its viability in biotech, is one such alternative.
5. Raise additional funds only on the basis of superior investment opportunities, not on the basis of available money.
6. Devise creative deal structures that ensure equitable incentives for investors and management.
7. Establish links to the global venture-capital network via alliances, joint ventures, reciprocal investing, co-investing, and exchange of people.

A FINAL WORD

The venture capital industry has reached a crossroads, and the direction it takes will have serious implications for its future. For practitioners, the roads lead to either opportunity or peril—

opportunity for those who focus on value-adding and peril for those who bring only capital to venture capital deals. For policy-makers, the crossroads represents an opportunity to shape the environment for entrepreneurship and venture capital for the twenty-first century in a way that can go far to revive America's compet-itiveness. Academics also have choices to make and new avenues to explore in their research and teaching. As fields of formal study, entrepreneurship and venture capital are in their adolescent stages; scholars have a chance to build solid intellectual foundations for both of them. The choices are there.

Mark Twain once remarked, "I was seldom able to see an opportunity, until it had ceased to be one!" Let us hope we will all have better vision.

Notes

Chapter 1

1. "The Economic Impact of Venture Capital," a joint study conducted by Coopers & Lybrand, Strategic Management Services, and Venture Economics, Inc., presented by R. Joseph Schlosser, managing associate, Coopers & Lybrand, at Venture Forum '90, October 25, 1990, San Francisco.
2. "The Most Entrepreneurial Place on Earth," *Inc. Magazine* (March 1990), pp. 60–61.
3. According to David L. Birch of Cognetics, Inc. as quoted in ibid., p. 60.
4. Special appreciation is extended to Bert Twaalfhoven, founder and chair of Indivers, who compiled the data for this chart. Twaalfhoven is an avid and generous supporter of the entrepreneurship studies at Harvard.
5. "Venture Performance," *Venture Economics,* 1989, p. 5.
6. Patrick Liles, "Sustaining the Venture Capital Firm," unpublished Ph.D. diss., Harvard Business School, 1969, p. 29. We have drawn heavily on this work here since it is the best single history of ARD.
7. *Boston Sunday Globe,* December 28, 1946.
8. Liles, "Sustaining the Venture Capital Firm," p. 31.
9. Ibid.
10. Gene Bylinsky, "General Doriot's Dream Factory," *Fortune,* August 1967, p. 130.
11. *Venture Capital Journal,* special report (July 1990), p. 14.
12. "Tough Times Seen for SBA's Venture Capital Program," *The Wall Street Journal,* January 24, 1990, p. B2.

13. "Venture Capital's New Look," *The Wall Street Journal,* May 20, 1988, p. B2.
14. "Venture Capital Dims for Start-Ups, But Not to Worry," *The Wall Street Journal,* January 24, 1990, p. B2.
15. David Warsh, "Harder Times Ahead for Venture Capital," *Boston Globe,* March 6, 1990, p. B1.
16. "Risky Business," interview with Ben Rosen, *Inc. Magazine* (March 1990), p. 20.
17. *Venture Capital Journal* (April 1990), p. 1.

Chapter 2

1. "Acquisition Exits Outpace IPOs for Third Year in A Row," special report, *Venture Capital Journal* (May 1990), pp. 13–15.
2. "The Tokyo Connection," *Inc. Magazine* (February 1990), p. 52.
3. Jeffry A. Timmons, *New Business Opportunities* (Acton, MA: Brickhouse Publishing, 1990), pp. vii–xi.
4. George Jenkins, "Venture Capital is Cautious: Who Will Fund Start-Ups?" *Harvard Business Review* (November–December 1989), p. 117.
5. Jeffry A. Timmons and David E. Gumpert, "Discard Many Old Rules About Raising Venture Capital," *Harvard Business Review* (January–February 1982), pp. 152–157.
6. "Risky Business," interview with Ben Rosen, *Inc. Magazine* (March 1990), p. 20.

Chapter 3

1. Thomas J. Soja and Jeffry A. Timmons, "Structural Changes and the International Growth of the Venture Capital Industry 1970–1989," working paper no. 90-071, Harvard Business School, 1990, p. 1.
2. "A Global View of the Venture Capital Industry, 1987–1988," *Venture Capital Journal* (December 1989), p. 10.
3. "LBOs Never Were Much Fun Anyway," *Venture Capital Journal* (July 1990), p. 18.
4. "Capital Commitments to U.K. Venture Capital Funds in 1989," *UK Venture Capital Journal* (January 1990), p. 7.
5. *Venture Capital Journal* (December 1989).
6. *Venture Capital in Europe: 1989 EVCA Yearbook* (Zaventem, Belgium: EVCA Secretariat, 1990), p. 11.
7. "A Global View of the Venture Capital Industry," p. 13.
8. *Annual Report 1989–1990* (Canberra, Australia: Management and Investment Companies Licensing Board, 1990), pp. 14–15.
9. "A Global View of the Venture Capital Industry," p. 17.

10. *Venture Capital in Europe: 1990 EVCA Yearbook* (Zaventem, Belgium: EVCA Secretariat, 1990), p. 10.
11. "Building a Competitive Strategy in Venture Capital," interview with Alan J. Patricof, *Asian Venture Capital Journal* (January 1990), p. 28.

Chapter 4

1. E. Braun and S. MacDonald, *Revolution in Miniature: The History and Impact of Semiconductor Electronics* (New York: Cambridge University Press, 1978), p. 38.
2. S. Ramo, "How We Can Regain Our Competitive Edge," *Scientific American* (May 1989), p. 148.
3. W. Shockley, "Statement on Technology and Economic Growth before the Subcommittee on Economic Growth of the Joint Economic Committee, U.S. Congress" (Washington, DC: U.S. Government Printing Office, 1976).
4. D. Hanson, *The New Alchemists: Silicon Valley and the Microelectronics Revolution* (Boston: Little, Brown, 1982).
5. Everett M. Rogers and Judith K. Larsen, *Silicon Valley Fever: Growth of High-Technology Culture* (New York: Basic Books, 1984), p. 102.
6. D. Lindorff, "The Venture 100: No Limits to Growth," *Venture* (May 1982), pp. 30–42.
7. Rogers and Larsen, *Silicon Valley Fever*, p. 105.
8. S. B. Quinn, "Managing Innovation: Controlled Chaos," *Harvard Business Review* (May–June 1985), pp. 73–85.
9. *The Economist*, January 25, 1983.
10. T. M. Doerflinger and J. L. Rivkin, *Risk and Reward: Venture Capital and the Making of America's Great Industries* (New York: Random House, 1987), p. 11.
11. Ibid.
12. James C. Worthy, *Portrait of a Maverick* (Cambridge, MA: Ballinger, 1987); "America's Most Admired Corporations," *Fortune*, January 6, 1986, pp. 16–17.
13. Worthy, *Portrait of a Maverick*.
14. Conversation in 1983 with Bill Congleton, then general partner of The Palmer Group venture capital firm.
15. Personal experience of one of the authors, WB, when he made a presentation to ARD's board.
16. Glenn Rifkin and George Harrar, *The Ultimate Entrepreneur: The Story of Ken Olsen and Digital Equipment Corporation* (Chicago: Contemporary Books, 1988), p. 13.
17. E. Romanelli, "Contexts and Strategies of Organization Creation: Patterns and Performance," working paper, The Fuqua School of Business, Duke University, 1987.

18. Rifkin and Harrar, *The Ultimate Entrepreneur,* p. 15.
19. Ibid., p. 34.
20. Ibid., p. 29.
21. Romanelli, "Contexts and Strategies of Organization Creation."
22. Tracy Kidder, *The Soul of a New Machine* (Boston: Atlantic–Little, Brown, 1981), p. 16.
23. Ibid., p. 15.
24. A. Smith, "Silicon Valley Spirit," *Esquire* (November 1981).
25. *Business Week,* January 14, 1991, pp. 101, 124; K. K. Wiegner and A. Senia, "Power Shift," *California Business* (October 1989).
26. "Calculating Reality," *Scientific American* (January 1991), pp. 101–109.
27. T. H. Nelson, *Computer Lib* (Chicago: Hugo's Book Service, 1974).
28. A. Osborne, *Running Wild: The Next Industrial Revolution* (Berkeley, CA: Osborne/McGraw-Hill, 1979).
29. Rogers and Larsen, *Silicon Valley Fever,* p. 11.
30. Ibid., p. 9.
31. Rifkin and Harrar, *The Ultimate Entrepreneur,* p. 195.
32. Ibid., p. 208.
33. Rogers and Larsen, *Silicon Valley Fever,* p. 12.
34. Rifkin and Harrar, *The Ultimate Entrepreneur,* p. 214.
35. W. A. Sahlman and H. H. Stevenson, "Capital Market Myopia," *Journal of Business Venturing,* vol. 1, no. 1 (1986), pp. 7–30.
36. P. David, "Congress Told US Ahead, Japan Second, Rest Nowhere," *Nature,* February 2, 1984, p. 402.
37. "Snapshot of a New Industry," *Nature,* February 2, 1984, p. 400.
38. R. A. Fildes, "Strategic Challenges in Commercializing Biotechnology," *California Management Review* (Spring 1990), pp. 63–72.
39. W. F. Hamilton, J. Vila, and M. D. Dibner, "Patterns of Strategic Choice in Emerging Firms: Positioning for Innovation in Biotechnology," *California Management Review* (Spring 1990), pp. 73–86.
40. M. D. Dibner, *Biotechnology Guide—U.S.A.* (New York: Stockton Press, 1988).
41. Fildes, "Strategic Challenges in Commercializing Biotechnology."
42. Doerflinger and Rivkin, *Risk and Reward,* p. 228.
43. "Promises, Promises, Promises," *The Economist,* October 5, 1991, p. 69.
44. D. G. Mitton, "Bring on the Clones: A Longitudinal Study of the Proliferation, Development, and Growth of the Biotech Industry in San Diego," in N. C. Churchill, et al., eds., *Frontiers of Entrepreneurship Research 1990* (Wellesley, MA: Center for Entrepreneurial Studies, Babson College, 1990); "Tracking the Trends in Designer Genes: A Longitudinal Study of the Sources and Size of Financing in the Developing Biotech Industry in San Diego," in N. Churchill,

ed., *Frontiers of Entrepreneurship Research 1991* (Wellesley, MA: Center for Entrepreneurial Studies, Babson College, 1991).

45. Ernst & Young. Reported in the *Boston Herald,* April 23, 1991, p. 27.
46. *Venture Capital Journal* (December 1990), p. 19.
47. " 'Antisense': A Drug Revolution in the Making," *Business Week,* March 5, 1990, pp. 88–89.
48. J. A. Schumpeter, *The Theory of Economic Development* (Cambridge, MA: Harvard University Press, 1934).
49. A. Maddison, *Phases of Capitalist Development* (New York: Oxford University Press, 1982).
50. W. J. Baumol, "Entrepreneurship: Productive, Unproductive, and Destructive," *Journal of Political Economics,* vol. 98, no. 5 (1990), pp. 893–920.
51. D. Gervitz, *The Entrepreneurs: Innovation in American Business* (New York: Penguin Books, 1985), p. 30.
52. David Birch, "A Look Back and a Look Forward at Entrepreneurs and Their Role in the Economy," paper presented at Babson College Research Conference, 1990.
53. *Business Week,* June 17, 1991, pp. 24–32.
54. As quoted by Doerflinger and Rivkin, *Risk and Reward,* p. 199.

Chapter 5

[Note: Notes 1–4 are the original notes for "Capital Market Myopia."]

1. Data on venture capital investment in the disk-drive industry were provided by Venture Economics, Inc., publisher of *Venture Capital Journal.*
2. Data on the disk-drive industry were provided by James N. Porter of DISK/TREND, Inc.
3. The highs for each of the companies were recorded in a relatively short time frame from May to July 1983. An exception was Miniscribe, which did not go public until November 1983.
4. For every $1.00 of sales, disk-drive companies needed approximately $0.80 in fixed assets and working capital. To sustain high rates of growth with normal profitability levels necessitates heavy reliance on outside capital. Low profits or losses combined with rapid growth create an untenable situation.
5. William A. Sahlman, from teaching notes on the hard-disk–drive industry case series.

Chapter 6

1. M. Boylan, "What We Know and Don't Know about Venture Capital," American Economic Association Meetings, December 28, 1981, and National Economist Club, January 19, 1982.
2. R. Premus, "Venture Capital and Innovation," study by the Joint Economic Committee of U.S. Congress, December 1984, p. 25.
3. H. H. Stevenson, D. F. Muzyka, and J. A. Timmons, "Venture Capital in a New Era: A Simulation of the Impact of the Changes in Investment Patterns," in R. Ronstadt et al., eds., *Frontiers of Entrepreneurship Research* 1986 (Wellesley, MA: Center for Entrepreneurial Studies, Babson College), pp. 380–403.
4. "Recent Venture Funds Perform Poorly As Unrealistic Expectations Wear Off," *The Wall Street Journal,* November 8, 1988, p. B2.
5. This range of numbers can be found in the following sources: W. A. Wells, "Venture Capital Decision-Making," Ph.D. diss., Carnegie-Mellon University, 1974; G. Kozmetsky, M. D. Gill, Jr., and R. W. Smilor, *Financing and Managing Fast-Growth Companies: The Venture Capital Process* (Lexington, MA: Lexington Books, 1984); Glenn Rifkin and George Harrar, *The Ultimate Entrepreneur* (Chicago: Contemporary Books, 1988).
6. W. Rotch, "The Pattern of Success in Venture Capital Financing," *Financial Analysis Journal* (September–October 1968), pp. 141–147.
7. D. Gevirtz, *The New Entrepreneurs: Innovation in American Business* (New York: Penguin Books, 1985), p. 130.
8. J. B. Poindexter, "The Efficiency of Financial Markets: The Venture Capital Case," Ph.D. diss., New York University, 1976.
9. R. B. Faucett, "The Management of Venture Capital Investment Companies," MBA thesis, MIT, 1971.
10. J. P. Hoban, "Characteristics of Venture Capital Investing," Ph.D. diss., University of Utah, 1976.
11. Poindexter, "The Efficiency of Financial Markets."
12. J. D. Martin and W. P. Petty, "An Analysis of the Performance of Publicly Traded Venture Capital Companies," *Journal of Financial and Quantitative Analysis,* vol. 18, no. 3 (1983), pp. 401–410.
13. L. Wayne, "Management's Tale," *New York Times Magazine,* January 17, 1988, p. 42.
14. R. G. Ibbotson and G. P. Brinson, *Investment Markets* (New York: McGraw-Hill, 1987), pp. 99–100.
15. Poindexter, "The Efficiency of Financial Markets."
16. Wells, "Venture Capital Decision-Making."
17. Stevenson, Muzyka, and Timmons, "Venture Capital in a New Era," pp. 387–393.
18. "Committee Issues Portfolio Valuation Guidelines," *Venture Capital Journal* (June 1990), pp. 1–2.

19. W. A. Sahlman and H. H. Stevenson, "Capital Market Myopia," *Journal of Business Venturing,* vol. 1, no. 1 (Winter 1986), pp. 7–30.
20. Poindexter, "The Efficiency of Financial Markets."
21. "Too Much Money, Too Few Deals," *Forbes,* March 7, 1988, p. 144.
22. "For Venture Capitalists, Too Much of a Good Thing," *Business Week,* June 6, 1988, p. 126.
23. W. Hambrecht, quoted in "New Record Set at NVCA Meeting," *Venture Capital Journal* (May 1987), pp. 1–2.
24. Kozmetsky, Gill, and Smilor, *Financing and Managing Fast-Growth Companies,* p. 38.
25. "Venture Capital Industry Resources," *Venture Capital Journal* (July 1984), pp. 4–6.
26. "The Growth of an Industry: Venture Capital 1977–1982," *Venture Capital Journal* (October 1982), pp. 8–10.

Chapter 7

1. T. A. Soja and J. E. Reyes, *Investment Benchmarks: Venture Capital* (Needham, MA: Venture Economics, Inc., 1990), p. 191.
2. R. Khoylian, *Venture Capital Performance* (Needham, MA: Venture Economics Inc., 1988), p. 6.
3. "Playing the Ponies," *PC World* (January 1988), pp. 110–114.
4. "Sevin and Rosen, Venture Capitalists, to Call It a Career," *PC Week,* July 2, 1987, pp. 125–132.
5. For the data that follow, we relied heavily on the following sources: W. D. Bygrave and M. Stein, "A Time to Buy and a Time to Sell: A Study of Venture Capital Investments in 77 Companies That Went Public," in R. H. Brockhaus, Sr., et al., eds., *Frontiers of Entrepreneurship Research 1989* (Wellesley, MA: Center for Entrepreneurial Studies, Babson College, 1989), pp. 288–303; W. D. Bygrave and M. Stein, "The Anatomy of High-Tech IPOs: Do Their Venture Capitalists, Underwriters, Accountants, and Lawyers Make a Difference?," in N. C. Churchill et al., eds., *Frontiers of Entrepreneurship Research 1990* (Wellesley, MA: Center for Entrepreneurial Studies, Babson College, 1990), pp. 238–250.
6. J. K. Morris, "The Pricing of a Venture Capital Investment," in S. E. Pratt and J. K. Morris, eds., *Pratt's Guide to Venture Capital Sources,* 9th ed. (Needham, MA: Venture Economics, Inc. 1985), pp. 108–111.
7. For example, T. J. Davis, Jr., and C. P. Stetson, Jr., "Creating Successful Venture-Backed Companies," in Pratt and Morris, eds., *Pratt's Guide to Venture Capital Sources,* pp. 119–128.
8. W. Sahlman, "The Changing Structure of the American Venture Capital Industry," paper presented at the National Venture Capital Association Meeting, Washington, DC, May 10–12, 1989.

9. Robert Levering, Michael Katz, and Milton Moskowitz, *The Computer Entrepreneurs* (New York: NAL Books, 1984), p. 457.

Chapter 8

1. Attributed to Frank Chambers, a veteran San Francisco venture capitalist who founded Continental Capital Corporation. Quoted in Everett M. Rogers and Judith Larsen, *Silicon Valley Fever: Growth of High-Technology Culture* (New York: Basic Books, 1984), p. 74.
2. Gene Bylinsky, "California's Great Breeding Ground for Industry," *Fortune* (June 1974).
3. "Venture Funds Raise $2.8 Billion in New Capital," *Venture Capital Journal* (February 1989), p. 21.
4. Rogers and Larsen, *Silicon Valley Fever,* pp. 64, 68.
5. This study was conducted by Jeffry Timmons, then professor of Entrepreneurial Studies at Babson College, Wellesley, MA; Stanley Pratt, Norman D. Fast, and Roubina Khoylian of Venture Economics, Inc., Needham, MA; and William D. Bygrave, then a professor at Bryant College, Smithfield, RI. It was sponsored by the National Science Foundation under IS182-13157, with support from Babson College. Any opinions, findings, conclusions, or recommendations expressed in this book are those of the authors and do not necessarily reflect the views of the National Science Foundation or our colleagues.
6. *Connectedness* is the term used by E. M. Rogers and D. L. Kincaid, *Communication Networks: Toward a New Paradigm for Research* (New York: Free Press, 1981). H. E. Aldrich and D. A. Whetten, "Organization-Sets, Action-Sets, and Networks," in P. C. Nystrom and W. H. Starbuck, eds., *Handbook of Organizational Design* [New York: Oxford University Press, 1981], pp. 385–408) use the term *density.* In network terminology, a pair of venture capital firms with a connection is called a *link.* If a pair has one or more co-investments, it is connected by a *direct link.*
7. For a group with N members, the maximum number of intragroup direct links is $N(N-1)/2$; for two separate groups with K and L members, the maximum number of intergroup direct links is KL.
8. Network theoreticians have developed measures to determine the centrality of organizations in networks (e.g., Aldrich and Whetten, "Organization-Sets, Action-Sets, and Networks"; Rogers and Kincaid, *Communication Networks).* We developed measures of centrality specifically for the venture capital industry (W. D. Bygrave, "The Structure of the Investment Networks of Venture Capital Firms," *Journal of Business Venturing,* vol. 3, no. 2 [1988], pp. 137–158).
9. Herbert A. Simon, "The Architecture of Complexity," *Proceedings of the American Philosophical Society,* vol. 106, pp. 467–482.

10. K. E. Weick, "Educational Organizations as Loosely Coupled Systems," *Administrative Science Quarterly* (March 1976), pp. 1–19.

11. M. S. Granovetter, "The Strength of Weak Ties," *American Journal of Sociology,* vol. 78, no. 6 (1973), pp. 1360–1380; and "The Strength of Weak Ties: A Network Theory Revisited," in P. V. Marsden and N. Lin, eds., *Social Structure and Network Analysis* (Beverly Hills, Sage, 1982), pp. 105–130.

12. Quoted in Gene Bylinsky, *The Innovation Millionaires: How They Succeed* (New York: Scribner's, 1976), p. 32.

13. The most active underwriters of all venture-capital-backed IPOs in 1990 were Alex. Brown & Sons; Smith Barney, Harris Upham & Co.; Donaldson, Lufkin & Jenrette; Hambrecht & Quist; and Robertson, Stephens & Company (*Venture Capital Journal* [February 1991], p. 17).

14. J. Rosenstein et al., "How Much Do CEOs Value the Advice of Venture Capitalists on Their Boards?," in N. C. Churchill et al., eds., *Frontiers of Entrepreneurship Research 1990* (Wellesley, MA: Center for Entrepreneurial Studies, Babson College, 1990), pp. 238–250.

15. C. Barry et al., "Venture Capital and Public Offerings," working paper, Texas Southern University and Southern Methodist University, 1988.

16. J. Rosenstein et al., "Do Venture Capitalists on Boards of Portfolio Companies Add Value Besides Money?," in R. H. Brockhaus et al., eds., *Frontiers of Entrepreneurship Research 1989* (Wellesley, MA: Center for Entrepreneurial Studies, Babson College, 1989), pp. 216–229.

17. Rosenstein et al., "How Much Do CEOs Value the Advice of Venture Capitalists on Their Boards?"

18. J. Booth and R. Smith III, "Investment Banking, Reputation, and Underpricing in Initial Public Offerings," *Journal of Financial Economics* (1986), pp. 261–281; R. Carter and S. Manaster, "Initial Public Offerings and Underwriter Reputation," working paper, Iowa State University and University of Utah, 1988.

19. D. J. Kramer, "The Entrepreneur's Perspective," in S. E. Pratt and J. K. Morris, eds., *Pratt's Guide to Venture Capital Sources,* 8th ed. (Needham, MA: Venture Economics, Inc., 1984), pp. 108–111.

20. *Venture Capital Journal* (March 1991), p. 19.

21. Fred Adler, quoted in *PC Week,* July 27, 1988, p. 132.

22. "New Record Set at NVCA Meeting," *Venture Capital Journal* (May 1987), p. 2.

23. *Business Week,* June 6, 1988, p. 126.

24. W. A. Wells, "Venture Capital Decision-Making," Ph.D. diss., Carnegie-Mellon University, 1974.

25. A. V. Bruno and T. T. Tyebjee, "The One That Got Away: A Study

of Ventures Rejected by Venture Capitalists," in J. A. Hornaday, J. A. Timmons, and K. H. Vesper, eds., *Frontiers of Entrepreneurship Research* 1983 (Wellesley, MA: Center for Entrepreneurial Studies, Babson College, 1983), pp. 289–306.

26. W. J. Baumol, "Entrepreneurship and a Century of Growth," *Journal of Business Venturing*, vol. 1, no. 2 (1986), pp. 141–145.

Chapter 9

1. We have based this section on Jeffry A. Timmons and Harry A. Sapienza, "Venture Capital: More Than Money?" in S. E. Pratt and J. K. Morris, eds., *Pratt's Guide to Venture Capital Sources*, 7th ed. (Needham, MA: Venture Economics, Inc., 1984), pp. 71–75. We are most appreciative to Venture Economics for permission to draw on this material here.

2. Timmons and Sapienza, "Venture Capital: More Than Money?" in S. M. Pratt and J. Morris, eds., *Pratt's Guide to Venture Capital Sources*, 14th ed. (Needham, MA: Venture Economics, Inc., 1990), pp. 36–41.

3. Don Valentine Interview, *Upside* (Palo Alto, CA: The Upside Publishing Company, 1990), p. 71.

4. Harry A. Sapienza, "Variations in Venture Capitalist–Entrepreneur Relations: Antecedents and Consequences," unpublished Ph.D. diss., University of Maryland, 1989, p. 259.

5. Ibid., p. 252.

6. Ibid., pp. 252–253.

7. Ibid., p. 253.

8. Ibid., p. 254.

9. Ibid., p. 255.

10. Ibid., p. 253.

11. Ibid., p. 257.

12. J. Rosenstein et al., "How Much Do CEOs Value the Advice of Venture Capitalists on Their Boards?" in N. Churchill et al., eds., *Frontiers of Entrepreneurship 1990* (Wellesley, MA: Center for Entrepreneurship Studies, Babson College, 1990), pp. 238–250.

13. Ibid., p. 245.

14. Ibid., p. 247.

Chapter 10

1. Michael S. Dukakis and Rosabeth M. Kanter, *Creating the Future* (New York: Summit Books, 1988), p. 19.

2. David L. Birch, "Choosing a Place to Grow: Business Location

Decisions in the 1970's" (Cambridge, MA: MIT Program on Neighborhood and Regional Change, 1981).

3. "What I Learned in the Eighties," *Forbes,* January 8, 1990, p. 100.
4. "The Economic Impact of Venture Capital," a joint study conducted by Coopers & Lybrand, Strategic Management Services, and Venture Economics, Inc., presented by R. Joseph Schlosser, managing associate, Coopers & Lybrand, at Venture Forum '90, October 25, 1990, San Francisco.
5. "A Golden Age for Entrepreneurs," *Fortune,* February 12, 1990, p. 120.
6. Details of this study are described in Chapter 8.
7. Dukakis and Kanter, *Creating the Future,* p. 15.
8. "MIT: Growing Businesses for the Future," report prepared by the Economics Department, Bank of Boston, June 1, 1989.
9. Richard C. Carlson and Theodore R. Lyman, "Silicon Valley: Some Success Factors in the Success Story," Public Policy Center, SRI International, 1985.
10. Donald Wolheim, *Advancing the Electronic Age* (Chicago: Encyclopaedia Press, 1962).
11. Carlson and Lyman, "Silicon Valley."
12. Brochure for the Center for Integrated Systems, Stanford University, Center for Integrative Studies.
13. Everett M. Rogers and Judith K. Larsen, *Silicon Valley Fever: Growth of a High-Technology Culture* (New York: Basic Books, 1984), pp. 30–31.
14. Ibid., p. 33.
15. Ibid., p. 35.
16. Richard Florida and Martin Kenney, "Venture Capital and High Technology Entrepreneurship," *Journal of Business Venturing,* vol. 3 (1988), pp. 301–319.
17. Ibid.
18. According to a report by the Massachusetts Board of Regents, 1988.
19. Florida and Kenney, "Venture Capital and High Technology Entrepreneurship," p. 315.
20. John Kao, "Note on Venture Incubators," 487-057. Boston: Harvard Business School, 1987, p. 1.
21. James C. Worthy, *Portrait of a Maverick* (Cambridge, MA: Ballinger, 1987).
22. "More Incubators Used to Hatch Small Firms," *The Wall Street Journal,* January 24, 1990, p. B1.
23. "Home Grown Businesses Help to Revive Local Economies," *The Wall Street Journal,* January 24, 1990.
24. Ibid.
25. Massachusetts Technology Development Corporation, Annual Report 1989.

26. Massachusetts Capital Resource Corporation, Annual Report 1989.
27. J. Maddox, "End of Cold Fusion in Sight," *Nature* (July 6, 1989), p. 15.
28. Michael Schrage, "Pork Barrels and Science Funding," *Boston Sunday Globe,* October 7, 1990, p. A2.
29. Ibid.
30. Rogers and Larsen, *Silicon Valley Fever,* pp. 43–61.
31. Everett M. Rogers, "High Technology Companies That Are University Spinoffs," in Wayne S. Brown and Roy Rothwell, eds., *Entrepreneurship & Technology: World Experiences and Policies* (Harlow, Essex, UK: Longman Group, 1986), p. 134.
32. "The Most Entrepreneurial Cities in America," *Inc. Magazine* (March 1990), p. 41. Rankings are based on job generation, rate of significant new business startups, and percentage of young companies enjoying high growth rates.
33. Robert Levering, Michael Katz, and Milton Moskowitz, *The Computer Entrepreneurs* (New York: NAL Books, 1984), p. 451.

Chapter 11

1. R. Premus, *Venture Capital and Innovation,* report prepared for U.S. Congress, Joint Economic Committee, Washington, DC, December 1984.
2. "Risk Business," *Inc. Magazine* (March 1990), p. 28.
3. "Observations and Insights," *Venture Capital Journal* (December 1984), p. 1.
4. For example, Premus, *Venture Capital and Innovation.*
5. Harvard University's Benjamin M. Friedman even claims that capital gains taxes have no effect on venture capital; see "A Benign Tax Increase—The Myth That Won't Die," *Business Week,* January 9, 1989, p. 22; "Don't Expect Any Capital-Gains Tax Cut to Nourish Startups," *Business Week,* April 24, 1989, p. 20.
6. "Do Venture Capitalists Really Need a Tax Break?," *Business Week,* April 8, 1985.
7. "Observations and Insights," *Venture Capital Journal* (March 1985), p. 2.
8. J. B. Poindexter, "The Efficiency of Financial Markets: The Venture Capital Case," Ph.D. diss., New York University, 1976.
9. W. D. Bygrave and J. Shulman, "Capital Gains Tax: Bane or Boon for Venture Capital?," in B. A. Kirchhoff et al., eds., *Frontiers of Entrepreneurship Research 1988* (Wellesley, MA: Center for Entrepreneurial Studies, Babson College, 1988), pp. 324–338.
10. William D. Bygrave, "Venture Capital Investing: A Resource Exchange Perspective," Ph.D. diss., Boston University, 1989.

11. W. D. Bygrave and J. A. Timmons, "An Empirical Model for the Flows of Venture Capital," in J. A. Hornaday et al., eds., *Frontiers of Entrepreneurial Research 1985* (Wellesley, MA: Center for Entrepreneurial Studies, Babson College, 1985), pp. 105–125.

12. Premus, *Venture Capital and Innovation,* p. 9.

13. W. D. Bygrave et al., "Rates of Return on Venture Capital Investing: A Study of 131 Funds," in Kirchhoff et al., eds., *Frontiers of Entrepreneurship Research 1988,* pp. 275–289.

14. Premus, *Venture Capital and Innovation,* p. 9.

15. T. Tyebjee and L. Vickery, "Venture Capital in Western Europe," *Journal of Venturing* (Spring 1988), pp. 123–126.

16. Premus, *Venture Capital and Innovation,* p. 67.

17. Ibid., p. 66.

Chapter 12

1. Michael E. Porter, *The Competitive Advantage of Nations* (New York: Free Press, 1990), pp. 125–126.

2. David Birch, "A Look Back and a Look Forward at Entrepreneurs and Their Role in the Economy," paper presented at Babson College Research Conference, 1990.

3. D. J. Brophy, "Venture Capital Research," in D. D. Sexton and R. W. Smilor, eds., *The Art and Science of Entrepreneurship* (Cambridge, MA: Ballinger, 1986), p. 120.

4. W. Scheirer, "Innovation in Small Firms," in *Issue Alert* (Washington, DC: U.S. Small Business Administration, Office of Advocacy, July 1986); Z. J. Acs and D. B. Audretsch, "Innovation in Large and Small Firms: An Empirical Analysis," *American Economic Review,* vol. 78, no. 4 (1988), pp. 678–690.

5. "The Brakes Go On in R&D: Spending Cuts Could Harm U.S. Competitiveness," *Business Week,* July 1, 1991, pp. 24–26.

6. Ibid.

7. "Living Standards Fall as U.S. Fails to Compete," *Boston Herald,* July 10, 1991, p. 3.

8. "Can John Akers Save IBM?," *Fortune,* July 15, 1991, p. 45.

9. Paul Wallich, "The Analytical Economist: David or Goliath?," *Scientific American* (October 1990), p. 125.

10. C. H. Ferguson, "From the People Who Brought You Voodoo Economics," *Harvard Business Review* (May–June 1988), pp. 55–62.

11. George Gilder, "The Revitalization of Everything: The Law of the Microcosm," *Harvard Business Review* (March–April 1988), pp. 49–61.

12. Wallich, "The Analytical Economist," p. 125.

13. Gilder, "The Revitalization of Everything," p. 50.

14. Ibid., p. 61.
15. "Intel's High-Powered Marketing in Chips War," *Computer Shopper* (September 1991), p. 117.
16. Gilder, "The Revitalization of Everything," p. 50.
17. James C. Worthy, *Portrait of a Maverick* (Cambridge, MA: Ballinger, 1987), p. 30.
18. Rosabeth Kanter, *When Giants Learn to Dance: Mastering the Challenge of Strategy, Management, and Careers in the 1990s* (New York: Simon & Schuster, 1989), p. 344.
19. Quoted by Tom Peters in the video *The Shape of a Winner* (Boston: *Inc. Magazine*, 1988).
20. Kanter, *When Giants Learn to Dance*, p. 361.
21. "Revenge of the Nerds in Biotech Land," *Business Week,* August 5, 1991, p. 26.
22. "The Brakes Go On in R&D."
23. Robert Reich, *The Next American Frontier* (New York: Penguin Books, 1983), p. 230.
24. Ibid., p. 159.
25. Dinesh D'Souza, *Illiberal Education* (New York: Free Press, 1991).
26. "Time Is Not on America's Side," *Business Week,* July 22, 1991, p. 12.
27. "The Best B-Schools," *Business Week,* November 28, 1988, p. 78.
28. *1988 Harvard Business School Placement Report,* Harvard Business School, 1988.
29. Everett M. Rogers and Judith K. Larsen, *Silicon Valley Fever: Growth of a High-Technology Culture* (New York: Basic Books, 1984).
30. Electronics Industries Association statistics. Quoted in the *New York Times,* January 20, 1991, section 3, pp. 1, 6.
31. "Commercial Biotechnology: An International Analysis" (Washington, DC: U.S. Congress, Office of Technology Assessment, 1984).
32. P. David, "Congress Told US Ahead, Japan Second, Rest Nowhere," *Nature,* February 2, 1984, p. 402.
33. Porter, *The Competitive Advantage of Nations,* pp. 617–682.
34. Quoted by Thomas H. Peters and Robert H. Waterman, Jr., *In Search of Excellence* (New York: Harper & Row, 1982), p. 107.
35. R. A. Fildes, "Strategic Challenges in Commercializing Biotechnology," *California Management Review* (Spring 1990), pp. 63–72.
36. The quotes by Edison, Wright, Watson, Einstein, and the Committee of the British Parliament are excerpted from *Perspectives* (Winter 1989), pp. 1–2, issued by IAA Trust Company, Bloomington, IL.
37. This 1888 statement was reproduced in *Scientific American* (March 1988), p. 10.
38. Glenn Rifkin and George Harrar, *The Ultimate Entrepreneur The Story of Ken Olsen and Digital Equipment Corporation* (Chicago: Contemporary Books, 1988), p. 199.

39. Ibid., p. 199.
40. J. G. Bednorz and K. S. Muller, *Zeitschrift für Physik* (B64, 1986), pp. 189–193.
41. As reported by Fildes, "Strategic Challenges in Commercializing Biotechnology," pp. 63–72.
42. "Cheap Solar Power: Has the Dream Come True?," *Business Week,* August 12, 1991, p. 49.
43. "The New Alchemy: How Science Is Molding Molecules into Miracle Materials," *Business Week,* July 29, 1991, pp. 48–55.
44. "The U.S. Has a New Weapon: Low-Cost Capital," *Business Week,* July 29, 1991, pp. 72–73.
45. Ibid.
46. "The Tax That Ate the Economy," *The Wall Street Journal,* June 24, 1991, p. A10.
47. Kevin Phillips, "From Riches to Rags," *Northwestern University Magazine* (July 1991), pp. 17–19. Adapted from his Ford Hall Forum address, Boston, April 28, 1991.
48. *Boston Herald,* September 7, 1991, p. 18.
49. "The Tax That Ate the Economy," p. A10.
50. *Venture Capital in Europe: 1991 EVCA Yearbook* (Zavetem, Belgium: EVCA Secretariat, 1991), p. 144.
51. Ibid.
52. Fildes, "Strategic Challenges in Commercializing Biotechnology," pp. 63–72.
53. Alan Patricof, "Reviving Venture Capital's Appeal," *Pensions and Investments,* October 14, 1991, p. 14.
54. Patrick Liles, "Sustaining the Venture Capital Firm," unpublished Ph.D. diss., Harvard Business School, 1969.
55. *Venture Capital Journal* (March 1991), p. 19.
56. Ibid.

About the Authors

William D. Bygrave, M.A, D.Phil. (Oxford), M.B.A. (Northeastern University), D.B.A. (Boston University), is the Frederic C. Hamilton Professor for Free Enterprise at Babson College.

As an academic, he teaches and researches entrepreneurship. He has written more than fifty papers on topics that include nuclear physics, hospital pharmaceuticals, philosophy of science, venture capital, and entrepreneurship. One of them was chosen as the best article published in *Entrepreneurship Theory and Practice* in 1989. For his physics doctorate, he investigated the internal structure of medium-weight nuclei. For his business doctorate, he studied the U.S. venture capital industry; his dissertation, *Venture Capital Investing,* received the 1989 Heizer Award from the Academy of Management. He serves on the review boards of three entrepreneurship journals.

As a practitioner, he founded a Route 128 venture-capital-backed high-tech company, managed a division of a NYSE-listed high-tech company, co-founded a pharmaceutical database company, and was a member of the investment committee of a venture capital firm.

Jeffry A. Timmons is nationally and internationally recognized for his work in entrepreneurship, new ventures, and venture capital. He is first to hold a joint appointment at the Harvard Business School (where he teaches Entrepreneurial Finance) as the first MBA Class of 1954 Professor of New Ventures, and at Babson College as the first Frederic C. Hamilton Professor of Free Enterprise Development. He has written or co-authored ten books, including *Venture Capital at the Crossroads* (Harvard Business School Press, 1992), *New Venture Creation* (Irwin, 3d ed., 1990), and more than one hundred articles and papers, including six articles in *Harvard Business Review,* on these topics. He is co-founder and director of several companies, including Boston Communications Group, owners of cellular and telecommunications-related ventures, an adviser to BCI Advisors, a $285-million growth capital fund and to Ernst & Young's national Entrepreneurial Services Group in the United States and the United Kingdom. He was the first outside director of Cellular One in Boston, and has served as an investor, director, and adviser to several emerging companies. He is also an adviser to the Ewing Marion Kauffman Foundation. He is a graduate of Colgate University, where he now serves as a trustee, and received his MBA and doctorate from the Harvard Business School.

Index

343